Personal Construct Psychology and Education

EDUCATIONAL PSYCHOLOGY

Allen J. Edwards, Series Editor
Department of Psychology
Southwest Missouri State University
Springfield, Missouri

In preparation:

Patricia A. Schmuck and W. W. Charters, Jr. (eds.). Educational Policy and Management: Sex Differentials

Phillip S. Strain and Mary Margaret Kerr. Mainstreaming of Children in Schools: Research and Programming Issues

Published

Maureen L-Pope and Terence R. Keen. Personal Construct Psychology and Education

Ronald W. Henderson (ed.). Parent–Child Interaction: Theory, Research, and Prospects

W. Ray Rhine (ed.). Making Schools More Effective: New Directions from Follow Through

Herbert J. Klausmeier and Thomas S. Sipple. Learning and Teaching Concepts: A Strategy for Testing Applications of Theory

James H. McMillan (ed.). The Social Psychology of School Learning

M. C. Wittrock (ed.). The Brain and Psychology

Marvin J. Fine (ed.). Handbook on Parent Education

Dale G. Range, James R. Layton, and Darrell L. Roubinek (eds.). Aspects of Early Childhood Education: Theory to Research to Practice

Jean Stockard, Patricia A. Schmuck, Ken Kempner, Peg Williams, Sakre K. Edson, and Mary Ann Smith. Sex Equity in Education

James R. Layton. The Psychology of Learning to Read

Thomas E. Jordan. Development in the Preschool Years: Birth to Age Five

Gary D. Phye and Daniel J. Reschly (eds.). School Psychology: Perspectives and Issues

Norman Steinaker and M. Robert Bell. The Experiential Taxonomy: A New Approach to Teaching and Learning

J. P. Das, John R. Kirby, and Ronald F. Jarman. Simultaneous and Successive Cognitive Processes

Herbert J. Klausmeier and Patricia S. Allen. Cognitive Development of Children and Youth: A Longitudinal Study

Victor M. Agruso, Jr. Learning in the Later Years: Principles of Educational Gerontology

The list of titles in this series continues on the last page of this volume.

Personal Construct Psychology and Education

Maureen L. Pope
Institute for Educational Technology,
University of Surrey
Guildford

Terence R. Keen
Garnett College
Roehampton
London

1981

ACADEMIC PRESS
A Subsidiary of Harcourt Brace Jovanovich, Publishers
London New York Toronto Sydney San Francisco

ACADEMIC PRESS INC. (LONDON) LTD.
24/28 Oval Road
London NW1

United States Edition published by
ACADEMIC PRESS INC.
111 Fifth Avenue
New York, New York 10003

British Library Cataloguing in Publication Data

Pope, M.
Personal construct psychology and education. —
(Educational psychology series)
1. Personality tests
I. Title II. Keen, T. R. III. Series
370.15'02413 LB1051

ISBN 0-12-561520-5

LCCN 81-66376

Typeset by Dobbie Typesetting Service,
Plymouth
Printed in Great Britain by
St Edmundsbury Press, Bury St Edmunds, Suffolk

Foreword

In this book Maureen Pope and Terry Keen have brought together their common interests in personal construct psychology and teaching to give us exciting new insights into the process of education. Views of education are diverse and there are many contrary opinions about which models of the learning process and philosophies of education should prevail. Pope and Keen suggest that we should accept and put to good use this diversity of viewpoints and encourage constructive alternatives in education. This is in keeping with the philosophy of George Kelly who saw each individual acting as a personal scientist forming alternative construct systems and moving between them. We can take advantage of the current emphasis in education on personal relevance to provide an adaptive system in schools and colleges based on individual needs and learning styles.

The authors discuss some of the practicalities of adapting and using in the educational setting Kelly's repertory grid technique for eliciting a personal construct system from an individual. The problem of how to extract information from a grid is tackled, with the two authors presenting differing preferences for the two commonly used methods of principal components analysis and clustering.

Readers will enjoy the case studies which show how personal construct techniques have been used in education. Terry Keen has devised a method of teacher appraisal which can be carried out and kept private by the individual teacher himself. He describes the TARGET methodology (Teaching Appraisal by Repertory Grid Elicitation Techniques) with some of its extensions. Some of his more recent work suggests a new approach to cognitive complexity which had particular application in the grid elicitation process where one can estimate to what extent "new" constructs are being given. Maureen Pope has been concerned with initial teacher education and in particular how the student teachers react to, learn from, and value their periods of practice in schools. More recently she has extended this work into the areas of management, training and recruitment in industry and in schools.

It is over a quarter of a century since Kelly introduced personal construct psychology to the world, and only now is it being realized how applicable it is to education and learning in the widest sense — in schools and colleges, in management, and in clinical psychology. Most recently published books on personal constructs have concentrated on management and psychology applications, and this is the first I have seen which gives such a fresh approach to many old problems in both the practice and philosophy of education. This book is particularly significant in presenting Kelly's ideas in a form which demonstrates their application to education.

March 1981 Mildred Shaw

Preface

Existing literature on educational psychology has omitted to place what we consider to be adequate emphasis on the work of George Kelly and subsequent developments of personal construct theory. There are a number of excellent volumes on aspects of personal construct psychology. However, to date these have largely attracted readers who are either working in clinical psychology and related fields or who are engaged in research where repertory grid techniques are being used. Educationalists in schools and colleges and those involved in management education tend not to be amongst the specialists groups to which the contents of current books on personal construct psychology have been directed. We have written this volume in the hope that it will go some way towards meeting the demands of educationalists we have met who have suggested to us that such a book would be helpful to them. We hope therefore that in this volume students of education, practising teachers, those involved in management education and psychologists interested in educational applications of personal construct psychology will find something to interest them.

At the outset we have tried to give an overview of some perspectives on education which have evolved from various psychological theories and philosophical approaches, some of which will undoubtedly be familiar to the reader. As an alternative approach we have presented those aspects of Kelly's theory which we feel to be most relevant to those involved in education in its widest sense. It has not been our intention to cover personal construct theory in detail. The reader will find several references to other texts which will give further elaboration of Kelly's theory.

We have attempted to provide the reader with a flavour of recent developments in personal construct psychology and grid methodology in the hope that this will encourage many readers to reflect on the relevance of such an approach for education and that many will feel able to evaluate the techniques themselves by further practical application.

Much of what we have written in this book has emphasized that there are many possible perspectives that one can take on education and that each of us will have a personal set of ideas which will influence how we approach the task of educating others. We hope that this book will encourage readers to reflect on their "personal constructs" in relation to education.

Maureen L. Pope
Terence R. Keen

March 1981

Acknowledgements

One cannot produce a book of any kind without a great deal of help and support by many people. We gratefully acknowledge, therefore, the help of all our friends and colleagues, our families for their tolerance and especially Linda and Margaret who have typed and re-typed the various draft and final manuscripts!

We wonder what George Kelly might say if he could now see how his personal construct psychology has developed, and how he might review our book. Whilst we might hope such a review would be favourable, there is no doubt in our minds that it is he who must be acknowledged as the fundamental stimulus for the volume, and we are very grateful for this.

Clearly, we cannot mention everyone who has contributed or assisted in the production of this volume, but we would especially like to mention the following for their help: Academic Press for commissioning the work; our colleagues at Stantonbury Campus and University of Surrey for tolerating our indulgence; Pru, Nicky and Martin, and Mike, Adrian and Kathlyn for supporting us (our families); Linda Lucas and Margaret Richards for typing the work; David Peters for compiling the index; Laurie Thomas and Brian Lewis for academic stimulation and support; all the authors and researchers noted in our bibliography without whom the work could not have happened; and Mildred Shaw and colleagues at the Barbican Research Group for their continual nagging which forced us to finish the work!

To Laurie and Brian

Contents

Part One

In recent years there has been increasing discontent with the models of learning upon which education and training are based. Much of the emphasis in the following chapters is on education in schools and colleges, although it is suggested that the issues raised are equally relevant to education/training in the wider sense, and at work or play. Indeed Hayes (1978) suggested a closer alignment of education, training and work, and indicated that "learning-to-learn" is as important a concept for industry and commerce as it is becoming to be within schools and colleges. There is growing recognition within industry of the need for establishing the personal strategies used and the values held by the learner in relation to any particular learning task. New techniques are evolving which encourage the individual learner to confront these aspects and to take an active and responsible part in the learning process.

Each of us has an implicit model of the learning process which will have an impact on our behaviour as learner or teacher/trainer. The first part of this section reflects on some of the more prevalent theories of education which have been adopted as a base by teachers and trainers alike.

The theories underlying the practice of educational research are also intimately linked to general educational ideologies. These educational ideologies embody theories on the nature and development of man. As Bruner (1966) pointed out, instruction can be seen as an effort to assist or to shape growth, and any theory of instruction is in effect a theory of how growth and development are encouraged. Any theory about teaching is thus inextricably linked to an underlying view or model of the nature of the learner. A teacher/trainer may conceive of the nature of the learner as passive or active, meaning-seeking, impulse-driven, fixed or constantly developing. Whichever model is adopted will influence that teacher's teaching strategy and aims.

Much of the current debate on education revolves round fundamental differences in the models of learning held by the individuals concerned. Many educationalists argue that a major problem is that at any point in time educational issues tend to be dominated by one particular viewpoint or "frame of reference" so that education becomes monolithic in structure (Joyce, 1972). Those involved in education often adopt rigidly opposing positions which militate against a more constructive and flexible approach. *There is now a growing recognition that alternative models can co-exist and enrich rather than detract from development in education.* Some educational researchers are seeking new approaches — recognizing that past educational research has been conducted on too narrow a base. Snow (1974) discusses these issues in relation to research on teaching and suggests that we should be concerned with

> Adapting methodology to match the complexity of students and situations in schools . . . . Hopefully in future programmes of research, alternative kinds of designs will be used and various hybrids will be invented so that the advantages and disadvantages of each can be counter-balanced and more clearly understood. (pp.288–9)

Part 1 of this book considers some of the alternatives in education. Chapter 1 looks at some of the major themes inherent in differing educational ideologies and relates these to particular models of the nature of knowledge and the psychological development of man. In Chapter 2 some of the current issues within the area of educational research are raised. It is suggested that alternative methodologies are needed if we are to adopt the perspective of the person in educational research (Morris, 1972).

Repertory grid techniques evolving from the work of George Kelly (1955) are proposed as one possible alternative mode of inquiry within educational research. Aspects of Personal Construct Psychology which seem to have a direct bearing on current concerns in education are discussed in Chapter 3. Of particular concern is that of the personal perspective of the learner. Repertory grid techniques are proposed as an alternative methodology which will allow both the researcher/teacher and participant subject/learner a means of monitoring and reflecting on the idiosyncratic frames of reference which the learner evolves. Rather than the imposition of a monolithic approach to educational issues, a Kellian framework allows for diversity of viewpoints and constructive alternatives in education.

1

Alternative Perspectives on Education

Inevitably, any attempt to categorize perspectives on education will do an injustice to the great diversity of viewpoints on education held by particular individuals. Nevertheless, the following categorization represents one possible way of construing the alternative themes presented within differing perspectives on education. It is suggested that there are at least four major schools of thought in the development of Western educational ideology, each exhibiting a continuity based upon particular assumptions of psychological development and philosophies of the nature of knowledge. These assumptions, together with political and economic constraints, largely determine pedagogic practice in schools and colleges and provide a framework for educational research. Some of the major theoretical issues underlying each approach will be indicated in this chapter and the practical application of these theoretical stances within schools and colleges will be discussed. These schools of thought may be termed:

(a) cultural transmission;
(b) romanticism;
(c) progressivism;
(d) de-schooling.

Since cultural transmission is rooted in the classical academic tradition of Western education, we shall consider this first.

CULTURAL TRANSMISSION

Theorists of this persuasion would see the primary task of the educator as the transmission of information, rules or values collected in the past. The educator's job is the direct instruction of information and rules. For example, Robert Maynard Hutchins (1936) wrote,

> Education implies teaching. Teaching implies knowledge. Knowledge is truth.

> The truth is everywhere the same. Hence, education should be everywhere the same. (p.66)

In the classical tradition it was thought that by studying the great works of literature, philosophy, science and history, the student learned the "truths" of his cultural heritage. Much of the basis of modern educational technology and behavioural modification approaches to education can be seen as variants of this cultural transmission approach. Knowledge and values are seen as located in the culture and are internalized by children imitating adult behaviour models or through explicit instruction and the use of such training procedures as reward and punishment. The criterion of successful education for such theorists is the student's ability to incorporate the responses he has been taught and to respond to the demand of the system. The major objectives are literacy and mathematical skills which are seen as necessary for adjustment to technological society.

Their philosophical approach is that absolute truth can be accumulated bit by bit, subject by subject. Knowledge is repetitive and objective and can be measured by culturally shared test procedures. This approach is exemplified by the "Black Paper — Fight for Education", edited by Cox and Dyson (1969). The learner is seen as naturally lazy and must be prodded into action by external incentives. Thus, they say,

> Exams make people work hard. Much opposition to them is based on the belief that people work better without reward and incentive, a naivete which is against all knowledge of human nature. (p.56)

The view of absolute truth accumulating corresponds to the basic principles of philosophic realism. In the Realist's view the world exists independently of man and is governed by laws over which we have little control. Most scientific realists deny the existence of free will and argue that the individual is determined by the impact of the physical and social environment on his genetic structure. John Locke assumed that the mind of the individual at birth was a *tabula rasa*. For Locke the intellect was essentially passive and acquired its content and structure through the impact of sensation through the senses. The world we perceive is not a world that we have recreated mentally but is the world as it is. The epistemological position of the Realist is that true knowledge is knowledge that corresponds to the world as it is. The task of the school and college would seem to be the instruction of a body of knowledge whose truth had been repeatedly confirmed.

The Lockean tradition is central to psychological theories of development which stress the *passivity of man's mind*. This emphasis is found in all types of associationism, behaviourism, stimulus-response psychology, contingency theories, etc. One might suggest that the appropriate metaphor for the view of man put forward by cultural transmission educational ideology, is that of the machine. The machine can be anything from the wax upon which the environment makes its mark (Locke) through to the computer. The environment is seen as "input" whose information is more or less *directly* transmitted to and accumulated in the "organism". The resulting behaviour is the "output". Using this mechanistic metaphor, cognitive development can be seen as the result of guided learning and teaching and behaviour is the result of an association between stimulus and response (Hull and Spence, 1946, Classical Learning Theory).

Skinner (1968) views teachers as architects and builders of student behaviour. Skinner defines learning as a change in the probability of response. He explains all human behaviour in terms of respondents and operant reinforcement. On the basis of his animal laboratory work he has set out a detailed methodology for the timing and spacing of scheduled reinforcement. Through progressively changing the contingencies of reinforcement in the direction of the desired behaviour (as defined by the experimenter) learning is seen to occur. Education change is evaluated from *performances*, not from *changes in thoughts or feelings*. Thus Skinner (1971) stated,

> We can follow the path taken by physics and biology by turning directly to the relation between behaviour and the environment and neglecting . . . states of mind . . . we do not need to discover what personalities, states of mind, feelings . . . intentions — or other prerequisites of autonomous man really are in order to get on with a scientific analysis of behaviour. (p.15)

This "Black Box" or "Empty Organism" approach with its emphasis on man's behaviour being controlled by his environmental situation, flourished in the decades following the 1920s. Theorists holding to a cultural transmission educational ideology find much support in the Realist's philosophy and the psychological theories put forward by the behaviourists, neo-behaviourists and contingency theorists. However this dominant position has been challenged by three major contenders — the Romanticists, the Progressivists and the De-schoolers.

ROMANTICISTS

The Romanticists stress that what comes from within the child is the most important aspect of development. Thus the pedagogical environment should be permissive enough to allow "inner good" to unfold and "inner bad" to come under control. The emphasis is on "health" and "growth" and working through aspects of emotional development which may not be allowed expression in the home. Rousseau's *Emile*, although written over two hundred years ago, contains what many consider are the fundamental principles behind modern educational ideas. Believing that man is born naturally good, Rousseau considered that by lifting social and pedagogical restraints, one would preserve natural goodness. Rousseau's "Negative Education" was not to be an education of transmitted norms, but one based on the psychological principles of natural development of the child and a non-directive approach on behalf of the teacher. The writings of G. S. Stanley-Hall in the early twentieth century suggested that before we let pedagogy loose on children we would have to overcome the fetishes of the alphabet and of the multiplication tables and must reflect that but a few generations ago the ancestors of all of us were illiterate. He maintained that there were many who ought not to be educated and that these would be "better in mind, body and morals if they knew no school". The type of school to which Stanley-Hall was referring was that in which the transmission of public knowledge was instilled without reference to the thoughts and feelings of the child and the perceived relevance of such knowledge to him. This stress on emotions, thoughts and feelings can be seen to be part of a romantic philosophy which was prevalent in the nineteenth century and whose epistemology involved the discovery of the natural and inner self.

The Romanticists probably come closest to the Idealist school of philosophy which holds that ultimate reality is spiritual in nature rather than physical, mental rather than material. Whilst not denying the existence of things in the "Real World" the idealists believe that these are part of a more fundamental incorporeal reality, although individual idealists, e.g. Plato and Kant, disagreed as to the nature of the ultimate reality and the relation of the spiritual being to that reality.

Idealist educators instil a closer intimacy between the person and the spiritual elements of nature. However, within the idealist tradition, different philosophers have produced different theories of knowledge. Thus for Plato, since the material world is only a distorted copy of a more perfect reality, the impressions which come *directly* via the senses must be uncertain and incomplete. True knowledge for Plato was the result of the process of reasoning, since this process transcends the material world and can discern pure spiritual reality. More modern idealists in the Kantian tradition maintain that knowledge is the imposition of meaning and order on sense impressions. This latter view of knowledge is held by many Progressivists but the goals of the two philosophies are distinct. For Idealists their aim is communion with the ultimate reality, the Progressivists, within the context of moral relativism, acknowledge no such ultimate goal.

Romantic ideology would seem to be supported by maturationist theories of psychological development, e.g. Freudian psycho-analytic theory and Gessellian maturational theory. While individual rates of development may be inborn, cognitive and emotional development is seen to depend on the unfolding of the biologically given although remaining vulnerable to fixation as in the Freudian sense, or frustration by the environment.

Rousseau in *Emile* made a plea for recognition that "Childhood had its own ways of seeing, thinking and feeling; nothing is more foolish than to try to substitute our ways". Accordingly we must "Hold childhood in reverence, watch him, study him constantly". A similar idea was expressed by Freud (1913) in *The Claims of Psycho-analysis to the Scientific Interest — the Educational Interest*; he said,

> Only someone who can feel his way into the minds of children can be capable of educating them and we grown up people cannot understand children because we no longer understand our childhood. (p.189)

Whilst the Progressivists and Romanticists are in agreement in their rejection of the cultural transmission approach, Progressivism is based on a different set of theoretical assumptions, both psychological and philosophical.

PROGRESSIVISM

John Dewey is usually cited as the founder of the Progressive School Movement. Two of his most quoted books are *Schools of Tomorrow* (1915) and *Experience and Education* (1938). Progressivism holds that education should nourish the person's natural *interaction* with a developing society or environment. Unlike Romantics they do not assume that development is an unfolding of an innate pattern or that the educational aim is the creation of a conflict-free environment in order to foster healthy development. They see development as a progression through ordered sequential stages and their educational goal is the eventual attainment by the child of a higher level or stage of development in adulthood.

In 1895 Dewey and McLellan said,

> Education is the work of supplying the conditions which will enable the psychical functions as they successively arise to mature and pass into higher functions in the freest and fullest manner.

Thus the educational environment for the Progressivists should be one which actively stimulates development through the presentation of a milieu in which the organizing and developing force in the person's experience is *the person's active thinking*. Thinking is stimulated by cognitive conflict. Like the cultural transmission theorists, they emphasize knowledge as opposed to feelings and experience but they see the acquisition of knowledge as an act of change in the pattern of thinking brought about by *experiential* problem solving situations. The Progressivists view morals, values and the nature of knowledge to be in constant change.

Progressivism in its pure form declares that education is always in the process of development. Education is not a preparation for living but it should be life itself. Like Rousseau, Dewey and his followers maintained that learning should be directly related to the interests of the person; motivation to learn should come from within the person rather than knowledge should be imposed upon him. The teacher is seen more as a guide or adviser in a process whereby the person reconstructs the subject matter in accordance with its perceived relevance to his own life. Learning should take place through problem solving rather than the inculcating of subject matter. Knowledge itself is seen as "a tool for managing experience"; as Dewey said, "Men have to do something to the things when they wish to find out something" (1916). For knowledge to be significant one has to do something with it and hence it must be linked to experience. For the Progressivists, education is not limited to a recollection of information obtained from the teacher or a textbook, it involves "perpetual grappling" with the subject matter. In this sense, grappling is not only the physical handling of material, but it involves the critical thinking process of reconstruction of previous ideas and discovery.

The teaching method upheld by Progressivism encourages student–student interaction as well as student–teacher interaction. The teacher is interested in students developing their own criteria regarding the quality and relevance of ideas and he allows this to develop by minimizing his role as an arbiter of what is acceptable. His aim is not the transmission of "nuggets", but rather the facilitation of the process of "learning how to learn".

The particular philosophy aligned with Progressivism is that of Pragmatism. It is mainly a twentieth century philosophy which has grown out of the British empircist tradition which maintains that we know only what our senses experience. A basic principle of Pragmatism is that the world is neither dependent on nor independent of man's idea of it. Reality is the *interaction* of the human being with his environment; it is the sum total of what we *experience*. The emphasis is on an *active* man reaching out to make sense of his universe by engaging in the reconstruction and interpretation of his *own* experiences. Pragmatists agree that knowledge is produced by *transaction* between man and his environment and that truth is a property of knowledge, but they disagree as to what can be defined as truth. William James maintained that an idea is true if it has a favourable consequence for the person who holds it. On the other hand, Dewey insisted that an idea was true only if it had a satisfactory consequence when objectively and if possible scientifically tested. Most would agree, however, that the core of universal ideas are redefined and reorganized as their implications are played out in experience and as they are confronted by their opposites in argument.

Psychological theories which support these ideas are those which discard the dichotomy between maturation and environmental determinism in learning. For example, Piaget claims that mature thought emerges through a process of development that is neither direct biological maturation nor direct environmental pressure, but a reorganization of psychological structures resulting from organism-environment interactions. Cognitions are seen as internally organized wholes or systems of internal relations through which events in the person's experience are organized. For Piaget the processes of "accommodation" and "assimilation" are not passive processes which can result from a programme of reinforcement. Such a programme would only change the person's behaviour and cognitive structure if it was assimilated by the person in terms of his present mode of thinking. For Piaget the teacher's role is to facilitate movement to the next stage of development by exposure to the next higher level of thought and conflict requiring active application of current thoughts to problematic situations.

Jerome Bruner (1966) also pointed to the necessity for the learner to relate new material to relevant ideas already established in his cognitive structure, for him to apprehend in what ways it is similar to and different from related concepts and to translate it into a personal frame of reference, consonant with his idiosyncratic experience.

The "symbolic interactionists" maintain that in a fundamental sense the "self" is a product of a person's interaction with others. A person's self-concept develops in relation to reactions of other people to that person and he tends to react to himself as he perceives other people reacting to him (Cooley, 1964, pp.168–210). This view has been extended by G. H. Mead and role theorists who recognize that the self in a social structure is that which arises through communication. By anticipating the other's reaction to him and his reaction to the other's reaction, a person is able to examine and evaluate several possible courses of action and choose a particular course. A person's behaviour is seen to be influenced by such interactions, not based upon the action of the other *per se* but on the meaning which the person assigns to the other's acts. Thus individual action and development is seen to be constructed in relation to the other, and not simply determined by, outside forces or evoked by internal impulses.

Whether the psychological theories are emphasizing cognitive development, as in the case of Piaget, or social development as in the case of role theorists, the emphasis is on interaction with the environment. These theories are in accordance with Progressivism which sees education as an interaction process rather than as a totally child-centred process as in the case of the romantics, or society-centred promoting the discipline of social order as seen by the cultural transmission theorists.

DE-SCHOOLING

The last three sets of philosophical and psychological assumptions represent perhaps the three main streams of development of Western educational ideology; however, it is necessary to mention a fourth emerging stream — namely De-schooling. Rousseau and Stanley-Hall both argued that the inculcation of knowledge could be harmful to the student. Ivan Illich (1971), who is perhaps one of the best known de-schoolers, has pointed out that, in his opinion, most of the really important and useful things learnt are learned outside the classroom, i.e. from friends or from interested others. They seldom learn such things from certificated teachers or under the process of compulsion. He recommends abolishing the school as a unit and reorganizing learning by bringing together, within a given area, those who want to teach and those who want to learn. There already exists in the Parkway Programme in Philadelphia a model along the lines Illich suggests. It is known as the "School without walls". Staff make arrangements with pupils to meet them for sessions in museums, factories, libraries or in their homes. The school is in fact the whole city of Philadelphia. A further example can be found in Great Britain at Stantonbury Campus where for one day in twenty the formal curriculum is abandoned in favour of group activities, selected by choice of staff and students, who meet with a common desire to learn.

Illich is not alone in his attack on education as we know it today, although few would go so far as total demolition of schools. Charles E. Silberman in *Crisis in the Classroom* (1971) claims that the school has been given too much credit as an agent of social change. The future school for Silberman is one in which the rights of children are observed, where learning methods are varied, where children can work and are expected to work on their own, at their own pace and at work of their own choosing. It is to be an institution which can offer children advantages which their locality may lack and also one in which the leaving age is open ended, since this is to be a school for the whole community where children and adults of all ages may come and go as they please. There are already prototypes of this type of school that may be more frequent in the future.

The "free school" of Liverpool is one where attendance is voluntary. In the private sector of British education, A. S. Neill's Summerhill and Dartington Hall are examples of schools based on revolutionary philosophies of education. Countesthorpe College is a state school which has recently become a symbol for radicalism in English secondary education. Many of its procedures have evolved from current practice in primary schools in Leicestershire, notably the "integrated day". Much of its theoretical basis was drawn from the Nuffield Resources for Learning

Project. The project director, L. C. Taylor, in *Resources for Learning* (1971), put forward the "Resources" viewpoint:

> If the school is at all frequently to be the arena for personal exploration and significant experience, then its teaching and timetabling practices will need radical overhaul. (p.21)

Countesthorpe has taken up the gauntlet with a purpose-built circular educational complex where students in the 14–18 age group make use of the resource media available, whilst also providing a "youth and general social area" containing a crèche for local mothers and the use of the resources for other members of the community. Stantonbury Campus, at Milton Keynes, is another state-financed "community" school with a different style to Countesthorpe but, in its way, revolutionary. The Stantonbury experience is described in an Open University publication supporting the university's course on curriculum development. One of the authors of the present work (Keen) was previously employed as a Deputy Head of the Campus.

This accent on the rejection of the typical territorial definitions found in conventional schools and colleges is found in the current educational ideology of those seeking alternative education. Recent works on this topic include Everett Reimer's *School is Dead*; John Holt's *How Children Fail*; Paul Goodman's *Compulsory Miseducation* and Neil Postman and Charles Weingartner's *Teaching as a Subversive Activity*. The majority of these theorists will acknowledge the attempts of progressivists to initiate active enquiry on behalf of the learner but they feel that the pedagogy that has resulted still leaves a lot to be desired. Postman and Weingartner (1971) make this point very forcibly in a chapter headed "Pursuing Relevance" in their book *Teaching as a Subversive Activity*. Thus they write,

> There is no way to help a learner to be disciplined, active and thoroughly engaged unless *he* perceives a problem to be a problem, or whatever is to be learned to be worth learning. It is sterile and ridiculous to attempt to release the enquiry power of students by initiating studies that hold no interest for them. (p.59)

Much of the thought expressed in the above mentioned works is reminiscent of existentialist philosophy. Existentialists reject the traditional view that philosophy should become detached. They say that philosophy should be reason informed by passion because it is in passion and in states of heightened feeling that ultimate realities are disclosed. They reject the notion of the "Natural development of man". In his book *Existentialism* Jean-Paul Sartre (1947) said,

> Not only is man what he conceives himself to be, but he is also what he wills himself to be after this thrust towards existence. Man is nothing other than what he makes himself. (p.18)

For the existentialists, man has responsibility for his own being. What he becomes is of his own choosing and his freedom in his potential for action. A person must act according to his strongest feelings and be prepared to take the consequences which will result from his actions. Knowledge is essentially phenomenological — a person's knowledge depends on *his* understanding of reality.

For the existentialist it is not sufficient that a body of knowledge from a textbook or given out by the teacher is accepted unquestioning by the student. The student must find them true for himself. He must be able to incorporate them within his view of the world. In *Between Man and Man* Martin Buber (1965) wrote about what he believed to be the tyranny of impersonal knowledge. For him teaching should be a true dialogue in which the teacher is not simply a mediator between the student and the subject matter. Rather than become a means for the transmission of knowledge, the teacher should offer knowledge, i.e. he must familiarize himself fully with the subject he teaches so that this subject becomes part of his own inner experience which he can then present to the student as something issuing from himself. The teacher and student can then meet as persons as the offered knowledge is not alienated from the teacher's real world of feeling. The student may reject or accept the teacher's interpretation of the subject matter, the responsibility is his. The aim of the teacher should be the establishment of an atmosphere of mutual trust in which the teacher sees the student not as a category or in evaluative terms, e.g. as in "bright" or "dull", but as a person.

Many existentialists, Buber included, would maintain that as it now stands the school is a powerful reinforcer of alienation in modern society.

Some psychologists share this concern with alienation and failure of real communication between people. In addition they regret the lack of emphasis on the person and his "view of the world" which is seen in some psychological theories of development — in particular those of the behaviourist and neo-behaviourist schools. Harry Stack Sullivan, R. Laing, D. Bateson and Carl Rogers have all been influential in raising the interpersonal encounter as an important topic within psychology. The writings of Laing and Rogers in particular lay great stress on personal experience as the origin of action. Their views on personality, psychological development and methodological issues in psychology bear a great resemblance to the thinking of existential philosophers. R. D. Laing is quite specific in his connections with the works of Heidegger, Jean-Paul Sartre, Merleau-Ponty, Friedrich Nietzche and Soren Kierkegaard. Thus in his book *The Politics of Experience*, R. D. Laing is talking about personal experience:

> It is tempting and facile to regard "persons" as only separate objects in space, who can be studied as other natural objects can be studied . . . . one will never find persons by studying persons as though they were only objects. (p.20)

Carl Rogers in *On Becoming a Person* (1961) and *Freedom to Learn* (1969) takes up this perspective of the personal with specific reference to the learning situation. Rogers differentiates between two processes in learning: *teacher-based* (the traditional cultural transmission approach) and *learner-based* learning.

Learner-based learning is self-initiated, has a quality of personal involvement and is evaluated by the learner, i.e. he knows whether or not it is meeting his needs. This significant learning is pervasive, i.e. it makes a difference in behaviour, attitudes and personality of the learner, and its essence is meaning. The knowledge/truth that evolves in self-discovered learning is "private" knowledge — truth that has been personally appropriated and assimilated in experience. According to Rogers this "personal" knowledge cannot be directly transmitted from the teacher to the student. This is not to say that the "public knowledge" or facts, ideas, etc., that the teacher is trying to impart can never become personal knowledge. What Rogers is saying is that the process is not one of direct impersonal association between the issues to be learnt (stimuli) and knowledge of them (response). If the public knowledge to be imparted is personally appropriated by the learner and has significant influence on his behaviour and attitudes, then public knowledge becomes personal knowledge. Whilst distinguishing between the two processes, Rogers makes a value judgment that personal knowledge should be the aim of the educational process. For Rogers, personal knowledge is facilitated by a specific type of interpersonal encounter between the teacher and student.

The encounter he advocates is similar to that found in the client-centred, non-directive therapeutic process that Rogers uses in his psycho-therapy. A main feature of this encounter is the quality of regard one for the other. The teacher needs to have regard for what the individual student is, i.e. independent of his ability, interests, social class etc. Labels should be abandoned. Only within the context of unconditional acceptance may students feel free to express the best and most creative aspects instead of the regurgitation of imposed knowledge. This type of interpersonal encounter does not necessitate sentimentality or *laissez-faire* attitudes within the school, rather it encourages self-directed discipline and the setting of students' limits rather than the imposition of rules.

In summarizing the emerging ideology of de-schooling, several points are worth noting. Firstly, its proponents vary in their aims — on one hand we have Illich, who advocates total demolition, and on the other Postman, who is aiming for a revolution within the system which can allow for relevant education which will facilitate the growth of "strategies for survival" and ability to cope with the ever-changing facets of our society. Secondly, there is the agreement that the cultural transmission approach is inappropriate to the needs of the person and modern society. Thirdly there is the acceptance of many of the principles put forward, for example by Rousseau and John Dewey. However, there is a rejection of the biological model found in much of the writings of the Romanticist. Whilst accepting the act of "questioning" and "learning by doing" approach of the Progressivist two main criticisms are put forward by the De-schoolers. One is the disproportionate emphasis on the structure of cognitive processes rather than on the meaning content. The other is that despite innovations within the educational system, the hierarchical power structure remains static. For the De-schooler "relevant" education will only take place within a framework in which the power structure barriers are broken down between staff and students and between the school and community at large.

THE PRACTICE OF THEORY

The De-schoolers argue that the "cultural transmission" view of knowledge with its teaching-learning situation as one of dominance and submission, still prevails. The teacher and the textbooks are seen as the prime sources of knowledge. In the main the "facts" are transmitted from the teacher to the student. Interaction between students is minimal. The "facts" (stimuli) are absorbed by the student and when an association has been made the desired response, i.e. reproduction of the facts, is obtained, learning is considered to have taken place. Proof of the learning is usually measured by an examination or test at a later date. In some situations the facts are rehearsed by the student in an endeavour to "hammer them home". However, this rote and drill method is in disrepute even within traditional schools.

The traditional teaching method is often referred to as expository presentation or "receptive" learning method, which emphasizes the student's role as the passive receiver of information rather than the active participant. Progress along the lines the teacher wishes is constantly monitored and shaped with a series of rewards (stars, classmarks, etc.) and punishments (lines, detention, etc.). A dominant idea is that students do not have sufficient self direction to work out educational programmes in collaboration with their teachers. The students have little or no control over the manner in which they are taught and the curriculum content — leadership is autocratic and non-participative (Lewin *et al.*, 1958). The essence of the traditional approach is the transmission of objective knowledge to a passive learner within a hierarchical structure. This can be seen in the following quote from an article in *Where* (September 1972) in which a Headmaster gives his view of what a school should be. He said,

> I believe that a school ought to be an autocratic institution, and that the Head should have virtually absolute powers . . . . the basic duty of schools is to

> induce literacy and numeracy . . . . I believe that the principle of "divide and rule" is a sign for education as for empires, and that to blur and confuse areas of study by "general" this and "integrated" that or "inter-disciplinary" the other only results in blurring the teacher and confusing the pupil. I believe solidly in examinations as the best test for pupils' competence.

This credo is the antithesis of the Romantics. Whilst it is true that the writings and methods of Froebel, Montessori and Neill have had some influence within the state system, especially in the primary school, their influence has been more readily accepted within sectors of private education. The late A. S. Neill (whose school Summerhill is an example of the Romantic ideal) in *That Dreadful School* wrote,

> Possibly the greatest discovery we have made in Summerhill is that a child is born a sincere creature. We set out to leave children alone so that we might discover what they were. (1937, p.17)

The aim of Summerhill is to provide for children an environment in which they are assured of love, understanding and freedom. Winnicott would probably refer to it as a "facilitating" environment. It is Neill's premise that if the emotions are permitted to be really free the intellect will look after itself. The imposition of learning interferes with happy growth. Thus no child is obliged to go to lessons. Dartington Hall school has an ethos similar to that of Summerhill. The school was founded in 1926 as an exploration in a liberal and experimental approach to co-educational schooling. Major features are its democratic process of decision-making, close staff/pupil relations and, absence of hierarchies and its efforts to reduce unnecessary pressures or external controls. Again, it seeks to provide an environment in which the personality of each child can develop fully and at its own pace unhindered by "distorting external pressures". The aim is the growth of emotional as well as intellectual aspects of the person. Dartington believes that fulfilment in education is best found in the context of freedom.

Assimilation of such ideas as, for example, the provision of a freer environment, and the need for emotional as well as intellectual growth has been slow within the State system. "Free expression" and "play methods" are fairly common within the nursery and infant schools but from junior school onwards the external pressures of examinations etc. take precedence.

The "activity" methods of the Progressivists have had somewhat greater impact. By 1920 there were already such experiments as the "Laboratory Plan" (Dalton, Massachusetts). The Dalton plan did not involve a change in curriculum or subject content but was a method of working. True to the "learning by doing" philosophy, Helen Parkhurst, the founder of the Dalton plan, wrote:

> The basic principle of the Dalton plan is that the pupil is made responsible for

> his own work and progress; he is made to feel that it is his own concern rather than the teacher's, that it is his own job, the success of which depends on his skill, initiative and industry. Having made him responsible for the job he must be allowed freedom to organise his work, his materials and his time (in short, his school life) and to secure whatever help from his teachers, his books etc., he finds necessary for the successful completion of his task. (p.139)

Tasks are set in a series of "assignments" in which the purpose, problems to solve, and the skills to acquire are set out. Some schools in England, for example Bryanston, use essentially the same principles as laid down by Helen Parkhurst. Project work and systems used in team-teaching resemble Dalton's "assignments". The "integrated day" and "vertical streaming" common in our primary schools today, bear a close likeness to the Dalton plan of the 1920s. The "inquiry method", "hypothetical mode of teaching", or "inferential learning" methods with their project work or assignments, has probably had a more lasting influence on the educational procedure in England than the efforts of the Romanticists, for example Montessori who saw Progressivism as letting each pupil learn what he wanted to learn when he wanted to learn it. Justification was by choice alone. The Progressivism of Dewey and Parkhurst is much more pragmatic; while allowing for active participation in the acquisition of knowledge and some choice of subject, the choice is not necessarily completely free.

In addition to its practical appeal, the Progressivists' notion of active learning receives support from psychological research. Piaget's work on the child's conception of number gives backing to the abolition of rote and learning of tables and replacement with number rods, active manipulation of water, sand etc., in containers and the use of various forms of charting. Bruner and Olver's (1963) research into concept formation in children has led to an appreciation that the structure of the child's conceptual system is different from that of the adult, thus the necessity for subject matter to be presented to the pupil in a way which will fit his particular stage of conceptual development. The rise of modern information theories, e.g. those of Miller *et al.* (1960) and attention theories, e.g. those of Sutherland (1964) and the recognition of such paradoxes as Partial Reinforcement and the Overlearning Reversal Effect within classical learning theory, has led to a paradigm shift (Kuhn, 1962) within the field of learning. The main emphasis of Piaget, Bruner and the experimental psychologists has been the structure of cognitive processes rather than the emotional components of learning, e.g. the teacher–student relationship. Today in our schools there is a growing trend towards the acceptance of many of the principles of Dewey-type Progressivism. Indeed one could say that in educational practice the dogmas of cultural transmission, selection at eleven and streaming within schools, are giving way to the dogmas of Progressivism, non-selection and non-streaming.

Dogmatism can be a major block to development in education. Much non-productive argument in education is due to the adoption of opposing dogmatic viewpoints — this method or theory is correct, therefore all others are wrong. G. Kelly's meta-theory (*see* Chapter 3) recognizes all theories as temporary constructions which should be abandoned when another theory leads to a better prediction of events. His theory acknowledges the importance of the personal theories which we all erect to explain events in our experience and predict future happenings. This recognition allows one to break down barriers in education and to recognize that for different people, with different purposes and faced with different circumstances to predict, alternative constructions regarding the nature of education, teaching and learning will evolve. Thus dogmatic ideologies could give way to a more flexible approach to education which recognizes the viability of these alternative constructions.

At the beginning of this section we commented that any attempt to categorize perspectives in education would no doubt do injustice to the great diversity of viewpoints that do exist. The trainer/teacher no doubt has his/her own "implicit personality theory" view of the nature of knowledge and perspective on pedagogical practice. The trainee or student will also have some views which should be explored. The exploration of the "cognitive models" of the learner would seem a very relevant area for educational research and thus the "perspective of the personal" has become more prevalent in recent educational research projects.

In educational research the issues to be raised and the methodologies adopted to pursue them have themselves undergone shifts in perspective which in many ways parallel the changes in viewpoints outlined in this chapter. A common theme amongst educators today is one of disillusionment with much of the educational research of the past. The relationship between psychology and education in particular is under attack. As J. B. Biggs (1976) puts it, "Let us face it: the frustratingly long honeymoon is over" (p.274).

The time is obviously ripe for a reappraisal of education research and the search for alternative strategies has become the concern of many researchers. Some of the problems are discussed in the next chapter.

2

Educational Research: the Future?

Review of past educational research would seem to indicate a similar paradigm shift as is witnessed within psychology. Emphasis on the use of I.Q. tests and attainment tests was once dominant as witnessed by the many tests published by the National Foundation for Educational Research. This emphasis was backed by the major psychological theories of the pre-1950 era — those who valued "observable data" (Behaviourism) or who adopted a biological orientation. Since the 1950s there has been a steady stream of research findings (mainly by sociologists and social psychologists) which have questioned the use of I.Q. and similar tests as means of selection between schools or placement within schools. Many writers have emphasized that inter and intra school grouping can be seen as methods for maintaining the *status quo* and are a reflection of the hierarchical structure of our society (Yates, 1966; Jackson, 1964).

In 1960 Goodlad wrote in the *Encyclopaedia of Educational Research*:

> Perhaps the most controversial issue of classroom organisation in recent years is whether or not students of like ability should be grouped together for educational purposes. (p.223)

However, despite many passionate statements about inter or intra school selection, a definitive answer on the question "to stream or not to stream" has not been found. A. H. Passow (1966) in reviewing *The Maze of Research on Ability Grouping* commented that,

> The quantity is great (dating back forty years or more), the quality is irregular and the result generally inconclusive . . . . (p.161)

A decade later that comment was still apt. For example, Barker-Lunn (1970) reported the study of a sample of 72 matched primary schools. It was shown that in one half of the sample pupils in non-streamed schools made better progress than pupils in streamed schools, whilst in the other matched half the reverse was the case. Barker-Lunn concluded that the differences must be due to some unknown factor and "it is possible that teachers' attitudes have something to do with it". Passow (1966) suggested that

> Most experiments were concerned solely with attainments in scholastic subjects. Little or no attention was given in most experiments to assessing the effects of grouping on other aspects of pupil growth — attitudes, interests or personal development. (pp.165–6)

Keen (1979) in his doctoral research found that mixed ability *common attitude* groups were more likely to demand common pedagogic styles. The arguments for and against ability grouping generally involve the effects of such practices on personal and social development, but the purposes of most experiments have excluded these behavioural areas and dealt primarily with academic achievement.

Educational researchers have tended to concentrate more on the student with little or no regard for the teacher, e.g. Marklund (1962) reported that pupils in small classes do not show marked superiority in attainment when compared with those in large classes. He has been criticized by teachers for overlooking the effects on them of having to teach large classes. This lack of regard for the teacher would seem misguided since it is becoming increasingly evident that the viewpoint of the teacher has considerable effect on the learning process. (Rosenthal and Jacobson, 1968; Barker-Lunn, 1970; Nash, 1973.) The perspective of the personal (Morris, 1972) is leading to an increase in the study of such factors as attitudes, social adjustment, friendship choices and perceptions of pupils and teachers. The failure of educational research to find a definitive answer to such questions as "to stream or not to stream" does not surprise one when one reflects that educational research has largely consisted of mass sampling techniques where certain variables, notably I.Q. or social class, of a sample have been measured and related to performance under such "controlled" environments as selective or comprehensive schools or streamed versus non-streamed classes. It is our belief that this emphasis on "the system" is bound to fail since the important factors are the viewpoints of the teacher, students and others concerned with the learning process within the system which are most relevant. We are observing and measuring the wrong things. As Biggs (1976) points out,

> There is a growing body of opinion that the existing technology of psychometrics is largely irrelevant to education; from the application of psychometric techniques of analysis to the construction of tests. (p.280)

He agrees with Snow (1974) who pinpointed the source of the problem in the fact that educational researchers have been obsessed for years by "systematic" research designs borrowed from agricultural research. In the last analysis it is the people within a particular school which will determine the outcome of education within it.

As Roy Nash (1973) points out, it is ironic that reliance upon group tests, questionnaires and mass sampling techniques has pushed educational psychology into the very area where these customary techniques can least adequately cope. He quotes Burstall (1970) who concluded that

> In a complex of factors determining a pupil's achievement, it must surely be recognised that the teacher's attitudes and expectations are of paramount importance. (p.11)

There are numerous pen and paper tests of teachers' values and attitudes, e.g. the Minnesota Teacher Attitude Inventory (1951) but these are open to several criticisms:

(a) They put the teacher in a test position which is at once a distorting influence. If people believe that they are being judged as good or bad on the basis of their responses it is easy for them to present a desirable picture of themselves.

(b) They tend to produce only global measures of such things as permissive teacher attitudes and may be limited indicators of actual classroom behaviour.

(c) The item content may be dated or indeed inappropriate for some groups of subjects.

There is growing dissatisfaction with research into teaching which has been based on inventories and attitude scales which use the experimenter's criteria, often without reference to the particular situation in which they are applied. Morrison and MacIntyre (1969) comment on the extensive diversity of criteria used to judge teacher effectiveness. Such criteria as teachers' knowledge of educational psychology, teachers' knowledge of methods of curriculum construction, teachers' knowledge of subject matter, teachers' intelligence, teachers' values, and teachers' emotional and social adjustment are amongst the criteria listed by the American Educational Research Association (1952). However, Morrison and MacIntyre (1969) point out that research into teaching has neglected the fascinating diversity of personal goals that teachers, pupils and others within the education system may hold. These criteria may be at odds with those of the experimenter "with his hat on" who enters as a stranger in the situation, and who is often seen as an agent of a controlling authority.

Barr *et al.* (1961), summarizing a massive amount of American research into teacher effectiveness, pointed out that

> There is plenty of evidence to indicate that different practitioners observing the same teacher teach, or studying data about her, may arrive at very different evaluations of her; this observation is equally true of the evaluation experts; starting with different approaches, and using different data gathering devices, they, too, arrive at very different evaluations. (p.150)

In more recent years attempts have been made to devise observation schedules which attempt to capture a more naturalistic appraisal of events in the classroom. One of the most widely used is the Flanders system aimed at systematically analysing the spontaneous verbal interaction between teachers and children. Such interaction analysis schedules are useful mainly in formal settings, for obtaining a description of events. However, they are less appropriate in more unstructured situations. The categories themselves are open to question since many of them are too broad, and there may be other dimensions which could have been included.

Hamilton and Delamont (1974) note that systematic observation schedules tend to focus on surface aspects of interaction and neglect underlying features which may have more meaning. Barnes *et al.* (1969) emphasized the need to consider the child's interpretation of a word or question used by the teacher. There may be a mismatch between this interpretation and the intended meaning of the teacher. The Flanders system has been criticized heavily by Adelman and Walker (1975) who comment:

> We do not consider that interaction analysis provides information appropriate or adequate for any but the most limited of educational ideologies. The system is 'virtually unusable in informal contexts'. (p.220)

The Ford Teaching project (Elliot and Adelman, 1973), an action research project aimed at monitoring the practices of 40 teachers in 14 East Anglian schools, is an interesting example of co-operation between teacher and researcher. The project emphasizes the need for teacher and researcher to jointly devise a research instrument appropriate for use in informal contexts. The terms used in this "conceptual map" were gradually refined and evaluated by the teachers with respect to its usefulness for describing their pedagogies. This project attempts to overcome the mismatch between the intended meaning of the actor and the interpretation of the recipient. Pupils, teachers and observers constantly feed back interpretations, so that misunderstandings and miscommunication are highlighted. By taking the pupils and teachers as full partners in the research enterprise the Ford Teaching project has developed an action-research methodology which many teachers have found useful for self-monitoring of inquiry/discovery pedagogy.

This recent emphasis on developing new forms of interaction analysis and micro-teaching has been welcomed by educationalists as an attempt to bring the locus of inquiry where it can have most effect. Wragg (1974) hopes that such techniques will accelerate the move towards active self-directed learning, both for teachers and pupils. But he warns

> To expect that the introduction of micro-teaching, interaction analysis, role-playing or simulation will of themselves vastly improve the quality of teaching, both within the institution and of the students being trained, would be akin to hoping that birthday toys would make an unhappy child

contented, irrespective of the relationships within his family. (p.193)

Human resources are of the utmost importance and, as Wragg points out, the student's own perceptions of the original lesson and his interpretation of sources of feedback will determine how he reteaches after a micro-teaching session.

There is then a growing emphasis on the person — a particular teacher or a particular student's opinions, attributes or decisions have become a prime focus of interest for those advocating education built on "humanistic" foundations.

Reidford (1972) comments on the dilemma facing those wishing to adopt a humanist approach to educational research. He maintains that educational research has been mostly worthless. The major preoccupation of educational researchers has been to test hypotheses which are highly likely to be confirmed. As Reidford points out, few educational research journals are interested in publishing studies whose results indicate that the hypothesis investigated has not been confirmed.

In education research the tendency has been the adoption of research strategies where prediction and control are paramount. The aim of such research has been to discover "laws" which can be generalized to other populations. A decade ago Bakan (1967) discussed the need to reconstruct psychological investigation. He argued that mastery via prediction and control and studied ignorance of the meanings of the subject's protocol language meant that the mystery of the psyche is not entered. He commented that "The mystery-mastery complex is the neurotic core of contemporary psychological research enterprise." (p.46)

If the aim of research is to discover laws, it assumes unchanging nature of those who are to be controlled. The scientist-subject distinction endows the scientist with autonomy, rationality etc. whilst denying the same processes in the "naive" subject. Bakan maintains that this approach inhibits understanding. The cultural norm is that research consists of the testing of pre-conceived hypotheses — as Bakan puts it, what a student needs is a "testable hypotheses, beg, borrow or steal". It is argued that researchers should be more open-minded as to the areas they investigate and the methodologies they use. Good research into the unknown cannot be well designed in the usual sense of the term.

Entwistle (1976) argues that the tight control of stimuli in traditional approaches to learning experiments has results in a tendency to trivialize human learning in order to discover fundamental general principles. However, the fundamental principles of stimulus-response learning may not be of much help to the teacher who is dealing with more complex learning issues. Entwistle suggests that conventional approaches to the study of learning have limited horizons and that alongside these conventional approaches we need to consider realistic complex human learning in more natural settings and this will necessitate unconventional research strategies.

The disruption of the scientist–subject distinction provides an alternative framework for research. In discussing his "conversational model" Mair (1970) suggests that

> As psychologists we seem to have an alarming tendency to transform important human characteristics into problems, weakness and sources of error. This largely seems due to a continuing, if often blurred, adherence to a view of science quite inappropriate to the subject matter we seek to understand. (p.182)

Educational research has largely based itself on a notion that if a sufficient number of relevant facts are assembled the laws governing these facts will reveal themselves. It is perhaps not surprising that this has been the dominant mode of research in education since it is predicated on the cultural transmission view of education discussed in Chapter 1, which has dominated Western educational thought. We indicated in Chapter 1 that there are alternate views on education and these viewpoints may need the invention of alternate methodologies. The current "perspective of the personal" adopted by many educators raises issues and problems which cannot adequately be tackled by the traditional empirical mode of inquiry (Nash, 1973).

There is now a growing body of British researchers who are developing alternate methodologies. A collection of recent developments is given in *Frontiers of Classroom Research* edited by Chanan and Delamont (1975), Sheldrake and Berry (1975) and Laurillard (1979). We suggest that George Kelly's theory and methodology form a coherent approach which is consistent with many of the current ideas on education. Despite this, relatively little use has been made within the educational sphere of the techniques he evolved.

However, since embarking on this book we have noticed that there has been a growing trickle of citations of Kelly's work within the educational journals. J. Britton (1976), discussing behaviour modification, says,

> There is in behaviour modification, that is to say, a method educators may use, but there is in it no ethic for the educational process. For my part, therefore, I would go with George Kelly whose methods are themselves exponents of the philosophy that provides the ethic. (p.3)

Educators are thus beginning to recognize potential application of a personal construct approach to education which may have significant impact on the educational research of the future. Biggs (1976) maintained that the honeymoon between psychology and education was over. We would suggest that the marriage between a psychology based on the idea of absolute truth and education is finished. However we argue that psychology based on personal construct theory offers a new relationship with education — one in which the views of those actually involved in the educational process are paramount and not subordinate to the elegance of experimental design. We explore this relationship in the next chapter.

3

Personal Construct Psychology in relation to Current Issues in Education

> Personal Construct Theory has also been categorised by responsible scholars as an emotional theory, a learning theory, a psycho-analytic theory (Freudian, Adlerian, and Jungian — all three), a typically American theory, a Marxist theory, a Humanistic theory, a logical positivistic theory, Zen Buddhistic theory, a Thomistic theory, a Behaviouristic theory, an Apollonian theory, a pragmatistic theory, a reflective theory, and no theory at all. It has also been classified as nonsense, which indeed, by its own admission, it will likely some day turn out to be. (Kelly, 1970a, p.10)

When discussing personal construct theory, Kelly himself took great delight in raising the ambiguity of categorical systems which sought to place his viewpoint within one framework or another. In this chapter we seek not to categorize Kelly's personal construct theory but to abstract aspects of Kelly's work which appear to us to have bearing on some of the issues raised in the preceding chapters. This abstraction represents, of course, our own perspective and preoccupations. We do not intend to cover in detail Kelly's theory nor do we seek to encapsulate it in the proverbial nutshell. The reader is referred to the writings of George Kelly, e.g. Kelly (1955, 1969a, b, 1970); Bannister (1970, 1977); Bannister and Fransella (1971); Bannister and Mair (1968) and Bonarius (1965) as a basis for his or her reconstruction of the extent and implications of personal construct psychology. Consideration will be given here to aspects of Kelly's work which may relate to the educational process.

PERSPECTIVE OF THE PERSONAL

Many writers on educational issues, e.g. Blumer (1966), Hargreaves (1972) and Morris (1972), have argued that it is time that recognition be given to the perspectives of the people engaged in classroom interaction. Blumer

(1966) writing on educational research, suggests that

> Since action is forged by the actor out of what he perceives, interprets and judges, one would have to . . . . take the role of the actor and see his world from his standpoint. (p.542)

This "perspective of the personal" is central to the work of George Kelly. It is implicit in the title of his theory — personal construct theory — and explicit in his writings, e.g. "We start with a person. Organisms, lower animals and societies can wait" (Kelly, 1970a, p.9) The fundamental postulate of personal construct theory, now more popularly called personal construct psychology (PCP), is that "a person's processes are psychologically channelised by the ways in which he anticipates events". For Kelly, man's behaviour is not driven by instincts (as in psycho-analytic theory) nor is it determined by the schedules of reinforcement and associations between stimulus and response (as in Skinnerian and Behaviourist theories). There have been many analogies used in psychology: man: the telephone exchange, man: the hydraulic system, and recently man: the computer. Kelly's analogy was man the scientist. Man the scientist and scientist the man are both engaged in a process of observation, interpretation, prediction and control. According to Kelly, each person erects for himself a representational model of the world which enables him to chart a course of behaviour in relation to it. This model is subject to change over time since constructions of reality are constantly tested out and modified to allow better predictions in the future. Thus for Kelly the questioning and exploring, revising and replacing in the light of predictive failure which is symptomatic of scientific theorising, is precisely what a person does in his attempts to anticipate events. The person can be seen as a scientist constantly experimenting with his definition of his existence. For Kelly man is himself "a form of motion" — thus he denies the necessity of "carrot and stick" or "impulse driven" theories of motivation. Man is constantly attempting to make sense of his environment and man's anticipation of future events is "both the push and pull of the psychology of Personal Constructs" (Kelly, 1955, p.49). Kelly does not deny the importance of early experiences or present environmental circumstances, but he suggested that it was more important to know what and how a person thinks about his present situation than to know what his early childhood experiences were or what environmental circumstances he now finds himself in.

The "Progressive" movement in education emphasizes the activity of the person struggling to impose meaning on his experiences and rejects the notion of a passive receiver of knowledge. The following quote from Berman and Roderick (1973) indicates some assumptions re curriculum which appear to us to be compatible with Kelly's viewpoint.

> Curriculum has long been thought of as that which is taught to somebody

> else . . . . The view of these writers is that curriculum must put the person at the centre of what is learned. Curriculum development and subsequent research on the curriculum will then see the person as the meaning maker and plan curricula experiences which enable the child to consider, contemplate, and expand his meanings. Critical to curriculum development, then, is the ascertaining of what is happening to the individual child as he interacts with persons, materials, time and space within the context of the school and the classroom. (p.3)

This emphasis on the person as the meaning-maker is central to Kelly's position. In order to understand a person's behaviour it is necessary to know how he construes his particular situation. Kelly argues that persons differ from each other in their construction of events (individuality corollary). Lambert *et al.* (1973) discussed the limits of structural analysis of the education system which has become prevalent in recent years. A major assumption of this approach is that the structural variables of a school are directly related to aspects of its pupils' society. In Chapter 2 we noted that research on the pros and cons of particular structural aspects of schools, e.g. streamed versus unstreamed, has produced contradictory findings. A Kellian viewpoint would reject social determinism — as Kelly said, "Societies can wait". Kelly would not presume that members undergoing a similar education system or belonging to particular groups would necessarily share the same system of construing. However, he did admit the possibility of shared areas of personal meaning and this was made explicit in his commonality corollary,

> To the extent that one person employs a construction of experience which is similar to that employed by another, his processes are psychologically similar to those of the other person. (Kelly, 1970a, p.20)

However, it is Kelly's stress on the personal nature of meaning and the elevation of the person to the central focus of inquiry that aligns him with much of contemporary theorizing on education.

RELEVANCE AND RESPONSIBILITY

In the section on De-schooling in Chapter 1, we postulated the viewpoints of theorists, e.g. Postman and Weingartner (1971) and Rogers (1969) who argue that it is important we realize that significant learning will only take place if the learner perceives personal relevance in the matter being learned. Thomas and Harri-Augstein (1977a) argue that,

> For education to be an enriching experience the meanings that emerge must become personal and they must be significant or important in some part of the person's life. .... the viability of the personality meanings attributed to each depends upon how richly the individual

incorporates them into his experience and tries them out in living. (p.9)

Berman and Roderick (1973) hold a similar viewpoint. In their discussion on curriculum development, they make the distinction between public knowledge, i.e. that which exists in books, films, museums etc., and personal knowledge. They suggest that

> It is only, however, when knowledge has meaning for the person so that he can take an idea and turn it to see its many facets that real learning has taken place. (p.8)

Kelly recognized learning as a personal exploration and saw the teacher's role as helping

> to design and implement each child's own undertakings . . . . To be a fully accredited participant in the experimental enterprise she must gain some sense of what is being seen through the child's eyes. (Kelly, 1970b, p.262)

What is relevant to the person is of importance and for education to be a joint venture between the teacher and learner it would be beneficial if each had some awareness of the other's personal constructs. As Kelly's sociality corollary states,

> To the extent that one person construes the construction process of another he may play a role in his social process involving the other person.

The perspective of the student as well as that of the teacher is important, although traditionally learning has been defined mainly from the latter's perspective (Jahoda and Thomas, 1965). For the existentialist the ultimate responsibility for learning rests with the student — man has responsibility for his own being. The existentialist rejects the notion of unquestioning acceptance by the student. The responsibility lies with him to incorporate public knowledge within his own view of the world. Knowledge should be part of a person's inner experience and is therefore emotional as well as intellectual. This point was stressed by Kelly in that, for him, the distinction usually made between cognition and affect was inappropriate.

Central to Kelly's theory is the notion that man may construe his environment in an infinite number of different ways depending on his imagination and the courageousness of his experimentation. Man is not stimulus-bound but he may well be bound by his construal of the world. "Man is nothing other than what he makes himself", which is a tenet of existentialist philosophy, could equally well be applied as a tenet of personal construct psychology. Kelly was perhaps somewhat reluctant to accept the label "existentialist". However, in his dislike of labels, his view of construing as having an emotional as well as cognitive base, his accent on freedom and responsibility of the individual and on relevance of events to the individual, he highlights areas of concern which are also of importance to the De-schoolers, many of whom are Existentialists. Kelly was no doubt correct in his warnings about the pernicious nature of categorization. For example, one can see that freedom, relevance and activity of the learner, which are inherent in Kelly's work, are also central issues for the Progressivists. So looking at Kelly's writings from these angles one could say he is aligned with the Progressivists. In whatever pigeon hole one tries to put him, however, relevance and responsibility are of prime concern.

RELATIVITY OF KNOWLEDGE

Kelly described his epistemological position as that of *Constructive alternativism*:

> Constructive Alternativism holds that man understands himself, his surroundings and his potentialities by divising constructions to place upon them and then testing the tentative utility of these constructions against such *ad interim* criteria as the successful prediction and control of events. (Kelly, 1966, p.1)

Whilst Kelly does not deny the existence of reality he maintains that it is presumptuous to claim that a person's constructions of reality are convergent with it:

> The fact that my only approach to reality is through offering some responsible construction of it does not discourage me from postulating that it is there. The open question for man is not whether reality exists or not but what he can make of it. (Kelly, 1969a, p.25)

For Kelly, events are subject to "As great a variety of constructions as our wits would enable us to contrive." (1970a, p.1). He rejected an absolutist view of truth and contrasted his position with that of *Accumulative fragmentalism* — the notion that knowledge is a growing collection of substantiated facts or "nuggets of truth". His philosophical position is opposed to that of the Realist (see Chapter 1). Even the most highly developed scientific knowledge can be seen to be subject to human reconstruction.

For Kelly the construction of reality is an active, creative, rational, emotional and pragmatic affair. Man the scientist evolves a set of constructions which he tests out and may ultimately discard in favour of a new set of constructions if the former fails to adequately anticipate events. Kelly pointed out that all theories are man-made hypotheses which may fit all the known facts at any particular time but may eventually be found wanting in some unforeseeable respect and be eventually replaced by a "better theory". An example from physics is the reappraisal of Newton's theory by Einstein. However, Einstein's theory is not the ultimate truth and Einstein himself regarded his theory as defective and spent much of his life trying to find a better one. In putting forward his theory, Kelly suggested that as a theory it would be subject to revision since it is itself an example of a human construct and so can be seen as an hypothesis waiting to be put to the test.

This view of theory, science and knowledge is echoed in the writings of Karl Popper (1963). He sees science and knowledge as progressing through a series of "conjectures and refutations". Kuhn (1970) analyses the progress of science and suggests that growth of knowledge occurs when the dominant paradigm of the day is challenged by the revolutionaries who step outside the limits of present theory and engage in what Kuhn calls "extraordinary science". Kuhn suggests that professional scientists are educated in the "normal" scientific mode which involves solving problems within the limits of the theory the scientist has been taught. The theory itself is not questioned. If problems are not solved the theory is not invalidated, the scientist merely lacks ingenuity! Popper (1970), in reply to Kuhn, suggests that normal science in Kuhn's sense does exist but it is the activity of the non-revolutionary, the none too critical professional, the student who accepts the dogma of the day. In discussing Popper's philosophy of science Magee argues that it could

> Scarcely be more undogmatic . . . . it holds that we never actually *know* — that our approach to any and every situation or problem needs to be always such as to accommodate not merely unforeseeable contributions but the permanent possibility of a radical transformation of the whole conceptual scheme. A great deal of disillusionment with science and reason which is so widespread in our age is based on precisely such mistaken notions of what science and reason are. (Magee, 1973, p.68)

Kuhn and Popper, like Kelly, are both arguing for the relative nature of knowledge. In recent years this relativity of knowledge has become a major concern of educationalists and sociologists in particular. Postman and Weingartner (1971) take up this point:

> We now know that each man creates his own unique world, that he, and he alone, generates whatever reality he can ever know. . . . . The purposes and assumptions and, therefore, the perceptions of each man are uniquely his . . . . Among other things, this means that no man can be absolutely certain of anything. The best anyone can ever do is say how something appears to him. (p.100)

These words echo the view of knowledge put forward by Kelly and could be seen to be a re-statement of his fundamental postulate and individuality corollary. Recent views on the sociology of knowledge emphasize man's active construction of experience and offer a clear challenge to the static, analytic conception of knowledge. The social phenomenology of Schutz (1967) has been most influential in this respect. Schutz suggests that action is mediated by a complex interpretational process within the constituted biography of the individual. Reality is interpreted in terms of the provinces of meaning which make up the individual's "stock of knowledge", which is his *Lebensfelt*. This stock of knowledge seems similar to Kelly's view of a construct system — it is continually changing through the processes of constitution and accommodation in the same way as validation and invalidation lead to elaboration and reorganization in a person's construct system. Schutz, however, emphasizes that the individual's "frame of reference" is a social product in that confirmation or disconfirmation of it is likely to come from his "consociates" — those with whom the individual has most social contact — with whom he is jointly engaged in reality-construction. This emphasis on the social nature of reality construction is the point at which Kelly and Schutz's ideas diverge. However, as Holland (1970, p.131) points out, Schutz's language bears an uncanny resemblance to personal construct psychology. He gives, as an example, "The individual's commonsense knowledge of the world is a system of constructs of its typicality" (Schutz, 1953).

The writings of Schutz and Berger and Luckmann (1967) have had significant effect on assumptions regarding the sociology of education. As Esland (1971) points out,

> If knowledge is dereified, it is, then, a much more negotiable commodity between teacher and pupil . . . . There is no reason to suppose that these will remain within the "boundaries" of what are now heuristically labelled as "subjects". New configurations of knowledge are likely to emerge from the combinations of questions which arise in the learning situations . . . . the boundaries are only human constructs and can, therefore, be broken. (p.96)

The similarities between this position and that of Kelly's is most apparent when we compare it with Kelly's view of the relativity of categorization — "subjects" being a case in point — and his view of teaching and learning as a process of negotiation between the joint experimenters in the venture, i.e. the student and teacher.

In recent years the area of curriculum development has become a focus of attention in education. Issues such as the relativity of knowledge and the recognition of the importance of the learner's, as well as the teacher's perspective have had a profound influence. Those advocating humanistic foundations of education suggest that we should recognize that learning is more than an intellectual exercise. Joyce (1972) suggests that curriculum planners have increasingly become servants to a system, largely impersonal in nature, which serves primarily to teach children the technological culture and to fit them into the economic and status system of a monolithic society. Joyce suggests that the curriculum should become pluralistic and should represent many domains of possible development. Attention should be paid to the creative and performing arts, education for greater interpersonal sensitivity and affairs of international concern. A goal of curriculum planning should be

> To create environments which enable individuals to actualise themselves on their own terms — emotionally, intellectually, and socially. (Joyce, 1972, p.169)

Postman and Weingartner (1971) made the point that change is occurring so rapidly that we can no longer foresee the information that would be necessary for a student to have in order to be successful in his world. It is for this reason education curriculum should include helping students to deal with change — the teaching of strategies for survival. They suggest that it is of vital importance that the teacher act as a facilitator of discussion, a resource for finding information and a stimulator of problem solving. We live in an increasingly complex and uncertain world marked by accelerating technological and social change. It is suggested that educational procedures developed during an era of relative stability and certainty are no longer able to provide the student with the skills he needs to exist effectively in contemporary society. It is for this reason Schroder *et al.* (1973) suggest that an emphasis on process goals rather than exclusively on content goals of education is needed. Diversity of strategy should be encouraged. Jordan (1973) commented

> How to learn is in itself something that has to be learned, though is rarely "taught" in traditional schools . . . . the development of learning competence enables the child to become an active determiner of his own destiny and gives him the fundamental power of extending and releasing all other potentialities. (p.87)

Jordan was putting forward a critique of American education but his comments could equally be applied to this country. Emphasis on "learning-to-learn" is not yet widespread in our schools and colleges although N.F.E.R. are currently investigating this area. Thomas and Harri-Augstein (1977b) have made significant contribution to this area by researching and developing methodologies for allowing an individual to become aware of his learning processes — in particular processes involved in reading, writing, discussing and listening. Thomas and Harri-Augstein's theoretical debt to George Kelly is well documented (Thomas, 1977).

Concomitant with the growing awareness of the need to extend curriculum to incorporate the notion of relativity of knowledge and to provide a medium through which personal strategies can be evolved, there is a growing emphasis on the need to reappraise educational research methodology.

RECONSTRUCTION OF EDUCATIONAL RESEARCH

In Chapter 2 we sketched the disillusionment felt by many educators with the traditional emphasis on psychometric and nomothetic studies found in educational research. With the emphasis on personal knowledge in emergent curricula, these research methods become inappropriate. Berman and Roderick (1973) suggest that these research methodologies are congruent with principles inherent in what they call *reactive* curricular frameworks, and suggest that if one recognizes the role of the emerging objectives of the student in relation to the curriculum, one must entertain studies that have been predicated on a conceptual framework that suggests a carefully delineated in-depth study of what happens to individuals in terms of processes as they interact with the components of their environment. Blumer (1966) criticizes traditional educational research for its viewing of the actor from the perspective of an outside detached observer. What is needed is a methodology which allows the person to elaborate on his personal meaning of events.

These concerns were central to Kelly's views on research and led to the development of his repertory grid techniques which will be discussed in detail in later chapters. Kelly was quite clear in his antagonism towards a psychology which sees man as reactive rather than constructivist:

> A psychology that pins its anticipations on the repetitions of events it calls "stimuli", or on the concatenations of events it calls "reinforcements", can scarcely hope to survive as man's audacities multiply. (Kelly, 1969a, p.31)

If one adopts a construct theory approach to research, one rejects the assumption that "laws of nature" will eventually evolve after a collection of an enormous amount of data. As Bannister and Fransella (1971) point out,

> Construct theory does not argue simply that it would be very difficult to fathom the nature of man in practice — most psychologists would admit that. It argues that it is a meaningless ideal, since the nature of individual men and of mankind is evolving and therefore can never finally be explained by any theory. (p.190)

This clearly sets a personal construct theory approach to research in opposition to those who hold that through large scale nomothetic studies one will determine the "nature of the beast". It does however lend itself to support the methodology of the individual case (Chapman, 1974, pp.5–21). Kelly's viewpoint is clearly in line with arguments put forward for example by Bakan outlined in Chapter 2 of this book, who argues against a rigid subject experimenter boundary. Kelly saw research as a co-operative enterprise. He urged his students

> Not to overlook what their subjects have to contribute, for psychological research, as I see it, is a co-operative enterprise in which the subject joins the psychologist in making an enquiry. I am very sceptical of any piece of human research in which the subjects, questions and contributions have not been elicited or have been ignored in the final analysis of results. (Kelly, 1969b, p.132)

Kelly acknowledged that many of his views were similar to those who put forward a plea for a humanistic approach to psychology. However, he suggested that much of what passed for humanism was "backward-wishing" rather than "forward-seeking". He suggested that it would be a mistake for those who wished to depart from the dehumanizing tradition of psychological research to abandon technology. He suggested that humanistic psychology should devise appropriate technologies to realise its objectives: "humanistic psychology needs a technology through which to express its humane intentions" (Kelly, 1969b, p.135). This statement is, we feel, of great significance for psychology. There has been a tendency to divide psychology into "hard" and "soft" psychology, hard psychology implying rigorous experimental procedures requiring rigorous statistics for the analysis of the data. Soft psychology, on the other hand, recognizing the individuality of the person, often adopts the extreme position of rejecting any systematic attempt to explore this individuality. Kelly's theory and methodology offers a bridge between these divisions which are in themselves arbitrary. Hudson (1968) notes the attractiveness of work such as that of Kelly in this respect: "It frees the experimenter from the rival hegemonies of the billiard ball and putty". (p.84)

In Chapter 1 we discussed the relationships between particular assumptions of psychological development and philosophies of the nature of knowledge and suggested that these assumptions play a part in determining pedagogic practice in schools and colleges. In addition, these assumptions provide a framework for educational research. The work of George Kelly would seem to offer both a theory and a methodology based on an epistemological position which would support much of the current emphasis in education on personal relevance and endeavour, relativity of knowledge, expansion of the curriculum and extension of the objectives of educational research. Salmon and Bannister (1974) advocate a similar position and suggest that education could be reappraised "in the light of personal construct theory".

However, despite the fact that Kelly's theory and methodology form a coherent approach which is consistent with many of the current ideas on education, relatively little use has been made within the educational sphere, of the techniques he evolved.

It is Kelly's philosophy of constructive alternativism that we feel is of greatest interest for the educationalist. If one adopts this philosophy one can provide an adaptive educational system which assumes many ways of succeeding and multiple goals from which to choose. An educational system in which individual learning styles are important and educational research is predicated on the individual's perspective. Constructive alternativism invites innovation and rejects dogma. As Allport (1955) suggested: "Dogmatism makes for scientific anaemia" (p.18). Rather than be bound by the "tyranny of fact" and tradition, a personal construct approach to education would suggest a forward thrust towards recognition of constructive alternatives in education.

Part Two

Having looked at many of the differing educational ideologies in Chapter 1, and related these to psychological and educational research in Chapter 2, we directed our attention to personal construct psychology in Chapter 3. We indicated that personal construct psychology would embrace the different ideologies outlined in Chapter 1 and view them as alternative constructions of reality in relation to education.

In this section we shall turn our attention to repertory grid methods, which have their roots in personal construct psychology. In Chapter 4 we discuss the grid in general terms in order to assist the reader in deciding if he wants to use a repertory grid based methodology and to alert him to some issues which he ought to consider. In Chapter 5 we indicate how he might go about the task of collecting and analysing such data.

Some readers may find parts of Chapter 6 outside their range of interest and the mathematical issues discussed in relation to principal component analysis may be difficult to grasp. We suggest that those not interested in the mathematical issues may prefer to omit this section.

However, we have deliberately avoided lengthy academic debates, which the interested reader may pursue via the references, and instead we have focused on practical considerations of the strengths, weaknesses and problems associated with the use of the repertory grid.

4

Practical Considerations in the use of Repertory Grid Techniques

Repertory grid techniques evolved from Kelly's personal construct theory (1955). Kelly's original technique was the role construct repertory test which he used to investigate the role relationships between patients and their families, friends, etc. and for assessing the relationships between a patient's constructs about people. The repertory grid, however, is not a test but a methodology involving highly flexible techniques and variable application. Although in the past its main use has been to investigate constructs about people, there is no theoretical reason why the elements of grids should not include inanimate objects or even abstract ideas. Indeed Bannister and Mair (1968) and Fransella and Bannister (1977) summarized many of the forms and applications of repertory grid techniques which have developed beyond Kelly's own approach. The papers included in this work also bear witness to the variety of types of elements used in repertory grids at the present time.

The procedure has its theoretical roots in Kelly's definition of a construct: "In its minimum context is a way in which two elements are similar and contrast with the third" (Kelly, 1955, p.61). The notion of contrast has been emphasized by Fransella and Bannister (1977) who write:

> When we say that Bill Bloggs is honest, we are not saying that Bill Bloggs is *honest*, he is not a chrysanthemum or a battle-ship or the square root of minus one. We are saying that Bill Bloggs is honest, he is not a crook". (p.5)

A construct is a dimension which may evolve when considering a particular set of elements but can usually be applied to a further range of elements. The dimensionality of a construct allows one to extract matrices of inter-relationships between constructs and between elements.

For Kelly, constructs do not exist in isolation. Indeed his organization corollary makes explicit his view that constructs are linked with each other in a more or less coherent and hierarchical manner. The organization of constructs at any particular moment in time exerts a limit beyond which it is impossible for a person to perceive, and thus the organization of the constructs has a controlling influence on behaviour. Kelly noted the importance of eliciting more than one construct or dimension. Thus he wrote:

> An event seen only in terms of its placement on one dimension is scarcely more than mere datum. And about all you can do with a datum is just let it sit on its own continuum. But as an event finds its place in terms of many dimensions of consideration, it develops psychological character and uniqueness. (Kelly, 1969, p.118)

Many organizations are now adopting the repertory grid as a means of entering the phenomenological world of an individual by exploring the nature and inter-relationships between various elements and constructs elicited by the method. However, since there is no such creature as "The Grid", it is necessary to make certain methodological decisions *vis-à-vis* the format of a grid for any particular project. Five major considerations will be discussed at this point:

(1) Purpose.
(2) Choice of elements and constructs.
(3) Scaling.
(4) Elicitation procedure.
(5) Method of analysis.

PURPOSE

The "purpose" of the grid is a most important preliminary consideration before the process of eliciting elements can begin. Purpose has at least two aspects:

(a) What is the topic to be investigated?
(b) What is the intended use of the grid information?

The negotiation of these issues is a crucial aspect of any grid conversation and requires more care than is usually recognized by the new user.

What is the Topic to be Investigated?

Since the elements in a grid should be representative of the problem area to be explored, it is essential that adequate time is given to a discussion of this aspect of purpose. Even in situations where elements and constructs are provided rather than elicited this is an important consideration. The elements in a provided grid should be representative of the "universe of discourse" which is central to the problem area and similarly provided constructs should be dimensions which are appropriate to the particular purpose. Take for example an organization interested in collecting information on the personal constructs used in appraisal. One could say to the person who is to complete the grid, "the purpose of the exercise is to explore your views of people". However, a free exploration of the person's views of people in general may not be what is required. If the purpose is to obtain the person's views of subordinates and others which he may have to appraise in the course of his work, then this must be clearly understood and an appropriate set of elements elicited/provided which contains such people and omits others such as his wife, mother-in-law, friend from the golf club, etc. Similarly, the constructs elicited could vary dependent on the initial discussions of purpose. Once again, if the purpose was to allow the individual to express any of the constructs he might have about subordinates, this should be discussed. However, if the purpose is to explore the type of constructs the individual brings to bear when he is appraising his subordinates from the point of view of the adequacy of their performance in various activities at work, then this more specific purpose should be conveyed. In this way constructs such as "*plays a good game of tennis/lousy on the tennis court*" may well be excluded — unless of course the person truly felt such a construct was relevant when appraising his subordinates' activites at work! The art of conversational elicitation of elements and constructs is to help the participant to focus his attention on those aspects of his thoughts and feelings which are relevant to the purpose, without putting ideas or feelings into the participant's mouth. A clear negotiation and definition of purpose is therefore a very necessary first step and one which has an effect on the types of elements and constructs chosen, an issue which will be referred to again.

What is the Intended Use of the Grid Information?

This second aspect of purpose also has an impact on the format and procedure of grid elicitation. Examples of different uses of the grid, although not mutually exclusive, would be:

(i) a conversation with one's self;
(ii) gathering of information about an individual's views on a particular topic;
(iii) a comparison of the viewpoints of two people in terms of either:
 (a) degree of agreement between them, or
 (b) the degree to which either can gauge the other's point of view;
(iv) an exploration of the nature and sharing of construing within a group;
(v) a monitoring of changes in perspectives.

Each of these purposes calls for a slightly different approach. If, for example, the purpose of the grid exercise was for an individual to explore his or her own views about a particular topic area and these views were not necessarily to be transmitted to any other individual, it may not be necessary to have anyone eliciting the grid from this individual. For example, the PEGASUS and DYAD computer programs allow an individual to sit down at a computer terminal and go through a grid elicitation privately (see pp.57–63). In these instances, the individual can choose how explicit he wishes to be in naming the poles of his constructs and also the label identification of his elements.

Since the object of this exercise is that the process of grid elicitation allows the individual an opportunity to explore his views and thus raise his self-awareness, the information contained in the grid is for his or herself alone. If, on the other hand, the purpose of the grid elicitation is to gather information and come to some understanding of the views of an individual, an interactive and conversational approach is necessary. The person eliciting the grid must ensure that, as far as is possible, the intended meaning of a construct or an element has been understood. Although a person may from time to time have some difficulty in articulating a particular construct, the individual should be encouraged to write as clear a description as possible in order that a person reading the construct can gain a degree of understanding or, as in the case of (iii) above, another person could attempt to use the construct. This is also important when the individual is required to use the same construct and elements on different occasions over a period of time, as in (v) above. Similarly, if one takes the case of (iv) above, when one wishes to explore how different people within a group view the same set of elements, it is important that time is set aside for a negotiation and full discussion of a set of elements which each member of the group can identify with. If, for example, one is interested in exploring the similarity and differences amongst a group of training officers in terms of how they view a specific set of training techniques, one should not automatically assume that the labels given to these techniques as the set of elements are fully understood by each member of the group.

Similarly, if the group generates the set of elements one should endeavour to select from a pool of possible elements the set which the majority of the group feel represent items which they can construe. Without endeavouring to ensure this common base, any judgements about similarities and differences in the constructs which individuals in the group may bring to bear on the set of elements, could be inaccurate if not nonsensical. The intended use of the grid information is thus an aspect of "purpose" which imposes some constraints on the grid technique which will be implemented. One can construe uses of the grid which have as their prime focus awareness raising as representing the *Reflective Mode* and those occasions where the focus is primarily gaining information about a person as the *Extractive Mode* of grid application.

CHOICE OF ELEMENTS AND CONSTRUCTS

When considering the use of repertory grid techniques, one of the first questions often raised is whether one should provide the elements and constructs for an individual or whether these should be elicited from each individual on a personal basis. In its original use as a clinical technique, personal elicitation of elements and constructs was the method adopted — indeed purists would argue that the theoretical base for repertory grid techniques emphasizes individuality and that by definition constructs are *personal*. However, there has been an increasing tendency of late to detach the technique from its theoretical base and so the use of a standard form of repertory grid in which both the elements and the constructs are provided for the person rather than elicited from the individual concerned, is becoming more widespread.

Whether or not one provides or elicits elements and/or constructs may well depend on the initial purpose and mode of application. For example, if one is exploring the nature and sharing of construing within a group, it is often the case that a common set of elements are selected and provided for each individual — this could be followed by either provision or elicitation of constructs or a combination of both. It should be emphasized, however, that if one decides to provide elements/constructs then adequate groundwork should be done in order to obtain what one hopes are representative elements and constructs. This would entail a series of discussions with the type of people to whom the standard grid will be provided, so that the items selected for elements may represent a range of events which can be construed by such people, and that the nature of the provided constructs is in line with the sort of dimensions which would, in the main, be used by them when considering the elements chosen. There are, as we shall see later, statistical aids to assure representativeness.

Kelly himself insisted that in order to be useful and meaningful, test items should be representative of an individual's life events. There have also been several studies which have compared the usefulness of Elicited versus Provided constructs and there is some indication that people prefer their own constructs to those supplied by the investigator. In some cases provided labels may be identical with those normally used by the subject in practice, but on the other hand, they may be far removed or incomprehensible to a particular person.

O'Donovan (1965) suggested that one aspect of extreme ratings or polarization on rating scales was the significance to the subject of the stimulus provided. Bonarius (1970) reviews a series of experiments which suggested that subjects consistently use the more extreme poles of rating scales when using personal constructs rather than provided constructs in rating themselves and others. Landfield (1965) asked subjects to rank order a pool of contrasts consisting of his own personal construct dimensions and those constructs provided by his therapist. The rankings were based on how useful they had proved to be in describing people. The major finding from this study is that the personal constructs were ranked amongst the top five ranks, whereas the therapist's constructs were more often found within the bottom five ranks. Adams-Webber (1970) in summarizing his review of the research on elicited versus provided constructs in repertory grid technique, commented

> Although normal subjects prefer to use their own elicited constructs to describe themselves and others, both kinds of dimensions seem to be functionally similar when grid technique is employed to assess structural features of their cognitive systems. (p.53)

One should remember that whatever meanings words may have, they are assigned or ascribed to them by people. Thus when a person is provided with the investigator's labels on the construct poles, the meaning ascribed to those labels may not be isomorphic with the meaning the investigator assumes these labels hold.

Thus if one is forced through circumstances to use provided rather than elicited constructs, one should be conscious of the need for extensive preliminary work to establish a reasonable selection of constructs and the need for caution during the interpretation phase.

Whether elements are elicited or provided, it is important that they are representative of the area to be considered and that they span the range of items which are considered to be important for the person or persons concerned.

One is often asked "how many elements should a repertory grid contain?" There is no fixed standard required. However, in practice, small numbers of elements may give rise to a grid which is devoid of sufficient detail or interest in terms of content, whereas construing large numbers of elements can be a very tedious exercise and thus should be avoided. In practice it has been the experience of the authors that between eight and fifteen elements provide a useful basis for the elicitation of a reasonable grid. During conversational elicitation of the elements, the investigator may have to offer some guidance on the nature of the elements to be included in the grid. It is important at this stage that the investigator refrains from forcing his own views as to what the precise items should be. However, some discussion will be needed, perhaps especially with regard to the level at which the element items is pitched. For example, one may find that the elements which are initially suggested by a person are very abstract and they may have some difficulty in eliciting constructs with respect to elements at this level.

Initial suggestions in response to a request for element items representative of aspects of e.g. teaching, might be *Tolerance*, *Patience or interpersonal relationships*. This type of element may be difficult to construe especially on the first occasion one is completing a grid. Specific teaching events, teaching materials or techniques are more concrete and thus may be more suitable for initial grids.

There are occasions when the person may find it difficult to come forward with a reasonable list of elements — this may often be due to the fact that the elements which they are considering are too global. At this stage it is important that some negotiation takes place and the person is encouraged to break down some of these elements into more specific items. For example, a manager considering activities with which he was involved in his job may indicate that *interaction with people* is an important element. This covers many work situations and thus the manager could be encouraged to break this down into such elements as *selection interview*, *exit interview*, *board meetings*, *working lunches*, etc. as appropriate.

It is also important that one includes in the element set items which will encourage the person to think of contrast. For example, in a grid where one is interested in examining constructs about people at work in relation to their effectiveness it is essential to have as elements some people who are seen as "ineffective" as well as those seen as "effective". Similarly if one is eliciting constructs about learning events it is desirable that the set include "good" learning events and "bad" learning events, so that persons construing of good events can be seen in the light of how he/she construes "bad" events.

A further point of negotiation may arise with respect to the type of construct elicited. As has already been mentioned, the constructs elicited must be appropriate to the purpose of the investigation. There are occasions when it is appropriate to encourage the individual to offer any type of construct. However, there are other occasions when it is appropriate to encourage some negotiation regarding the type of construct about which the individual should be concerned.

It is possible to consider at least four different types of constructs:

(a) Sensory-perceptual.
(b) Behavioural.
(c) Inferential.
(d) Feelings/attitudinal.

If we are interested, for example, in a supervisor's appraisal of his subordinates we may be more concerned with behavioural, inferential and feelings/attitudinal type constructs than sensory-perceptual. If the supervisor proceeds to offer constructs which are all of the sensory-perceptual kind, e.g. *fat/thin*, *tall/short*, *swarthy complexion/pale complexion*, the investigator should encourage the individual to consider other types of constructs. This must be done of course with care, since these constructs are obviously of relevance to the individual and it is after all the person's constructs in which one is interested. The fact that the individual offers such sensory-perceptual constructs when asked to appraise his/her subordinates, is in itself of interest to note and may be a useful point for discussion — indeed feelings/attitudinal type of constructs may well come to the fore during such discussions if the individual stresses a preference for *fat, swarthy complexioned* subordinates!

If, on the other hand, the investigation was aimed at finding the personal constructs used by quality control inspectors on a production line, one may actually require that the individuals concentrate on sensory-perceptual construing. Gardner (1978) in his paper "Task Analysis: Can the grid help?", discusses the different types of constructs which can be elicited with respect to radar displays — "S" constructs refer to the appearance of the displays, "O" constructs relate to the implications of the displays, i.e. what they signify about the internal state of the radar, and "R" constructs referring to activities to be carried out on the basis of the radar display. In this paper he suggests that most uses of grid technique result in a predominance of "S" type constructs. He argues that for some purposes the investigator needs to structure the elicitation of constructs so that "S", "O" and "R" type constructs evolve.

There are two further points which should be raised in connection with the choice of constructs. The first is the issue of "range of convenience" of the construct. Kelly considered it essential that all elements in a grid must fall within the range of convenience of any construct included in the grid. Range of convenience refers to the assumption that, for any given individual at a given time, a construct will only apply to a finite number of elements. We may hold a construct or set of constructs which we can readily use for members of our own family which may not be appropriate when considering individuals at work, for instance *monopolises the bathroom/doesn't* . . . . In a grid containing family members and other persons an individual may find some difficulty and would be inclined to leave many blank spaces when completing the grid.

When one comes to relate such a construct to others in the grid one will produce a distorted or spurious set of relationships. Fransella and Bannister (1977) give a further example of a person who might sort his people into *attractive* and *unattractive* but for whom this is a construct whose range of convenience is limited to women. When this person is asked to ascribe the construct *attractive/unattractive* to a set of people in a grid, he may well put some of the women into *attractive*, some of the women into *unattractive* and all the men into *unattractive*, whereas this does not reflect the actual construing of the person concerned. If one elicits constructs conversationally and encourages discussion of difficulties such as the issue of range of convenience, one can seek alternative constructs which more appropriately apply across the elements and thus avoid too many situations where *non applicable* will have to be used.

Finally, there is the question of the number of constructs to be included in a repertory grid. There is no magic number to suggest, although as Kelly (1969) himself pointed out, it is important to elicit several constructs in order to explore an individual's world of meaning. There are of course some limits to consider, for example:

(i) The prime prerequisite is that the constructs elicited cover the range of constructs which the individual feels are important to the area under consideration. Construct elicitation should continue until the individual indicates that his repertoire of constructs for that particular range of events is exhausted.

(ii) The elicitation of constructs can be exhausting for both the person completing the grid and the person carrying out the grid interview. One should recognize this and not extend the grid interview beyond the limits of exhaustion for both parties.

(iii) In many circumstances there may be time limit constraints on behalf of either the individual or the person conducting the grid interview which may well impose a limitation on the number of constructs which are elicited at any one session.

(iv) For those who wish to make use of the various computer program facilities available for analysis of grids it is important to be aware of the limitations with respect to numbers of constructs which any individual program might impose.

Chapter 7 considers one statistical guide to assist an administrator in deciding when further construct elicitation may cease to be of value.

Some investigators may feel it desirable to consider every possible permutation of triads when eliciting constructs by triadic elicitation, and may be concerned about the large number of constructs that might evolve if such a procedure was adopted. It is of course desirable that the elements are considered in various groupings but in practice an individual will often tend to repeat constructs and will have exhausted his sub-system of constructs for a particular area of investigation long before all possible permutations have been considered. *One is not aiming to encapsulate the whole of an individual's construct system but that part of it which is relevant to the defined purpose*. The number of constructs which are included in the final grid will therefore be a result of some or all of the limits which have been mentioned. It is important to remember triadic elicitation is an *aid* to formulating constructs but can often be abolished together when constructs "come to the respondent" freely.

SCALING

Kelly's original method incorporated the dichotomous form of the grid. Using this approach a person is asked to place each element on one or other of the two poles of the construct — the usual method is to ascribe either a tick or a cross under each element, as in Fig. 1.

✓	Mother	Father	Aunt Lou	Sara	Mr Grundy	Mrs Peabody	X
Good company	✓	X	X	✓	X	✓	Boring
Happy disposition	✓	X	✓	X	X	✓	Bad tempered
Etc.							

Fig. 1.

If an element could not be described by either pole of the construct a "not applicable" can be applied, although the reservations mentioned earlier under "range of convenience" should be noted. Using this method, one can, for example, gain information as to which group of elements are described by one pole of the construct, and which group are more adequately described by the opposite pole. This method was sufficient for many of Kelly's purposes, but it does not allow any finer discriminations to be represented.

In more recent years alternatives to this dichotomous form of the grid have been developed to broaden the potential of the method. Bannister (1959) noted that a feature of the dichotomous grid was the possibility of spurious relationships caused by lopsidedness, i.e. many ticks and few crosses, or vice versa, on a particular construct. In order to eliminate this, he proposed the split-half method whereby a person is required to place half the elements on the emergent and the other half on the implicit pole of each construct. Whilst this does overcome the problem of lopsidedness, it tends to constrain the person in that they often feel forced into making an artificial judgment. It may well eliminate important dimensions; for example, *kind/cruel* may be an important dimension to a person but they may classify very few people as *cruel*.

Perhaps the two most popular forms of the grid which have evolved in recent years are the "ranking" form and the "rating" form (Bannister and Mair, 1968; Fransella and Bannister, 1977). In these forms each construct is used as a scale along which the individual elements can be placed. For example, on a "ranking" grid with a construct *like/dislike*, the elements are ranked from the most liked through to the most disliked. The usual procedure is for the elements to be arranged in order of their distance from the emergent pole of the construct. Thus if there are eight elements, the element most like the emergent pole is ranked 1 and the element least like this pole is ranked 8. In some cases the implicit pole is not even named. However, as Humphreys (1973) points out, the implicit pole should be mentioned as it may well affect the ranking. He gives the following example:

> Suppose we have a case where two of the elements to be ranked are 'mother-in-law' and 'wife' and the emergent pole of the construct is labelled 'cool' — it seems quite likely that the ranking of these two elements would be different if the implicit pole was 'uncool' rather than 'warm'.

If one adopts a ranking form of the grid it is desirable therefore that both poles of the construct are discussed and entered on the grid form. In practice, some individuals find the ranking form somewhat tedious, especially if there are a large number of elements to be ranked — they find it difficult to rank-order large numbers and may be confused if tied ranks are allowed. The rating scale or grading method would seem to hold a number of advantages over the methods already described. In this form the person is given freedom to place any number of the elements in the various positions along a linear scale ranging from the emergent pole to the implicit pole. Thus each element will be assigned a rating which reflects its position on a particular construct. A 5-point or 7-point scale is usually employed and thus this method allows finer discriminations to be made than the dichotomous or trichotomous methods (i.e. when non-applicables are used), e.g. Fig. 2.

This rating form of the grid is often compared with Osgood's semantic differential technique (Osgood *et al.*, 1957). One major difference between these two techniques is that the dimensions used on the grid are usually those provided by the person, whereas the adjectives used in the semantic differential are fixed.

It is important when considering whether to use dichotomous, ranking or rating forms of the grid that one takes note of the population who will be

	Mother	Father	Aunt Lou	Sara	Mr Grundy	Mrs Peabody	
Good company	1	4	5	2	5	3	Boring
Happy disposition	1	4	2	4	5	1	Bad tempered
Etc.							

Fig. 2.

asked to complete the grids. The experience of the authors would indicate that the dichotomous method is useful in situations where one is dealing with:

(a) Children.

(b) Adolescents or adults who are anxious when asked to use numbers.

(c) Adolescents and adults whom one has reason to believe are intellectually unsophisticated.

(d) The purpose of the grid does not require the finer discrimination which a ranking or rating scale will allow.

For the majority of situations, however, a 5-point rating scale would seem to offer a finer discrimination than the dichotomous method allows, and will avoid some of the disadvantages which have been described of the ranking method.

ELICITATION PROCEDURE

Prior to the elicitation of a first grid from an individual or group of individuals, it is a sensible idea to discuss the procedures involved in element elicitation, construct elicitation and the use of the particular scale which will be implemented. It is useful if the individual can complete a small "dummy" grid in order to come to grips with some of the "mechanics" of completing a grid. This preliminary is often necessary since the completion of a grid is in itself an unusual task for many individuals and results or information in an initial grid may well be contaminated by the confusion of the individual as to what is required. An overriding assumption of many participants is that the procedures are a "test" and that there are "correct answers" which are required of them. In the early stages of the conversations with an individual completing grids it is important to place considerable emphasis on encouraging the participant to put forward his or her own ideas and feelings about the topic.

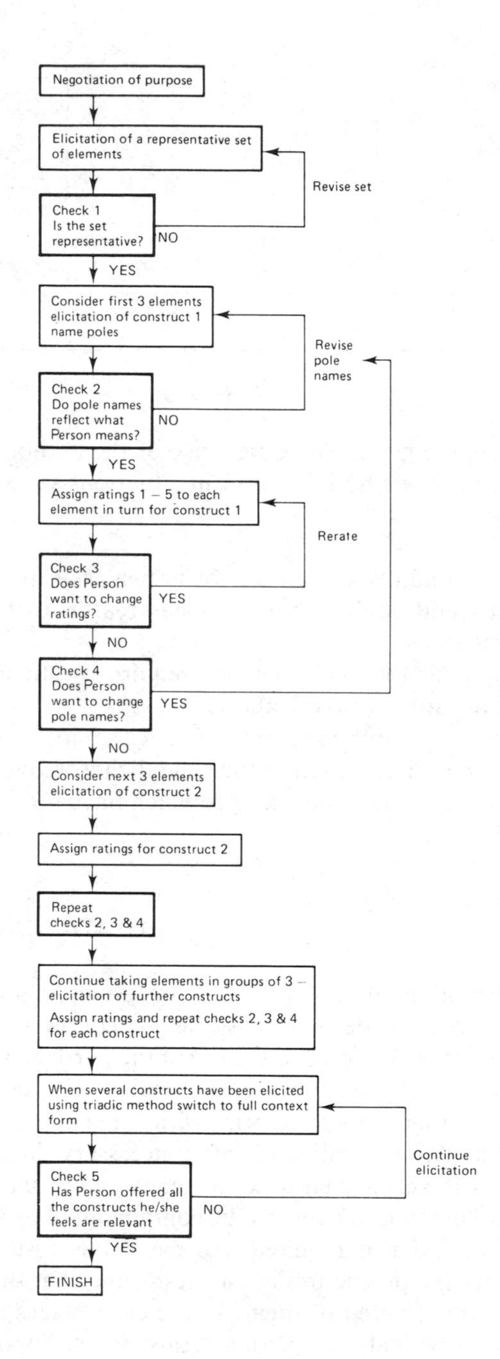

Fig. 3. Flow diagram for grid elicitation.

Given the individual nature of the particular interactions between the investigator and an individual during completion of a grid, it is not possible to give a formal account of what might traditionally be referred to as "instructions to subject". However, a flow diagram of one procedure for grid elicitation is given in Fig. 3. As has already been discussed, a major concern initially is the negotiation of purpose. Having defined a list of representative elements, the next step is the process of construct elicitation. In practice it is often useful to have each element written out on a separate card. This allows the individual to physically sort through the elements and to consider them in groups of three or more depending on the process of elicitation adopted by the investigator. Kelly (1955) described six approaches to the elicitation of constructs. However, the Minimum Context Form or "triadic method" is perhaps the most widely used, since it is closest to Kelly's theory as to how constructs are actually formed. Using this triadic method, the person is asked for a representative list of elements and then presented with three of these elements and asked to say in what way two of them are alike and thereby different from the third. The person is asked to give both the emergent pole, i.e. the way in which two of them are alike, and also the implicit or contrast pole, i.e. what makes the single element distinct from the pair. This construct is then recorded. The emergent pole and the contrast pole can be written on separate cards and placed at either end of a rating or ranking scale. Figure 4 shows a five-point rating scale with a construct pole at either end and the elements cards sorted and placed under the relevant rating. It is helpful if the rating scale, construct and element

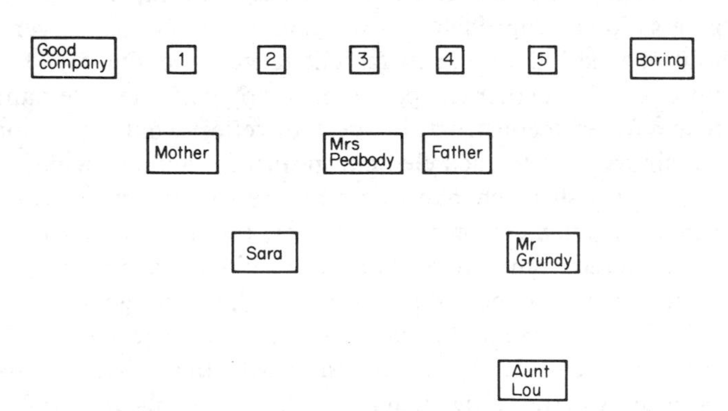

Fig. 4. Card sorting of elements on a typical construct.

cards are of different colours. This process continues, using different triads, until either the person cannot identify any new constructs or the administrator feels than an appropriate and representative set of constructs have been elicited.

1	Mother	Father	Aunt Lou	Sara	Mr Grundy	Mrs Peabody	5
Good company	1	4	5	2	5	3	Boring
Happy disposition	1	4	2	4	5	1	Bad tempered
I can get my own way with	2	5	1	3⁻	5	1	Firm
Easy to talk to	1	4	3	3	5	1	Does not listen
Intelligent	3	3	4	1	2	5	Dull
Strong physique	5	1	2	3	1	3	Feeble
Sticks to principles	3	1	5	1	1	3	Bends as the wind blows
Helps others	1	5	3	3	4	2	Self centred
Sociable	1	5	2	3	5	1	Keep to himself
I like being with	1	4	3	3	5	3	Prefer to keep out of the way

Fig. 5. Raw Grid.

When construct elicitation and assigning of ratings is completed a raw grid (Fig. 5) with its matrix of elements rated on each construct can be analysed in various ways which will be discussed in Chapter 5.

A conversational approach allows one to carry out several checks throughout the period of construct elicitation (see Fig. 3). Firstly, it's important to check whether the person is happy with the pole names which he/she places for each construct, i.e. do they reflect what the person means? After assigning ratings to each element in turn for any particular construct, the person may wish to change one or more of the ratings. In addition, having rated each element on the construct, the person may feel that this process has caused some change in the original meaning which he had ascribed with his pole names and thus may wish to change these pole names in order to fully represent the meaning which he/she was implementing when rating the elements. Free discussion with the individual also allows one to ascertain whether a particular construct is applicable to most of the elements within the grid. If a person is having difficulty applying a particular construct to the majority of his elements, this construct can then be omitted from the grid rather than forcing the person to enter a mid-point value on the scale for the other elements, which is one of the means adopted for dealing with non-applicables. If one carries out grid elicitation on a group basis, this individual discussion is often absent and thus when one collects grids for analysis one may be faced with situations where:

(a) Pole names are not clearly written or the meaning is difficult to interpret.

(b) Although two pole names have been given, the ratings on a particular construct may be all ones or all fives and thus since there is no contrast this is not truly a construct in Kelly's terms.

(c) One may have large numbers of empty spaces on the grid and may not be sure of the reason for the blanks. It may be due to indecision about which rating to give or it may be due to the fact that the element concerned is outside the range of convenience for the particular construct and thus a "non-applicable" should have been stated.

It is important, therefore, during any elicitation that the administrator stresses the need for clear naming of poles, attention to the idea of contrast and the importance of indicating either a rating or a "non-applicable" in each space in a group elicitation session. One should endeavour to circulate amongst the group in order to have conversations with individuals who may wish to discuss such issues. In some cases individuals may be asked to complete postal versions of a grid. This method is fraught with many difficulties, not least of which is the provision of clearly understood instructions to the individual as to what is required. Postal methods may give some indication as to the thoughts and feelings of an individual but a conversational approach will provide a much richer data base and a firmer ground for interpretation.

Although this triadic method has come to characterize grid methodology for many, there is nothing sacrosanct about the use of triads. Indeed, in Kelly's Full Context Form all elements were considered by the person and they were then asked to think of important ways in which groups of the elements were alike. For some people the triadic method is often an unfamiliar and difficult task. In order to get across the idea of a dimension or construct it is sometimes helpful to ask the individual to divide his or her pile of cards or list into two, so that in some way one pile or part of the list represents elements which are alike and the other pile or part of the list are also alike, but are the opposite or other end of the dimension. The importance of contrast should be stressed because, whichever method is used for construct elicitation, one occasionally encounters a situation where the construct poles given by a person represent two ends of what are, in fact, two dimensions.

Given a particular triad of people a person may offer the "construct" *good company/bad tempered* as the description of the pair and singleton. On attempting to use this construct for other people in the grid the person will have difficulty if some of the elements are *both* very good company and very bad tempered. The person may realize that this really represents two dimensions and thus can suggest, e.g. *good company/boring* and *happy disposition/bad tempered* as two constructs rather than the original description. To overcome this tendency Epting (1971) actually asks for the *opposite* when given the emergent pole.

Readers may find that the process known as "laddering" can be useful in construct elicitation. Kelly differentiated between "core" constructs which were very stable, more resistant to change and of central importance to the individual and "peripheral" constructs which might be more open to change and were at a different level in the overall construct system. Laddering is a technique for moving between levels. For example, if one was eliciting constructs about efficiency at work an individual might offer the construct *keeps good time/always late*. One can "ladder" up towards more central constructs by asking which pole of that construct is important to the individual and why. By asking the question why the individual will usually offer a further construct at a deeper level, e.g. *shows commitment/shows lack of commitment*. Why is *shows commitment* important? "Because it shows that the person values the job I ask him to do" and so on.

One can keep on pushing the individual to reveal very central issues by using further why questions but one must take care that one does not take the process too far if one is not prepared to offer the client support as one would be giving in a clinical or therepeutic interview. For most research purposes continued use of the why question may be inappropriate.

One can move "down" to more specific constructs by the use of the what or how questions. For example given a construct *I like/I do not like* one does not have a clear picture of the terms this individual might use when construing people he liked as opposed to disliked. One can say to the individual what is it about Joe Bloggs and Mary Smith that you like and this makes them different to Sam Jones? The individual might offer *speaks in seminar/silent in seminar* as the construct. This construct gives more specific information and is at a different level to the original. Generally speaking, use of what and how are useful questions in extractive modes of grid research whereas why can also be used if one has an on-going relationship with the client as in a therapeutic setting or in some "reflective" research projects.

One approach to construct elicitation (as outlined in Fig. 3) is to use the minimum context form at the start of the elicitation and after all elements have been included in at least one triad, the person can either choose his own triad or indicate an important dimension in which groups of the elements were alike and different from other elements. Indeed to continue with every possible triadic combination would be a long and tedious task for a person and involve considerable repetition for constructs. In addition, the particular triad selected by the administrator may miss an important dimension. Thus it seems desirable to allow the person some freedom to choose further dimensions without the constraints of triadic elicitation. However, one should be flexible in approach as much may depend on the particular circumstances of each grid interview. Stewart and Stewart (1976) give a very useful account of the method they use in their managerial effectiveness studies. Grid methodology is best seen as a flexible technique rather than constrained by a formal and detailed procedure.

METHOD OF ANALYSIS

Once one has elicited elements, and constructs, and perhaps assigned ratings, one has a matrix which is open to several different types of analyses. One can do a content analysis of the types of constructs offered which is based upon one's assumptions about the similarities of meaning of the constructs, as indicated by the verbal labels used. A visual inspection of the similarities between rows and between columns of ratings will give some indication of possible relationships between constructs and between elements in the grid.

The type of analysis will depend on the purpose of the study and the practical feasibility of implementing particular analyses. Some of the different analyses will be treated in depth in Chapter 5. However, at this stage we would like to offer some initial comments.

Although there is much to be gained by considering the raw data of a grid and visually or manually extracting relationships from it, the advent of computer program packages for the analysis of grids allows one to readily extract the simple formal structural relationships between elements, or between constructs, which may be obscured by the detailed raw data matrix. A summary of the various methods of computer analysis used at present can be found in Fransella and Bannister (1977), and are discussed in Chapter 5. Traditional methods of grid analysis have been factor analysis and principal component analysis (Slater, 1964). These analyses are based on two matrices of similarity measures — an element matrix which includes the measure of similarity of every element with every other element, and the construct matrix which shows the measures of similarity between all pairs of constructs. These measures of similarity are viewed as distances in space or dimensions. As these matrices get larger one may have difficulty conceptualizing the geometry of a n-dimensional space which might maximally require n-1 dimensions. Factor analysis extracts the major dimensions or factors and then proceeds to describe each item by defining its position along each dimension, thus yielding factor loadings. Most matrices can thus be expressed as a series of factor loadings which are significantly less in number than the similarity measures in the original matrix. One usually proceeds by considering this "simplified" expression of the raw data and placing a label on the major factors, in a similar manner to Eysenck's classification (1970) of neuroticism or extroversion.

Although this method is widely used it has some drawbacks. Firstly, the different forms of mathematical pushing and shoving can isolate different dimensions or factors. Secondly, some researchers feel it is presumptuous for the researcher to name the factors; they consider it best to allow the participant or subject to be involved in this process. Thirdly, it would seem that some people find it difficult to conceptualize or experience their construct system as a series of co-ordinate reference points along a limited set of axes. They find it difficult to conceptualize what has been done to their original data in order to arrive at this reductionist mapping of their system.

Recent programs developed at the Centre for the Study of Human Learning, Brunel University, are based on modifications of McQuitty's (1966) cluster analysis. Cluster analysis also works with the two similarity matrices but instead of extracting the major factors, groups or clusters of similar items are extracted and the patterning of the original data can be exhibited. FOCUS, developed at the Centre, see Shaw (1978), based on a type of non-inclusive two-way cluster analysis. This program produces a linear re-ordering of the elements to highlight similarities in the way in which they are construed and also re-ordered the constructs in a similar fashion. Analysis of grids, whether one uses manual or computer methods, will give a structure to the original responses which can be the basis for valuable further discussion with the individuals concerned.

However, one should be aware that, for some people, grid methodology may not be the best method of approach for certain purposes. For example, some report that they find assigning ticks or crosses, or numbers, is too formal and structured an approach and thus this constraint interferes with the "raising of awareness" which can be a major purpose in the use of grid techniques. For such individuals paper and pencil approaches are probably inappropriate and a freer discussion may be a more useful method. In order to evaluate changes in constructs, one could encourage such individuals to keep a diary of their thoughts and feelings. Warner (1971) described such an approach with trainee teachers who were asked to keep a "Journal of Introspection".

If one is using repertory grid technique, and especially if feedback sessions are aimed at getting the individuals to think more deeply about their constructs, it is important to be aware of the need for some system of ongoing support for the individual. There are times when appraising one's construing of people or events can be very disturbing and thus some ongoing empathetic support is needed throughout this period.

Before concluding this chapter it is necessary to point out another subtle danger. For many, numerical analysis seems to be equated with absolute truth. The existence of numbers in repertory grids, and the ensuing development of computer programs for analysis, must be treated with caution.

The repertory grid, with its heavy reliance on numerical analysis, has been used by some investigators as a definitive measure of the persons concerned. This is totally unjustified on both statistical and philosophical grounds. *The grid is perhaps best seen as a catalyst within a conversation between investigator and the individual.* It can allow insight into some of the ways in which the individual construes the particular aspects of his world which is being investigated. It is certainly not a psychological test which accurately pigeon holes the individual into a neat category system.

The process of grid elicitation is very time consuming and each grid may take between one and three hours to complete, and this often places an unacceptable burden on the administrator as well as on the "client". Additionally a high level of skill is required to "sense" the progress of the elicitation and to give "prompts" and assistance when required, but not to become over-directive in the approach. This kind of skill comes from practice and really cannot be learnt from books! The reader who is about to embark on such a data collecting exercise will, therefore, find it essential to have some "dry runs" eliciting grids to develop this sensitivity to what is actually happening during an elicitation session. It cannot be stressed too strongly that the grid is a powerful instrument and should not be used indiscriminately by folk who are not adequately prepared to use it.

Friends and colleagues will often give useful feedback as to when they are confused about requirements or may feel constrained or forced along a particular track by your comments. Listening to tape recordings of such initial grid interviews can be a salutary experience!

In the authors' view the most efficient way of learning to elicit a repertory grid is firstly to sit in on an elicitation session with an experienced researcher (or watch a video tape of such a session) and secondly to elicit some grid data oneself in the presence of a guide and mentor. Grid research is becoming popular and it is very likely that some university or college near every reader has at least one "user" who will be willing to give guidance and help. Both of the authors have run seminars and training sessions for interested potential users in education, industrial and commercial contexts, and the network of grid users is now quite extensive in the United Kingdom.

Before carrying out any investigation using repertory grids, it is important to consider the issues that have been dealt with in this chapter. Perhaps one should also add the proviso that prior to eliciting a grid from someone else, one should have undergone this experience oneself, as this is perhaps the best way of learning the pitfalls as well as the benefits of the repertory grid method.

5

Getting to Grips with the Data

In Chapter 3 we drew a distinction between personal construct psychology and the repertory grid. This is important as many users of the "grid" see it as the heart and soul of the theory. Nevertheless, to practising teachers, students and researchers about to embark on their projects, it is to the grid that many will turn. As has already been indicated there are three areas upon which such prospective "users" should dwell:

(a) Why am I about to use a grid?
(b) How am I going to collect my raw data (i.e. elicit my grids)?
(c) Am I going to be able to analyse the results in a significant way?

In our experience the rationale for grid usage may be very convincing and indeed there have been many areas of research where alternative methodologies just do not exist. It is therefore very easy to convince oneself of the value of using grids and embark on the data collecting stage without adequate planning. This chapter concentrates on ways of answering question (c) above assuming the reader has first convinced himself that there is no doubt that it is grid data he is after and that he has taken notice of the issues touched on in the preceding chapter.

COLLECTING GRID DATA

There are many ways in which grid data may be collected (elicited) and many of the popular techniques have been well documented in such volumes as *A Manual for Repertory Grid Technique* (Fransella and Bannister, 1977). In Chapter 4 we concentrated on the conversational elicitation where the grid "user" talks to his client usually on a one to one basis, and he completes a grid with a matrix of numbers representing the assigned ranks or ratings of the elements on each construct.

However, there is an alternative approach to the face-to-face grid elicitation which is becoming more widespread and capitalizes on the increased availability of small computers. The microprocessor revolution has made this alternative realistic for the researcher or practising teacher/manager who has access to a small microprocessor. Keen, whose original work had all been conducted on large installations, now works almost exclusively on a small 56K core 38OZ microprocessor manufactured by Research Machines at Oxford. The first of the interactive programs developed for the elicitation of a grid was called PEGASUS and developed by Shaw and Thomas at the Centre for the Study of Human Learning, Brunel University. Since then Shaw has modified the program and has a version suitable for small microprocessors. The PEGASUS program not only elicits the grid but goes on to analyse the data by clustering, for the purposes of this discussion we are directing comments only towards the elicitation part of the program.

The "client" who is providing the data sits alone with the computer and responds to prompts from the visual display unit or on a line printer. He is clearly completing a grid and the computer extends the element and construct sample as well as frequently checking that the respondent is sure about previous ratings. There is little doubt that such an approach overcomes most of the difficulties associated with conversational elicitation and yet it generates new problem areas which need consideration. PEGASUS is an acronym for Program Eliciting Grid And Sorts Using Similarities. It uses real time analysis of the structure of the developing grid to provide appropriate feedback during the elicitation.

Figure 6 illustrates a FOCUS-ed grid which is available at the end of a PEGASUS run. The 14-year-old student who produced this grid defined his purpose for using PEGASUS as a resource in helping him "to distinguish the books I have recently read". In the initial stages of the interaction this student used the constructs *Totally commercialized/Written as literature* and *Sensational/Plain* with a high degree of match.

The computer provided feedback concerning this match and encouraged the student to add an element which "Is either totally commercialized and plain *or* sensational and written as literature". The student opted to add the element *Catch 22*. The feedback given by the computer also points out matching or similar ratings of elements and gives opportunities to act on the information given at each stage. The computer is conversing with the "client" and the feedback assists him to explore, clarify and elaborate his own thoughts and feelings, much in the same way as if a "real live researcher" were conversationally eliciting the grid. Shaw in describing her own program says:

> The PEGASUS grid differs from the Kelly Repertory Grid in that it encourages the user to explore the differentiations he can learn to make rather

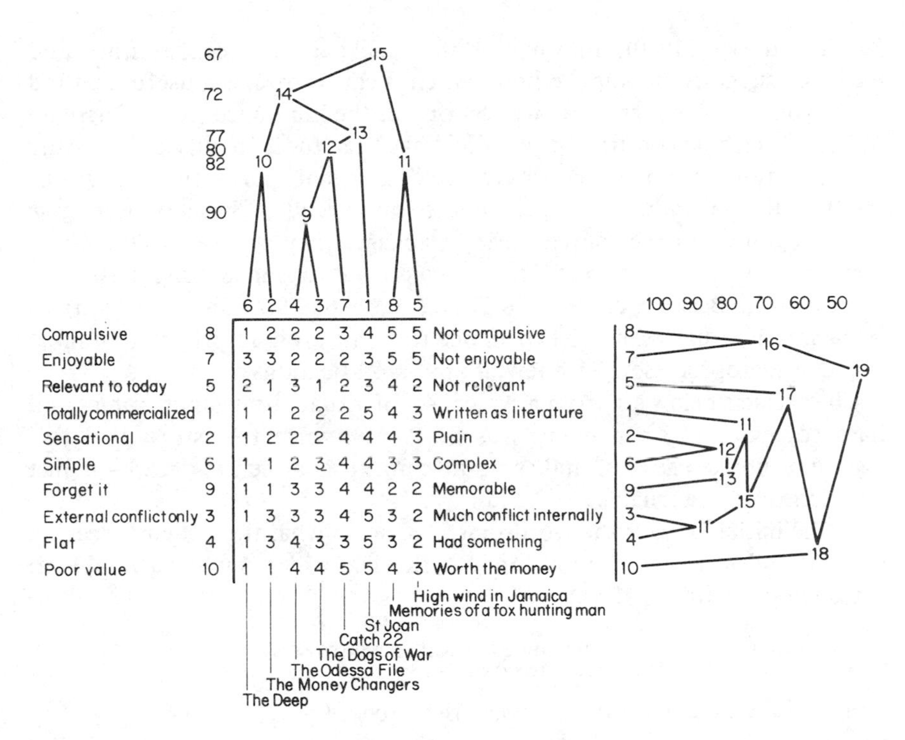

Fig. 6. FOCUS grid on books.

than just elicits those he does habitually make". (Shaw and Gaines, 1979, p.15)

This is certainly true, and PEGASUS has led the way towards this alternative kind of elicitation. However, the kind of conversation one has with one's wife, child, friend, associate is often somewhat unstructured, in that one thing leads to another, rather than reiterating previous comments in the light of new advances in the conversation. Having used PEGASUS, the authors felt the feedback was less than truly conversational, and whilst it was quite possible to complete a grid with no external guidance, the process seemed a little unnatural and used terms such as construct and element early in the elicitation. Such terms will be less than clear to a respondent unfamiliar with grid parlance!

Keen set out produce an interactive program which was more natural, did not use technical terms early on, and most importantly, "committed" the client to a high level of involvement without ever letting him know he was completing a grid! This was achieved by a dyadic (rather than the usual triadic) elicitation process. Keen worked on this and related tasks with a colleague from Western Australia who was in England on secondment

(Keen and Bell, 1980). Piloting of this package has been exciting and feedback suggests that the method, which is called DYAD is a useful method for anyone to elicit a grid. As we feel one of the hindrances to the increase of use of personal construct psychology has been the difficulty of accessing such programs, Keen and Bell have decided to make all of their programs freely available, without charge, subject to the request that any users give due recognition of the source of any packages they choose to use. Thus, there is a listing of DYAD, written in BASIC (a version of disc basic not dissimilar to Basic V called XDB Basic, Research Machines, Oxford) as Appendix 1. It has been our experience that this program will run on most popular microprocessors with few, if any, modifications.

The extracts below are from a typical set of visual display unit frames and hard copy output when DYAD is used. It is important to stress that this program, unlike PEGASUS, makes no attempt to analyse the data — it just elicits the grid in a reliable and valid way.

In the initial extracts the words correspond to what the "client" sees on the VDU whilst the final section contains the data which is made available to the client in "hard copy" form.

```
LET'S LOOK AT THE WAY YOU THINK ABOUT THINGS — INPUT THE NAME OF THE KIND OF THING
   (MAN, BOOK, DOG, ETC.) YOU WISH TO CONSIDER —
?BOOK
INPUT THE NAME OF A BOOK THAT YOU WOULD LIKE TO CONSIDER
?BIBLE
INPUT THE NAME OF A BOOK WHICH IS DIFFERENT IN SOME IMPORTANT WAY FOR YOU
?THE ASCENT OF MAN
WHAT IS THIS CHARACTERISTIC AS IT APPLIES TO THE BIBLE
?PHILOSOPHICAL
WHAT IS THE OPPOSING TRAIT OF THE ASCENT OF MAN
?FACTUAL
GIVE ANOTHER BOOK THAT PHILOSOPHICAL/FACTUAL ALSO APPLIES TO
?PLATO'S REPUBLIC
IF YOU WERE RATING THESE THINGS ON A SCALE OF 1 to 5
(WHERE 1 MEANS MORE LIKE PHILOSOPHICAL, AND 5 MEANS MORE LIKE FACTUAL)
HOW WOULD YOU RATE THEM?
RATING FOR BIBLE
?1
RATING FOR THE ASCENT OF MAN
?4
RATING FOR PLATO'S REPUBLIC
?2
DO YOU WANT TO ADD ANOTHER BOOK?
ANSWER 'YES' OR 'NO'
?YES
INPUT THE NAME OF A BOOK WHICH IS DIFFERENT IN ANOTHER IMPORTANT WAY FROM PLATO'S
   REPUBLIC
?ULYSSES
WHAT IS THIS CHARACTERISTIC AS IT APPLIES TO PLATO'S REPUBLIC
?SEEKING FOR TRUTH
WHAT IS THE OPPOSING TRAIT OF ULYSSES
```

```
?DEVELOPMENT OF A NEW LANGUAGE OF COMMUNICATION
GIVE ANOTHER BOOK THAT SEEKING FOR TRUTH/DEVELOPMENT OF A NEW LANGUAGE OF
  COMMUNICATION ALSO APPLIES TO
?KHARMA SUTRA
IF YOU WERE RATING THESE THINGS ON A SCALE OF 1 TO 5 (WHERE 1 MEANS MORE LIKE SEEKING
  FOR TRUTH, AND 5 MORE LIKE DEVELOPMENT OF A NEW LANGUAGE OF COMMUNICATION)
  HOW WOULD YOU RATE THEM?
RATING FOR BIBLE
?3
RATING FOR THE ASCENT OF MAN
?2
RATING FOR PLATO'S REPUBLIC
?1
RATING FOR ULYSSES
?5
RATING FOR KHARMA SUTRA
?4
DO YOU WANT TO ADD ANOTHER BOOK? ANSWER 'YES' OR 'NO'
?YES
INPUT THE NAME OF A BOOK WHICH IS DIFFERENT IN ANOTHER IMPORTANT WAY FROM
  KHARMA SUTRA
?ENCYCLOPAEDIA OF LOVE
WHAT IS THIS CHARACTERISTIC AS IT APPLIES TO KHARMA SUTRA
?FANTASY
WHAT IS THE OPPOSING TRAIT OF ENCYCLOPAEDIA OF LOVE AND SEX
?FACTUAL
GIVE ANOTHER BOOK THAT FANTASY/FACTUAL ALSO APPLIES TO
?DR. NO
IF YOU WERE RATING THESE THINGS ON A SCALE OF 1 TO 5 (WHERE 1 MEANS MORE LIKE
  FANTASY, AND 5 MEANS MORE LIKE FACTUAL) HOW WOULD YOU RATE THEM?
RATING FOR BIBLE
?1
RATING FOR THE ASCENT OF MAN
?5
RATING FOR PLATO'S REPUBLIC
?4
RATING FOR ULYSSES
?1
RATING FOR KHARMA SUTRA
?2
RATING FOR ENCYCLOPAEDIA OF LOVE AND SEX
?5
RATING FOR DR. NO
?2
DO YOU WANT TO ADD ANOTHER BOOK? ANSWER "YES" OR "NO"
?NO
YOU HAVE AN INTERESTING BOOK GROUP, YOU MAY HAVE REALIZED THAT THE LATTER
  ELEMENTS ADDED HAVE NOT BEEN RATED ON EARLIER TRAITS.
WOULD YOU LIKE TO GO BACK AND "FILL THESE IN"?
ANSWER "YES" OR "NO"
?YES
OKAY, REMEMBER TO RATE AS BEFORE WHERE 1 MEANS MORE LIKE THE LEFT-HAND TRAIT,
  AND 5 MEANS MORE LIKE THE RIGHT-HAND ONE. ENTER "0" IF THE TRAIT SEEMS TOTALLY
  INAPPROPRIATE FOR THE BOOK
FOR ULYSSES
RATING FOR PHILOSOPHICAL/FACTUAL
?2
FOR KHARMA SUTRA
RATING FOR PHILOSOPHICAL/FACTUAL
```

?2
FOR ENCYCLOPAEDIA OF LOVE AND SEX
RATING FOR PHILOSOPHICAL/FACTUAL
?5
RATING FOR SEEKING FOR TRUTH/DEVELOPMENT OF A NEW LANGUAGE OF COMMUNICATION
?3
RATING FOR FANTASY/FACTUAL
?5
FOR DR. NO
RATING FOR PHILOSOPHICAL/FACTUAL
?3
RATING FOR SEEKING FOR TRUTH/DEVELOPMENT OF A NEW LANGUAGE OF COMMUNICATION
?0
RATING FOR FANTASY/FACTUAL
?1
YOU HAVE CONSIDERED THESE ELEMENTS –
BIBLE
THE ASCENT OF MAN
PLATO'S REPUBLIC
ULYSSES
KHARMA SUTRA
ENCYCLOPAEDIA OF LOVE AND SEX
DR. NO
IN THESE WAYS –
PHILOSOPHICAL/FACTUAL
SEEKING FOR TRUTH/DEVELOPMENT OF A NEW LANGUAGE OF COMMUNICATION
FANTASY/FACTUAL
CAN YOU THINK OF ANY OTHER WAYS YOU SOMETIMES DISTINGUISH BETWEEN THEM?
ANSWER "YES" OR "NO"
?YES
OKAY, ENTER ONE END OF THE NEW CONSTRUCT
?PLEASANT TO READ
NOW THE OTHER
?ONLY O.K. FOR REFERENCE
NOW RATE THEM AS BEFORE. 1 MEANS MORE LIKE PLEASANT TO READ, 5 MEANS MORE LIKE ONLY O.K. FOR REFERENCE
RATING FOR BIBLE
?2
RATING FOR ASCENT OF MAN
?1
RATING FOR PLATO'S REPUBLIC
?1
RATING FOR ULYSSES
?2
RATING FOR KHARMA SUTRA
?2
RATING FOR ENCYCLOPAEDIA OF LOVE AND SEX
?5
RATING FOR DR. NO
?2
CAN YOU THINK OF ANOTHER SOURCE OF DIFFERENCES?
ANSWER "YES" OR "NO"
?NO
THANK YOU FOR YOUR INTEREST. I HOPE YOU ENJOYED THINKING ABOUT THE WAY YOU THINK ABOUT THINGS

A hard copy printout such as the one given below would be made available to the client or researcher. The resulting matrix can be either hand focused or computer analysed (see section on analysis).

YOUR AREA OF INTEREST WAS BOOK IN WHICH YOU CONSIDERED THE FOLLOWING ELEMENTS –
A BIBLE
B THE ASCENT OF MAN
C PLATO'S REPUBLIC
D ULYSSES

E KHARMA SUTRA
F ENCYCLOPAEDIA OF LOVE AND SEX
G DR. NO
AND YOUR THOUGHT ABOUT THEM IN THESE WAYS –
1 PHILOSOPHICAL/FACTUAL
2 SEEKING FOR TRUTH/DEVELOPMENT OF A NEW LANGUAGE OF COMMUNICATION
3 FANTASY/FACTUAL
4 PLEASANT TO READ/ONLY O.K. FOR REFERENCE
YOU RATED EACH ELEMENT ON EACH CONSTRUCT (WITH 1 MEANING MORE LIKE THE LEFT POLE OF THE CONSTRUCT, AND 5 MORE LIKE THE RIGHT) IN THE FOLLOWING WAY, THE COLUMNS REPRESENT THE ELEMENTS AND THE ROWS THE CONSTRUCTS

	A	B	C	D	E	F	G
1	1	4	2	2	2	5	3
2	3	2	1	5	4	3	0
3	1	5	4	1	2	5	1
4	2	1	1	2	2	5	2

By now the reader will have decided to collect his data either by acquiring the skills necessary to use the conversational technique or by using PEGASUS, DYAD or an alternative inter-active computer programme. We can therefore proceed to a consideration of the analysis stage.

GRID ANALYSIS

Once again the "new user" is faced with a choice of strategies, these may be diagrammed as shown in Fig. 7.

From a glance at Fig. 7 it will be clear that there are a number of key decision points which may be considered in turn. A major decision will be whether one will use:

(a) visual or simple analysis, or
(b) a sophisticated computer analysis.

We cannot prescribe any permanent recommendation, because different situations will demand different strategies. Until microprocessors became so readily available, one was compelled to use simple techniques if immediate feedback was required. It is likely that someone about to embark on the use of a grid method will still use simple techniques initially whilst a "feel" for the data develops, and indeed such techniques lead to a natural understanding of what grid data is really about. However, if access to some kind of computing facility is possible, it is likely that the greater degree of sophistication will attract most users quite soon. There is certainly no need to fear using computers as it is now quite possible to use "packages" for analysis which can be applied with little or no computing

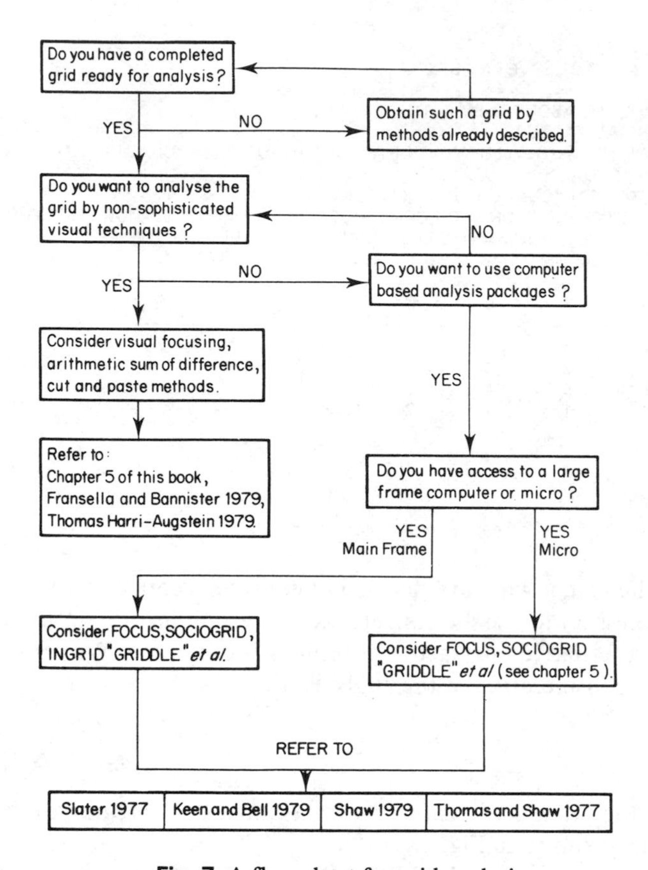

Fig. 7. A flow chart for grid analysis.

expertise. Many of these packages (e.g. GRIDDLE and TARGET, Keen and Bell, 1980; Keen *et al.*, unpublished data) provide a printout which clearly explains what the analysis means, (Bar charts in the case of TARGET and verbal descriptions in GRIDDLE) without further interpretation of numbers being required. Other packages (e.g. INGRID, FOCUS) provide printouts which contain Eigen Values, Trees, etc. which do need further interpretation).

Simple Visual Analyses

The simple visual techniques are certainly easy to use, and provided one is not attempting to build *complex* models of a respondent's construction of reality, do a very good job. They have the added advantage of assisting the newcomer to grow towards a greater understanding of the analysis process.

Three techniques will be outlined here:
(i) Visual/hand focusing.
(ii) Arithmetic sum of difference matrix.
(iii) Use of acetate sheets.

Visual/Hand Focusing

This technique was devised by Thomas *et al.* (unpublished data) at the Centre for the Study of Human Learning, Brunel University and is very simple to use if one follows the following steps.
Step 1. Inspect the raw grid matrix and isolate the pair of columns which have the highest match. This is done by taking pairs of columns and adding up when two ratings are identical in each column, e.g. in Fig. 8 the columns under E_5 and E_6 have ratings (in this case tick or cross) which match on 6/7 constructs. One can continue to make a note of high and low relationships by this visual method or proceed to steps 2–8.

	E_1	E_2	E_3	E_4	E_5	E_6
C_1	✓	✓	✓	X	X	✓
C_2	✓	O	O	O	✓	✓
C_3	✓	X	X	X	X	X
C_4	✓	X	X	O	✓	✓
C_5	✓	X	✓	O	✓	✓
C_6	✓	X	X	X	X	X
C_7	✓	X	X	O	✓	✓

Fig. 8. Raw grid.

Step 2. Cut up the raw grid into its component columns ensuring that the element number or name heads each column. For the grid in the example one would now have 6 element strips.
Step 3. Align the two strips with the highest match (in the example it is E_5 and E_6) and continue to match the other strips against E_5 and E_6 until a high match is noted, e.g. E_1 with E_6 and E_4 with E_5. One continues until one has re-ordered the elements so that elements given similar ratings are placed next to one another (see Fig. 9).

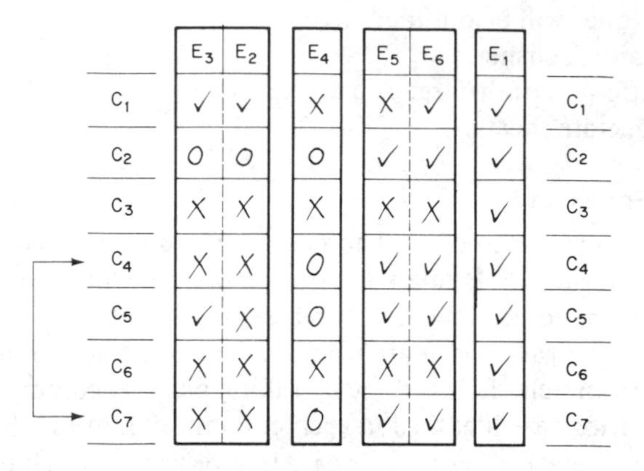

Fig. 9. Grid with elements reordered.

Step 4. Rewrite the re-ordered grid (as in Fig. 9). Now inspect the rows of constructs and isolate high matches., e.g. constructs C_4 and C_7.
Step 5. Rewrite the re-ordered grid with the ratings on each construct reversed (see Fig. 10). This is done because, since constructs are bipolar, it is possible that a high degree of match may be obtained if the construct was reversed.

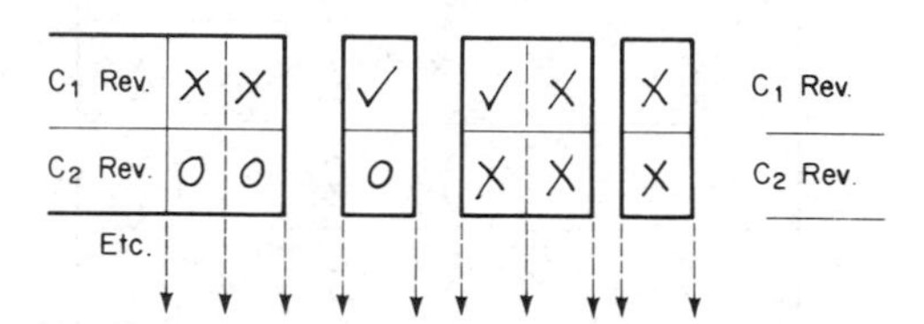

Fig. 10. Constructs rewritten with rating reversed.

Step 6. Cut up the rows ensuring that the construct name or number is attached. In the example one would have 14 rows: 7 rows of constructs as rated originally and 7 rows of reversed constructs.
Step 7. As with the elements, start with the highest matched rows, in the example C_4 and C_7, and continue to match up strips of constructs until the constructs are re-ordered in such a way that those which are similar to each other are placed next to one another. In the example none of the "reversed" constructs matched up better than the original ratings.
Step 8. The grid can now be rewritten and the result is a manual or hand-focused grid in which both elements and constructs have been re-ordered and the pattern of relationships is more easily noted (Fig. 11).

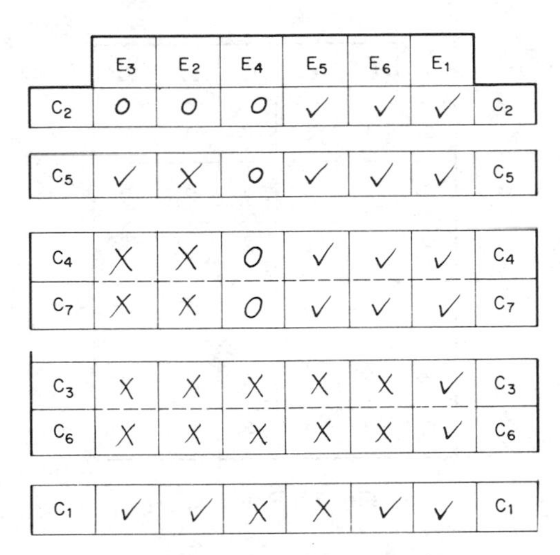

	E_3	E_2	E_4	E_5	E_6	E_1	
C_2	O	O	O	✓	✓	✓	C_2
C_5	✓	X	O	✓	✓	✓	C_5
C_4	X	X	O	✓	✓	✓	C_4
C_7	X	X	O	✓	✓	✓	C_7
C_3	X	X	X	X	X	✓	C_3
C_6	X	X	X	X	X	✓	C_6
C_1	✓	✓	X	X	✓	✓	C_1

Fig. 11. Grid focused manually — elements and constructs reordered.

This is a very useful method when one wants immediate feedback of a tick-and-cross-type grid and one is interested in relationships between elements and between constructs in addition to the content of the verbal labels given to the constructs. However, things are more complex when one is dealing with ranked or rated data. The arithmetic sum of differences matrix will help with such data.

Arithmetic Sum of Difference Matrix

In many ways this is similar to the visual/manual focusing technique but additional steps are required. For example, given a raw grid (as in Fig. 12), the first step would be to match up the columns of elements by calculating the differences in rating on each construct for each pair of columns, and summing these differences for each pair of elements. These sums of differences can be placed in a matrix (see Fig. 13). By inspecting the matrix for the smallest difference one can isolate the pair of elements with the highest match — in the example it would be elements 4 and 2 which have a summated difference of 1. One can now proceed, with the aid of the matrix, to rewrite the grid so that the elements are re-ordered (Fig. 14). As before (Step 4) one is now ready to deal with the re-ordering of the constructs. One now needs to sum the differences in ratings along the rows and produce another matrix of the sums of differences between pairs of constructs. Using this matrix one can rewrite the grid with the constructs re-ordered as in Step 8 for manual analysis. The reader should note that, as before, each

	E_1	E_2	E_3	E_4	E_5
C_1	1	3	2	3	5
C_2	2	5	3	5	5
C_3	1	3	4	3	2
C_4	2	4	3	4	5
C_5	4	2	1	2	3
C_6	2	1	5	2	3

Fig. 12. Raw grid.

	E_1	E_2	E_3	E_4	E_5
E_1		12	12	11	13
E_2			10	(1)	7
E_3				9	13
E_4					6
E_5					

Fig. 13. Matrix of sums of difference between element pairs.

	E_1	E_2	E_4	E_5	E_3
C_1	1	3	3	5	2
C_2	2	5	5	5	3
C_3	1	3	3	2	4
C_4	2	4	4	5	3
C_5	4	2	2	3	1
C_6	2	1	2	3	5

Fig. 14. Elements re-ordered in a "rated" grid.

construct will also have to be rewritten with the ratings reversed so that the matrix which one would be calculating for the example given would be a 12 × 12 matrix (see Fig. 15).

	C_1	C_2	C_3	C_4	C_5	C_6	C_{1R}	C_{2R}	C_{3R}	C_{4R}	C_{5R}	C_{6R}
C_1		6	5	4	8	9		12	5	10	8	9
C_2			9	2	12	11	12		9	12	6	7
C_3				7	9	6	5	9		7	5	10
C_4					10	9	10	12	7		4	7
C_5						7	8	6	5	4		5
C_6							9	7	10	7	5	
C_{1R}								6	5	4	8	9
C_{2R}									9	2	12	11
C_{3R}										7	9	6
C_{4R}											10	9
C_{5R}												7
C_{6R}												

Fig. 15. Sum of differences between constructs as originally rated and with ratings reversed.

In this example one can see that in the case of construct 5 one would get lower sums of differences with each of the constructs if this construct was reversed (compare C_5 with C_1 - C_6 and C_{5R} with C_1 - C_6). In rewriting the grid C_5 would be reversed and therefore the pole descriptions (construct labels) need to be rewritten so that the left hand pole name becomes the right-hand pole name and vice versa. For example, if construct 5 was originally

	E_1	E_2	E_4	E_5	E_3	
Good	4	2	2	3	1	Bad,

in the re-ordered grid the ratings would be reversed, i.e.

E_1	E_2	E_4	E_5	E_3
2	4	4	3	5 .

Thus to keep the same intention of meaning the labels "good" and "bad" have to be reversed, i.e.

	E_1	E_2	E_4	E_5	E_3	
Bad	2	4	4	3	5	Good.

The grid in the example can now be rewritten as a focused grid with the patterns of relationships in the data more clearly revealed (Fig. 16).

	E_1	E_2	E_4	E_5	E_3
C_2	2	5	5	5	3
C_4	2	4	4	5	3
C_1	1	3	3	5	2
C_3	1	3	3	2	4
C_{5R}	2	4	4	3	5
C_6	2	1	2	3	5

Fig. 16. Focused grid — elements and constructs re-ordered.

As the reader will now be aware, this process of calculations can be very time consuming, especially with large grids. It is often this aspect alone which leads the user to seek an appropriate computer package which not only relieves the tedium of such calculations but will also do additional more sophisticated analyses.

Use of Acetate Sheets

As was indicated in Chapter 4 there are many purposes for which grid data might be elicited. One such purpose might be to monitor change in construing of one individual between separate occasions. Using acetate sheets one can get a quick visual representation of areas of change. This method is appropriate for tick and cross data.

If the original ticks and crosses are entered in cells drawn on an acetate sheet and then a subsequent acetate sheet similarly filled in is placed over this original, one can clearly see where a tick is now a cross or vice versa. Alternatively, one can shade one half of the cell in one colour to represent the emergent pole of the construct and the other half in another colour to represent the implicit pole. When the two acetate sheets are placed one upon the other, areas of change are indicated by "complete" cells (see Fig. 17).

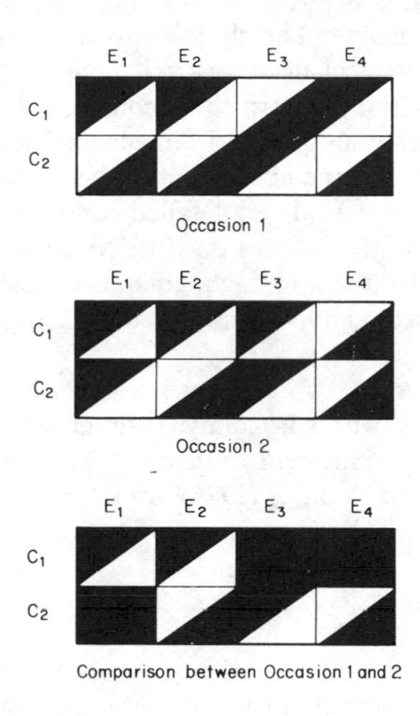

Fig. 17.

If Fig. 17 represented a small portion of an individual's grid completed on two occasions one can note that elements 3 and 4 have been given a different rating on construct 1 on the second occasion and similarly element 1 on construct 2.

This type of display can also be used to highlight similarity and differences between the construing of two individuals. If for example "occasion 1" above was a teacher and "occasion 2" was a student using the same constructs to construe the same element set then one could note there is a mismatch between the teacher and student in three areas i.e. E_3 and E_4 on Construct 1 and E_1 on Construct 2.

The acetate sheet display is therefore a particularly useful analysis technique for use in reflection of construct change for an individual and a means whereby differences between individuals can be highlighted and thus form the basis of negotiation.

Computer Analyses

After exploring simple visual techniques, let us assume the intrepid convert to the technique obtains access to a computing facility and now wishes to consider packages available. The choice now ceases to be simple in that, philosophical and statistical decisions will have to be made — does he require clustering techniques, principal component analysis, elementary linkage analysis, factor analysis, multi-dimensional scaling or others? Many respected researchers disagree about what is best! Rathod (1981) and Bell (unpublished data) have considered detailed comparisons, but frankly even these excellent comparative studies do little to assist the "user" about to start. Often, an unscientific approach, such as choosing the package most readily available is used, and like banking, once committed to one marque, one often resists change.

The authors represent two extremes: while both have used many techniques, Pope has worked mainly with clustering, while Keen has favoured principal component analysis. The clustering techniques developed by Shaw and Thomas (1976) are described below and principal component analysis is the basis of Chapter 6.

Clustering Techniques

The PEGASUS program mentioned earlier not only elicits a grid but goes on to analyse it by a clustering technique. FOCUS is a separate program (Shaw and Thomas, 1976) which analyses (but does not elicit) a grid by the same clustering technique. The FOCUS package produces a printout of:

(a) The original raw grid.

(b) A matching score matrix of the relationship between all pairs of elements.

(c) A matching score matrix of the relationship between all pairs of constructs (with ratings reversed as well as originally rated).

(d) A statement as to which constructs (if any) should be reversed.

(e) A re-ordered grid with tree diagrams attached which show the patterns of relationships in the data.

This focused or resorted grid retains the raw data but presents it in a re-ordered form to display the pattern of responses (see Fig. 18).

It has been our experience that individuals have little difficulty with print-out in this form. It is useful for feedback to an individual and the ensuing conversation often produces further very relevant information about the person's thoughts and feelings. During feedback one should encourage the individual to:

(a) Note high relationships between pairs or groups of elements.

(b) Consider personal reasons why pairs or groups within the total set may be alike or dissimilar.

(c) Consider the clusters formed in order to ascertain possible superordinate constructs.

Figure 18 shows a FOCUS-ed grid with the element and construct trees attached. The reader may find the following notes on some of the aspects of a focused grid of use when considering this figure. The clusters which occur are a basis for interpretation and feedback.

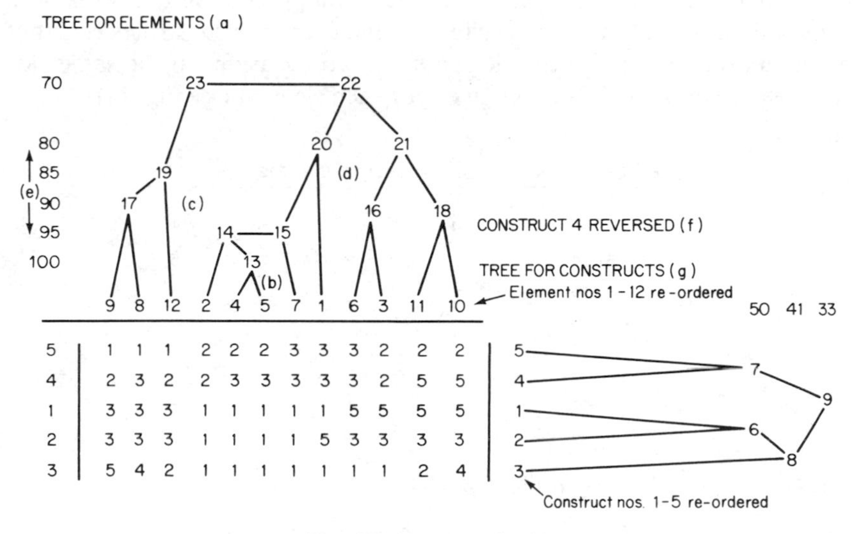

Fig. 18. A FOCUS-ed grid.

Notes

(a) The tree for elements shows the clustering or grouping of elements.

(b) A closely related pair, elements 4 and 5, are matched at 100% level, i.e. they have identical ratings on all constructs — see the other elements.

(c) A group of 3 elements forming a separate group.

(d) An element which is least linked to any other element — i.e. No. 1 in this case.

(e) As one "ascends" the tree the matching score or degree of relationship between the elements decreases, e.g. at Node 13 matching score is 100, at Node 19 matching score is 85.

(f) Where one has printed out a reversal of a construct this indicates that on that construct the original ratings have been reversed, i.e. 1 is now 5 and 5 is now 1, a 4 becomes a 2 and a 2 is entered into the focused grid as a 4. A

3 remains the same. In order to retain the original meaning of the ratings one must now reverse the pole names on that particular construct, for example, in this grid Construct 4 has been reversed. If the original pole names were *Good/Bad* this construct should now be given the reversed label of *Bad/Good*.

(g) The tree for constructs can be explored in a similar fashion to the element tree, i.e. note highly matched pairs or groupings of constructs.

As was mentioned in the discussion on the use of acetate sheets, one may be interested in monitoring the changes in an individual's construing over a period of time. One can exploit the FOCUS computer program to explore changes if a series of grids are elicited. If one keeps the constructs constant and enters the ratings for the elements on two occasions in the same raw grid one can compare the ratings given for each element (see Fig. 19).

	E1	E2	E3	E4		E15	E16	E17	E18	E19		E30
C1	3	4	1	5	....	4	5	2	3	5	....	4
C2	2	3	4	3	....	5	4	2	4	3	....	5
C3	4	5	2	5	....	3	2	2	3	4	....	3
	.	.	.	....			.	.	.	....		
	.	.	.	....			.	.	.	....		
C14	2	1	4		....	2	5	1	3		....	2
C15	3	3	4	3	....	3	4	3	4	1	....	5

Fig. 19. "Combined" raw grid.

Figure 19 represents a portion of a combined grid with 15 constructs and 15 elements on the first occasion. The ratings for elements 16–30 are those for elements 1–15 on the second occasion. Thus one can see that in element No. 15 ratings have changed very little compared with the change on element No. 1 ratings. By pooling the ratings in this way one can obtain a matching score matrix for elements. Figure 20 is a portion of a 30 × 30 element matrix which highlights the different matching scores obtained for each element with itself. In this example (Fig. 20) one can see that the 3 elements "atmosphere", "area in which I teach" and "long term commitment" have changed most between occasions 1 and 2.

One could also explore possible changes in each of the original set of constructs between the various occasions. This is achieved by holding the elements constant and entering two sets of ratings along each construct (one set being the ratings on one occasion and the second the ratings obtained on a subsequent occasion) in the same raw grid. See Fig. 21 where, for example, Construct 18 is the ratings for construct 3 on the second occasion.

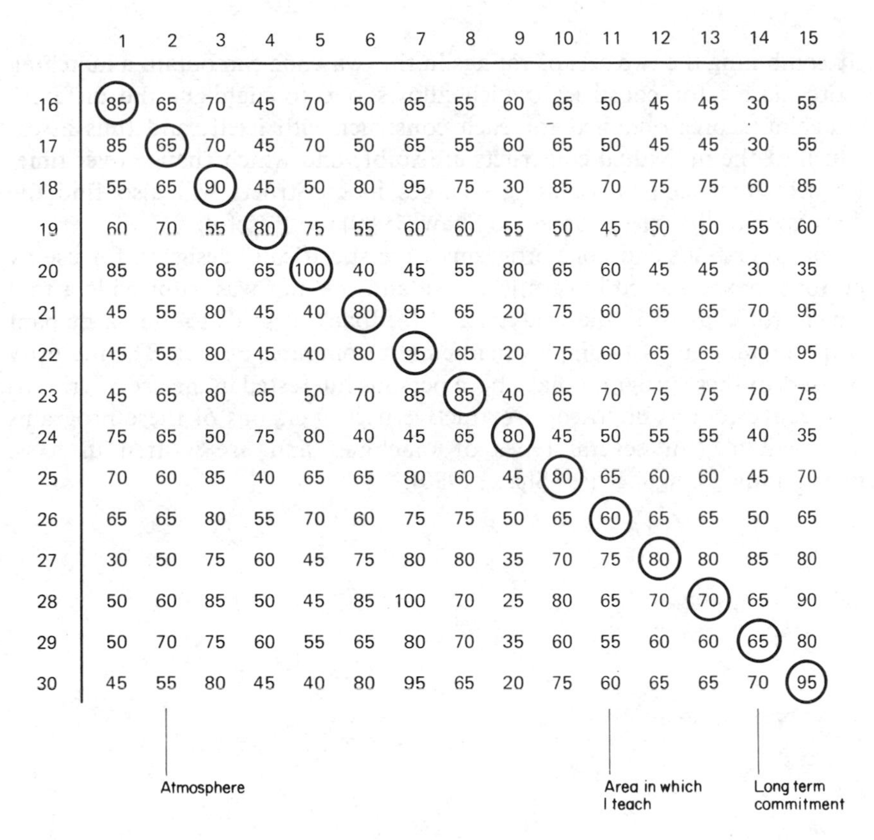

	1	2	3	4	5	6	7	8	9	10	11	12	13	14	15
16	85	65	70	45	70	50	65	55	60	65	50	45	45	30	55
17	85	65	70	45	70	50	65	55	60	65	50	45	45	30	55
18	55	65	90	45	50	80	95	75	30	85	70	75	75	60	85
19	60	70	55	80	75	55	60	60	55	50	45	50	50	55	60
20	85	85	60	65	100	40	45	55	80	65	60	45	45	30	35
21	45	55	80	45	40	80	95	65	20	75	60	65	65	70	95
22	45	55	80	45	40	80	95	65	20	75	60	65	65	70	95
23	45	65	80	65	50	70	85	85	40	65	70	75	75	70	75
24	75	65	50	75	80	40	45	65	80	45	50	55	55	40	35
25	70	60	85	40	65	65	80	60	45	80	65	60	60	45	70
26	65	65	80	55	70	60	75	75	50	65	60	65	65	50	65
27	30	50	75	60	45	75	80	80	35	70	75	80	80	85	80
28	50	60	85	50	45	85	100	70	25	80	65	70	70	65	90
29	50	70	75	60	55	65	80	70	35	60	55	60	60	65	80
30	45	55	80	45	40	80	95	65	20	75	60	65	65	70	95

Fig. 20. A portion of a 30 × 30 element matching scores matrix.

	E1	E2	E3	E4..........E15	
C1	3	4	1	5............4	
C2	2	3	4	3............5	
C3	4	5	2	5............3	Set I
⋮					
C15	3	3	4	3............3	
C16	5	2	3	5............4	
C17	4	2	4	3............5	
C18	2	2	3	4............3	Set II
⋮					
C30	4	3	4	1............5	

Fig. 21. Raw grid.

By combining the two sets of ratings in this way one can obtain a matching score matrix for constructs which allows one to highlight the different matching scores obtained for each construct with itself, and thus assess which of the individual constructs are stable and which change over time. Readers interested in assessing changes in constructs will also find the discussion of the CORE program in Shaw (1980) most useful.

FOCUS, PEGASUS and CORE programs were specifically designed for use by persons inexperienced in computer use and the aim was to provide a tool which would assist in the analysis and feedback of grids to the participant with the minimum of complex mathematic computer output. The majority of users of these programs have been persons interested in the use of grids as a refective tool as opposed to extractive uses. Versions of these programs are available for several types of machines and are written in BASIC programming language (see Shaw, 1980).

6

Principal Component Analysis

Only two programs will be considered here: the Keen and Bell (1979) GRIDDLE package and Slater's INGRID (1972). The GRIDDLE package was developed as an alternative to the well-known INGRID program to provide a readily available package which would run on a 56K core microprocessor, and it is written in BASIC. The authors accept that it contains imperfections which are being worked on for a new GRIDDLE 2 program, which will provide output in terms easily understood by the non-technical user. However, GRIDDLE, as it now exists, has proved itself to be of real value provided that limited interpretive skills are acquired by the user. To facilitate this development, user comments are required and prospective users should contact the authors. No charge is made for GRIDDLE 1, providing potential users acknowledge the source of the material when undertaking any publication or presentation by paper of work which has used the program.

One can direct attention to specific parts of the printout from which important relationships contained in the original grid may be identified. Figure 22 shows a typical printout.

GRID BEING ANALYSED

```
1 4 2 2 2 5 3
3 2 1 5 4 3 0
1 5 4 1 2 5 1
2 1 1 2 2 5 2
```

SUMMARY INTRACLASS CORRELATIONS

N. CONSTRUCTS	CONSTRUCT-R	ELEMENT-R
2	-0.196	-0.162
3	0	-0.163
4	0.192	-0.12

CONSTRUCT STATISTICS

	N	MEAN	SDEV	MIN	MAX
L1/R1	7	2.71	1.28	1	5
L2/R2	7	2.57	1.59	0	5
L3/R3	7	2.71	1.75	1	5
L4/R4	7	2.14	1.25	1	5

CONSTRUCT CORRELATIONS

1.00	−0.20	0.73	0.56
−0.20	1.00	−0.20	0.25
0.73	−0.20	1.00	0.22
0.56	0.25	0.22	1.00

	RMS	SMC	MSA
L1/R1	0.545	0.744	1.34
L2/R2	0.217	0.238	0.653
L3/R3	0.454	0.594	0.601
L4/R4	0.377	0.522	0.000

ELEMENT STATISTICS

	N	MEAN	SDEV	MIN	MAX
A	4	1.75	0.829	1	3
B	4	3	1.58	1	5
C	4	2	1.22	1	4
D	4	2.5	1.5	1	5
E	4	2.5	.866	2	4
F	4	4.5	.866	3	5
G	4	1.5	1.12	0	3

ELEMENT CORRELATIONS

1.00	-0.76	-0.74	0.90	0.87	-0.87	-0.67
-0.76	1.00	0.90	-0.53	-0.37	0.37	0.14
-0.74	0.90	1.00	-0.68	-0.47	0.47	0.00
0.90	-0.53	-0.68	1.00	0.96	-0.96	-0.60
0.87	-0.37	-0.47	0.96	1.00	-1.00	-0.77
-0.87	0.37	0.47	-0.96	-1.00	-1.00	0.77
-0.67	0.14	0.00	-0.60	-0.77	0.77	1.00

PRINCIPAL COMPONENTS FOR 4 CONSTRUCTS OF 4

EIGENVALUES

3 NON-ZERO EIGENVALUES

1	22.6	55.9	55.9
2	12.5	30.9	86.8
3	5.36	13.2	100
4	-0.12	-0.297	99.7

CONSTRUCT VECTORS

1	-0.30	0.69	-0.22	0.61
2	0.90	0.43	0.03	1.00
3	-0.05	0.05	0.96	0.93
4	0.31	-0.58	-0.15	0.46

ELEMENT VECTORS

1	0.20	-0.29	-0.13	0.14
2	-0.17	0.16	-0.78	0.67
3	0.21	-0.02	0.50	0.29
4	0.51	0.15	-0.18	0.32
5	0.32	0.03	-0.11	0.12
6	-0.07	0.50	-0.01	0.26
7	-0.50	-0.26	-0.06	0.33

Fig. 22. Part of a typical GRIDDLE printout.

After printing the grid being analysed the computer determines the intraclass correlations for elements and constructs. For the new user these may be ignored, although reference to Chapter 6 will indicate the potential value of such computations (see also Fransella and Bannister (1977) on cognitive complexity).

The construct statistics are then listed. The table has in order, as columns, the number of elements considered on that construct, the mean of the respondent's grading of those elements, the standard deviation and the minimum and maximum assigned score. Each successive row considers a new construct. Having completed the construct relationships, a construct correlation table is produced. This indicates the positive and negative relationships between all the constructs used.

The element statistics are then considered in precisely the same way with the printout indicating the element correlations in a similar matrix. Already the user will be able to extract much information which can be beneficially used in a consultation with his client. For a variety of reasons (which it would be inappropriate to explore in this volume, but which are considered at length in the GRIDDLE manual), the user might wish to exercise certain statistical options. These include:

(1) Remove grand mean effect.
(2) Remove construct means.
(3) Remove element means.
(4) Standardize by construct.
(5) Standardize by element.

The user can select the chosen statistical option, and subsequent analysis is based on a rescaled grid. *For the user who is doubtful of the meaning of any statistical operation it is best to omit the options altogether and continue using the basic grid.* The danger of using an option is exemplified by some evidence we found from one study where a researcher using Slater's INGRID analysis package had used the "remove construct means" option. In the grid concerned the respondent had scored zero on every construct for one provided element indicating that the element was unknown to him. The Slater package scans the constructs for such lack of variation but not the elements so the column was included in the analysis. Removing construct means resulted in the column of zeros becoming a column of small numbers (either positive or negative) with a very small standard deviation. Thus in the final analysis the element had a large vector on the first principal component, so not only did the statistical operation hide the fact that the element was not construed by the respondent but raised it to the highest level of significance. The GRIDDLE program checks for such potential errors even if options are chosen but the example is intended to highlight the importance of knowing the implication of opting for certain statistical operations. Eigen values are then compiled for 2 of n components, then 3 of n etc., to n of n components with tables of element and construct vectors listed.

The user who wishes to get some indication of a component description will scan each column of vectors (one column for each component) and select the three highest vectors, irrespective of sign for both elements and constructs. The component is thus defined as some amalgam of these construct labels and element titles. A profile not dissimilar to a TARGET profile (Keen 1976) can then be constructed. The INGRID (Slater, 1977) package offers similar options together, and these programs can be used to analyse grids with not more than 30 elements or constructs per grid. The program will analyse any number of individual grids one after another in sequence. The elements may be ranked or graded in terms of the constructs. Grading may be dichotomous, as favoured by the original form of Kelly grids, on a seven-point scale (as favoured by users of Osgood's "semantic differential"), on percentage scales, or on five-point scales as is popularly the case. Whatever the rating system adopted for evaluating the elements, it should be maintained for all the constructs in the same grid, and all the constructs should include all the elements in their range of convenience. For instance, if ranking is used all the elements must be ranked in terms of each of the constructs. Ranking reduces to grading when ties are allowed; that is to say, grids with tied ranks are analysed as graded. When using the Slater INGRID package, each grid is introduced by a pilot card giving, among other information, the number of constructs and elements, the rating system used and the options selected for the output. So grids with different numbers, systems and options can be included in the same sequence. Principal component analysis is incorporated. There is a set of tables at the end of the output, defining the relationships among the elements, and between the constructs and the elements in terms of direction cosines mathematically equivalent to correlation coefficients. Thus all the associations among the constructs and the elements are expressed in comparable terms and can be assembled and presented in a single table.

The mean and the total variation, i.e. the sum of squares of deviations from the mean, are calculated for each construct: the grand total of the variation for all the constructs (V) is accumulated; and the percentage contributed by each construct to V is derived.

If the respondent is applying the same grading scale consistently to all the constructs, the means, totals and percentages per construct will not differ greatly. Theoretically it may seem reasonable to suppose that the constructs in terms of which the respondent can discriminate better between the elements will be the ones which will have the larger totals and percentages; but in practice the ones with the larger totals may turn out to be those where the respondent discrimination is cruder. Elements may then be pushed out to one extreme or other of the construct scale and no finer distinctions made. They may be seen, for instance, as black or white with no intermediate shades of grey. Gross differences between means, totals and percentages are evidences that the same grading scale is *not* being applied consistently with all the constructs.

The researcher must decide whether to retain such differences between the constructs in the later stages of the analysis or to eliminate them by having the constructs normalized, i.e. rescaled so that they each have their total variation put equal to unity. (Note the authors' earlier caution.) Respondents who use the grading scale consistently for all their constructs differ from one another in the way they use it: some avoid both extremes on every scale; some gravitate towards one pole to avoid the other; some favour the extremes and avoid the midpoint. Such differences between respondents may be described by measures of bias and variability.

The following section, printed in italics, is considered optional for all but the most mathematically orientated reader determined to get to grips with the analyses.

Bias *increases when more elements are referred to one pole of a construct than the other. The difference between the mean for the construct and the midpoint of the grading scale measures the amount and direction of the bias in the grading scale. The direction cannot be treated as the same in all the constructs, but the amount of the bias can be accumulated for all of them and expressed as a standard deviation.*

A variance ratio, F, *may be calculated from this measure and the measure of variability, to test whether the amount of bias is significant.* F *is entered in a table of variance ratios. The test may not throw much light on the psychological interpretation of the observation, as evidence from another closely related measure indicates that a significant degree of bias is normal.*

Variability *increases as the elements are contrasted more widely on the grading scale. It reaches its maximum when the elements are evenly balanced at the opposite poles. If there is any construct in the grid where every element has been put in the same grade, it is discarded, but this is not true of any element where every construct is put in the same grade. The breakdown of the total variation about the construct means,* V, *into its subtotals per construct is the first of many given in the printout.*

Before the analysis is carried any further, the original grid is replaced by a table of deviations from the construct means, D, *which is not printed out. It may be visualized as a table with a row for every construct and a column for every element. The sum of the entries in every row is 0·0. The sum of their squares per row is displayed in the printout when ranking has been used or the option to normalize the constructs has been taken. Otherwise the sum of squares for each construct, i.e. for each row of* D, *remain unchanged. For the correlations the variances of the constructs must be normalized. Thus, geometrically speaking, the constructs are all assigned locations at an equal distance from a common origin, and differ only in being placed in different directions away from it. They lie on the surface of a hypersphere, and the difference between any two of them can be expressed as an angular or circumferential distance: the angle they subtend at the centre. An angle of 0° corresponds with a correlation of +1·0., an angle of 90° corresponds with a correlation 0·0., which implies that the constructs are independent of one another, and so on. The two constructs are located diametrically opposite one another: one provides the same scale of measurement as the other, but in reverse. In some contexts it is an advantage to consider the angular distances between constructs rather than their correlations: the average of a set of angles is itself an angle, whereas the average of a set of correlations is not itself a correlation. So the angle corresponding to each correlation is printed out alongside it. Such measurements can be used for comparing grids. For instance it would be possible to compare the average angular distances between the constructs* Like me as I am *and* Like I would like to be *in the grids of respondents from different classes, without necessarily using a standard set of elements for every grid or keeping the other constructs the same.*

The entries referring to each element in the table of deviations, i.e. the entries in each column of D, *are summed, so are their squares, and the results are listed. The cumulative total of all the sums of squares is also printed out giving the value of* V, *if it was not given previously because ranking was used or if it was redefined by normalization. All the constructs have the same total variation under ranking or normalization. The totals per element are also expressed as percentages of* V, *and listed with the element totals, opposite the element number.*

The sums of squares *for different elements may vary widely. A small sum of squares implies that the informant's attitude towards the element is indifferent; he has rated it neither high nor low but near the mean on all the constructs. Conversely, if the sum of squares is large the element must be an important one in the subject's construct system, whether his attitude towards it is consistently favourable or consistently unfavourable, or favourable in some respects and unfavourable in others. A large range of positive and negative quantities among the* totals *indicates a simple construct system where all the constructs tend to give convergent results; all running, for instance, from high to low along a common evaluation scale. A narrow range, however, does not necessarily indicate a much more complicated system: the constructs may all still relate to a common scale, only with some running in the opposite direction to the others. In either case, the elements will differ from one another mainly in one dimension, which will be the major axis of the construct system. Their distribution along the axis must always be balanced about a central point, but otherwise it may take on any form: it is not at all unusual to find many elements clustered at one end of an axis balancing a few or only one at the other. In a more complicated construct system the elements may spread out from the central point in several directions, the less important individually remaining closest to the centre and the more important spreading further away. The distance of an element from the centre is a function (the square root) of its sum of squares. If one salient element is sharply distinguished from the rest, the contrast between it and them may well form the most important axis in the construct system. For better or worse it sets the scale or standard according to which the rest are judged; thus the term trend-setting has been used to describe it.*

The distances between pairs of elements are worth examining as well as their individual distances from the centre. It is here that evidence of clustering or isolation will be found. The expected distance between two elements drawn from a construct system at random can be calculated. This quantity is displayed in the printout, and the observed distances between all possible pairs of elements are compared with it and displayed in a table of distances between elements.

Distances can be used for comparing grids in the same way that angular distances were formerly used. Myself as I am *and* Myself as I would like to be *can, for instance, be used as elements instead of the corresponding constructs mentioned above. The average distance between the two elements could then be used for comparing groups, without necessarily standardizing all the other specifications of the experimental grids.*

In the course of calculating the sums of squares for the elements and the distances between them, the squares and products of the deviations in D *are summed by element to form an* m *by* m *covariance matrix* D′D, *and it is to this matrix that the principal component analysis is applied.*

Like the grid from which it was obtained, the table of deviations, D, *has a row for every construct and a column for every element. In terms of Cartesian geometry, the column of entries for an element gives its location in a space where there is an axis for every construct, so the complete table defines the dispersion of the elements as a scatter of* m *points in the construct-space, which has* n *dimensions. The table can also be read by row: the entries for a construct locate it as a point in a space with an axis for every element, so the complete table also defines the dispersion of the constructs as a scatter of* n *points in an* m*-dimensional element space. The two views are strikingly different although they both belong to the same data.*

Principal component analysis is consistent with both views of the data. It provides a common co-ordinate system for the two dispersions and thus establishes the connection between the two techniques. Its most important advantage, however, is different: the components form an ordered series, each accounting for an independent part of the total variation from the largest to the least. In this respect principal component analysis is unique.

No axes, other than those of the components, can be used to analyse the total variation in this orderly way; any rotation of the axes sacrifices the advantage.

If the elements are given similar ratings on a large number of the constructs, the main differences between them can be shown on a single scale. Their measurements on it can be found by adding their ratings on the constructs in certain proportions. The scale which shows the greatest amount of variation is the axis of the first component. The amount of variation shown on it is given by the latent root, *which is a sum of squares accounting for part of the total variation about the construct means,* V. *The proportions in which the ratings for an element on the constructs should be combined to obtain its measurement on the scale of the component are given by a set of coefficients, one for each of the constructs, and called the construct vector. The measurements themselves are listed as element loadings.*

This is not the only way of considering the results. The importance of distinguishing between certain elements or groups of elements may govern the informant's choice and use of the constructs included in the grid. So it is just as reasonable to relate a component directly to the elements and define it in terms of an element vector, from which construct loadings can be derived. A principal component is completely defined by its latent root, its construct vector and its element vector.

The latent root *is a single numerical quantity which must be positive or zero; and the sum of the latent roots of the components is equal to* V.

The construct vector *is a set of coefficients, one for each of the constructs. It is listed in a column. The coefficients are normalized, that is to say, scaled so that the sum of their squares equals 1·0.*

The element vector, *similarly, is a normalized set of coefficients, one for each element. It is also listed in a column in the printout, though there are contexts in which it needs to be treated as a row of numbers.*

The element loadings for a component can be obtained from the element vector by multiplying the coefficients by the square root of the latent root; and multiplying the coefficients in the construct vector by the same quantity gives the construct loadings. Although vectors and loadings are related in this simple way they are both printed out.

A second component may then be computed to account for the residuals in D(1). *Like the first, it is specified by an element vector, a construct vector and a latent root. Element loadings and construct loadings are also obtained by rescaling the vectors so that the sums of their squares equal the latent root. The second component reduces* V(1) *as far as possible, namely to* V(2), *which may still not be zero. In that case a second table of residual deviations* D(2), *will still be left, including some non-zero entries, and the analysis will continue.*

Three, four or a good many more components may be needed to complete an exhaustive analysis, but it is unusual to find much variation left in an individual grid after three components have been extracted. Osgood (1963) is deeply committed to a particular formulation of the opinion that evaluative systems are three-dimensional.

The total number of positive components, t, *is limited by the number of constructs and the number of elements in the grid. When the grid is replaced by the table of deviations from the construct means,* D, *the dispersion of the elements is balanced about its central point. If there are only two elements their relative positions will be defined by two points on a straight line with the central point midway between them. The relative positions of the points for three elements can be shown on a surface of two dimensions at most, and so on. Thus the maximum number of dimensions into which a dispersion of* m *elements and* n *constructs can extend is one less than the smaller of* m *or* n.

The construct vector of the major component specifies the dimension within this space where most of the variation between the elements occurs; the vector of the second, the dimension where most of the remaining variation occurs outside the dimension of the first; and so on. The amount of variation is given by the latent root. Dimensions where no variation occurs will be specified by components with zero latent roots. So once again, t, *the number of components with positive latent roots, cannot exceed* m-*1 or* n-*1, whichever is the less.*

The well-known Bartlett test for principal component analyses in general (to decide whether the remaining variation after a given number of the major components have been extracted is scattered at random over the remaining dimensions), is applied to the data to determine the number of components significant at the 0·05 level. The results are not always helpful and indeed the authors find little evidence to support the application of this test in the INGRID *package. The test works backwards from the smallest roots to the largest; and there may be some dimensions in a grid where the variation is restricted as well as some where it is notably extensive. Indeed the two effects are likely to be concomitant. If there are a few exceptionally small roots the test may indicate that all the larger ones are significant, and confront the researcher with a perplexing problem in interpretation. What needs to be considered may be why the variation along some axes is so small, and the explanation may be quite a simple one — the informant may have failed to distinguish between some of the constructs or some of the elements.*

The dimensionality of a grid, as illustrated, cannot exceed n-*1 or* m-*1, whichever is the less. It may be further reduced, for instance, if the informant has given identical ratings to two of the elements, or if one of the constructs has been cut out because he has rated all the elements the same on it. If, for a given grid there are* t *dimensions (components) then the complete set of* t *latent roots is listed in order of magnitude. Their numerical values of their proportionate size as percentages of the total observed variation,* V, *are also given. The results of the Bartlett test follow in the printout. Each successive application of the Bartlett test is followed by the appropriate value of* chi-*squared, with the appropriate degree of freedom.*

The test does not apply to the first component. *Having identified that a given number of components may be considered significant at the prescribed level, certain detailed information is listed in the printout for each component.*

Loadings have great interest from many perspectives. The total variation of a component, that is to say its latent root, is the sum of the squares of its element loadings, and also the sum of the squares of its construct loadings. It can be analysed in both ways: either into the amounts due to constructs 1, 2, . . . n, *or into the amount due to elements 1, 2, . . .* m*; and both alternatives are equally valid. A component is in fact a measurement of one way in which the constructs and the elements interact: the way in which it concerns the constructs may be easier to understand that the way in which it applies to the elements, or vice versa; but both need to be considered for a complete interpretation.*

The sum of squares for an element is the sum of squares of its component loadings, and it can be analysed in this way. The residuals listed in the printout simplify such an analysis. The residual from the first component can be compared with the original sum of squares; the residual from the second with the residual from the first, and so on. A large proportional drop indicates that the evaluation of the element is largely in terms of the component concerned. Similarly the variation of a construct is the sum of squares of its component loadings, and can be analysed as such. Again the residuals in the printout simplify the breakdown. A large drop from one component to the next shows that evaluation in terms of the constructs tends to coincide (positively or negatively) with evaluation in terms of the component. Loadings can also be used for representing the results of a grid graphically. Although there are of course a limitless number of ways in which that can be done, two deserve special consideration as exact geometrical equivalents, the first has been considered as a means of checking the representatives of an element sample by Keen (1979).

The first is the dispersion of the elements in the component space within the construct space. As already explained, the entries in the same column of

D, *which all refer to the same element, together specify a point for the element in a space where the reference axes are defined by the constructs. The entire array of numbers in* D, *corresponds geometrically with a dispersion of* m *points in this space, which is* n*-dimensional. The distances between the points in it are the distances between the elements. Its dispersion is not equally wide in all directions within the construct-space. The construct vector of the first component specifies the axis of the dimension where the variation between the elements is widest. The constructs with the highest positive coefficients contribute most to defining it positively; the ones with the highest negative values to defining it in the opposite direction. (Or both directions may be defined by the emergent and the implicit poles of the same construct.) The orthogonal, i.e. independent dimensions with successively smaller variation are similarly defined by the construct vectors of the successive components. The locations of the elements in this component-space are given by their component loadings; and their dispersion can be mapped conveniently in two dimensions at a time. One then plots the position of the elements from their loadings, and it is natural to consider the two major dimensions first. As the map cannot show how far the scatter extends outside them, generally it can only be approximate. How close the approximation is depends on how much of the total variation is attributable to the first two components. This is frequently as high as 90%. If the distance between two elements given in* (d) *is much greater than the distance mapped, it must occur in dimensions defined by the construct vectors of one or more of the components not on the map. So it must show up in some other map, constructed in the same way, referring to some pair of components in the construct-space. Although it is natural to consider the major components first, components which show relatively small amounts of variation are not necessarily devoid of interest. There must be some reasonable explanation if variation is particularly restricted along some dimension in the construct-space. It may not be at all difficult to detect. Two constructs may be effectively the same or almost the same, e.g. the ratings of the elements may differ scarcely if at all in terms of two constructs such as* Good/Bad *and* Like/Dislike. *Or two elements, e.g.* Myself as I am *and* Myself as I would like to be *may be virtually indistinguishable in terms of the constructs used in the grid. In either case, little or no use may have been made of one of the dimensions available in the grid for distinguishing between the constructs or the elements. Why the informant fails to make such a distinction may be a question of interest. The most useful results to examine in search of explanation, apart from the graphs described already, are the table of correlations between the constructs, and the table of distances between the elements. Sometimes the explanation may be more obscure and involved; and sometimes practical* considerations may make it not worth seeking. What is unjustifiable is a general assumption that dimensions where variation is small can have no interest.

The second geometrical equivalent for the numerical entries on the grid, which can be shown by graph, is the dispersion of the constructs in the component-space within the element-space. The entries in one row of a grid, or of D, can be treated like the entries in one column. Taken together, all the entries referring to one construct specify a point for it in a space where the reference axes are defined by the elements, or, in other words, the element-space. The points for the n constructs in the element-space are all either exactly or approximately equidistant from a central point, and consequently must lie on or near the surface of a hypersphere. Its dimensionality depends on the number of components with positive latent roots; that is to say, it occupies a t-dimensional component-space within the m-dimensional element-space. Constructs with high loadings on the first component only will cluster together in one region on the hypersurface if their loadings are positive, and in the diametrically opposite region if their loadings are negative. Such distributions are easy to examine when they are represented geographically. If the positive pole for the first component is set on the equator of a geographical globe at longitude 0°, its negative pole will be on the equator where the international date-line, longitude 180°E or W, intersects it. Constructs with high loadings on the second component only will be located on the surface around points 90° away from the two poles of the first component, e.g. on the equator at longitude 90°E for positive loadings and longitude 90°W for negative loadings. Constructs with high loadings on the third component only must then be located around the points 90° away from those already occupied, e.g. at the North pole for positive loadings and the South pole for negative ones. The geographical model can only, of course, include three components; but if the first three components account for over 80% of the total variation in grids of the customary size, the model for them will usually give a very useful indication of the relationships between the constructs.

Polar co-ordinates of the constructs can be computed and these are displayed on the printout as H, V and R. The values of H and V (horizontal and vertical measurements in degrees) are the ones to be used for plotting the positions of the constructs. The radial measurement R is not used in map-making. To be precise, a construct can only be located on the surface of the sphere if its value of R is 1·00. Otherwise, it should be located beneath the surface, proportionately nearer the surface the larger its R. R has other interesting properties: it defines the multiple correlation between the construct and the first three components; and R^2 is the proportion of its total variation they account for. A construct with a very small R could *perhaps be treated as if it had disappeared beneath the surface completely, for most of its variation must occur in dimensions unmapped. (To refer to an earlier argument, it approaches the point of total uncertainty, i.e. the origin, see Keen, 1978.)*

Among grids in general, the absence of any simple regularities is perpetual. When they both refer to the same components, a map of the dispersion of the elements in the construct-space and one of the constructs in the element-space are two different views of the same variation, for the variation of a component in the construct-space is identical with its variation in the element-space. So if suitable conventions are adopted, either map may be projected onto the other. It would be very misleading, however, just to superimpose one onto the other, and map the constructs and the elements together as n + m *points in a common component-space. The constructs should be represented as direction-lines in the component-space; and the elements as direction-lines in the component-space within the element-space where the constructs appear as points. As the direction of a line from an origin can be indicated by a single point at any distance from it, the difficulty can be overcome; but the convention being adopted must be clearly understood.*

Such composite maps take advantage of a unique property of principal components, in that they provide a stationary co-ordinate system in both spaces, allowing the two dispersions to be aligned. They may reveal interesting and unexpected relationships between elements and coincident or diametrically opposed constructs. Diametrically opposite the point for a construct, another point can be marked on the globe for its contrast, and since the projection for an element should be regarded as a hypothetical construct referring to it rather than as the element itself, it too may be regarded as bipolar and represented by two points, the pro-element and the anti-element. To obtain the polar co-ordinates for the opposite pole of a construct or a pro-element; when H *is positive, one can subtract 180°; when* H *is negative one can add 180°; and change the sign of* V.

For the reasons explained earlier, the relationships between the constructs and the elements and of the elements with one another can all be expressed in terms of direction cosines. These are mathematically equivalent to correlation coefficients and like them, serve to describe how closely two variables are associated. The printout concludes with four tables listing results of this kind. All these measurements refer to the relationships of the elements and the constructs with one another in the whole component-space, and enable a mathematical model to be used in place of the physical model previously described.

Certain analytical techniques will be favoured by particular researchers, and it is our view that each user may best determine his preference by trial and error, as despite fundamental differences of technique there is rarely any difference in the conclusions drawn from several different analytical approaches to the same data.

This extended theoretical consideration of the way Slater's INGRID package produces its output has been included as Keen, who used INGRID extensively in the work reported in Chapter 7, has found such reports difficult to come by, although they are crucial for a potential user who needs a relatively straightforward guide to the interpretation of a printout he may receive from his local friendly computer centre!

Part Three

So far we have been dealing with ideas and theory but have not demonstrated exactly what personal construct psychology has to offer. In this section we attempt to do just that. The last four chapters deal, in turn, with the work of each of us (Keen, Chapter 7, Pope, Chapter 8) and then the work of others in the field (Chapter 9), and we conclude with a chapter discussing the future. By reading what we have been doing in Chapters 7 and 8, we hope you will begin to appreciate the power of the instruments based on repertory grids, and we hope we will be able to pass on some of our enthusiasm for such work. Chapter 7 is less detailed than the later ones but attempts to show how wide-ranging is the interest in grids. It should point out areas where further research is likely to be beneficial and where it will widen the horizons.

The final chapter intends to draw the whole book to a conclusion, which is anything but a full stop! We hope that many researchers will find some comments in our summing up which will stimulate them to undertake personal construct psychology research in their own field and so make further progress in this exciting and developing area.

7

Personal Construct Psychology in Job Improvement and Pedagogic Effectiveness

TEACHER APPRAISAL

The authors have both worked in Europe where teacher assessment is still an unusual feature in education. Practising teachers become very upset at the thought of regular assessments of their effectiveness, which promotion and tenure might depend upon. Equally, the professional associations quite rightly resist the introduction of such techniques when there is little evidence to suggest that the criteria of effectiveness defined by some existing assessment instrument are based on sound rationale. Our colleagues on the other side of the Atlantic already have promotion and tenure linked to such schemes (e.g. Biles, 1976, IDEA) and seem less neurotic about their application. Whether assessment of teaching effectiveness is already a fact of life (as in the USA) or a feared future innovation (as in the UK) there is little doubt that we must consider education from a cost-effective basis, particularly in time of financial constraint. Such a realistic approach demands that we, as practising teachers, look critically at the way we do our job at all stages from the kindergarten to the university.

Keen first considered this problem in 1975, arguing that we spend a vast sum of money training our teachers to be professional, but seeming unwilling to trust them to evaluate their own performance against appropriate criteria. It follows, from such a stand, that the provision of some technique which would enable a teacher to determine, from his own professional knowledge, how well he was performing was all that would be required. Such a technique would, of course, have to be non-threatening and confidential to the individual until such time as he chose to disclose its content to his peers or superiors. Thus, in a Buxton Working Mens Club, on the last evening of a conference, TARGET was born, (Keen, 1979; Hopwood and Keen, 1978; Biles *et al.*, 1976). TARGET is an acronym for Teaching Appraisal by Repertory Grid Elicitation Techniques.

The developmental work was exciting and the system is still fully operational and made available to practising teachers by Keen's "partner in crime" Warren Hopwood at Plymouth Polytechnic. The project had emerged directly out of Keen's doctoral research and was modified for practical application. In essence the teacher who chose to avail himself of a TARGET appraisal went to a TARGET Centre where, after being given a card with a personal "secret" number, he embarked on the completion of a repertory grid, the elements of which were a mixture of teachers he knew, himself and some video-taped extracts of observed teaching acts. Upon completion of the grid, which was administered in a conversational way by

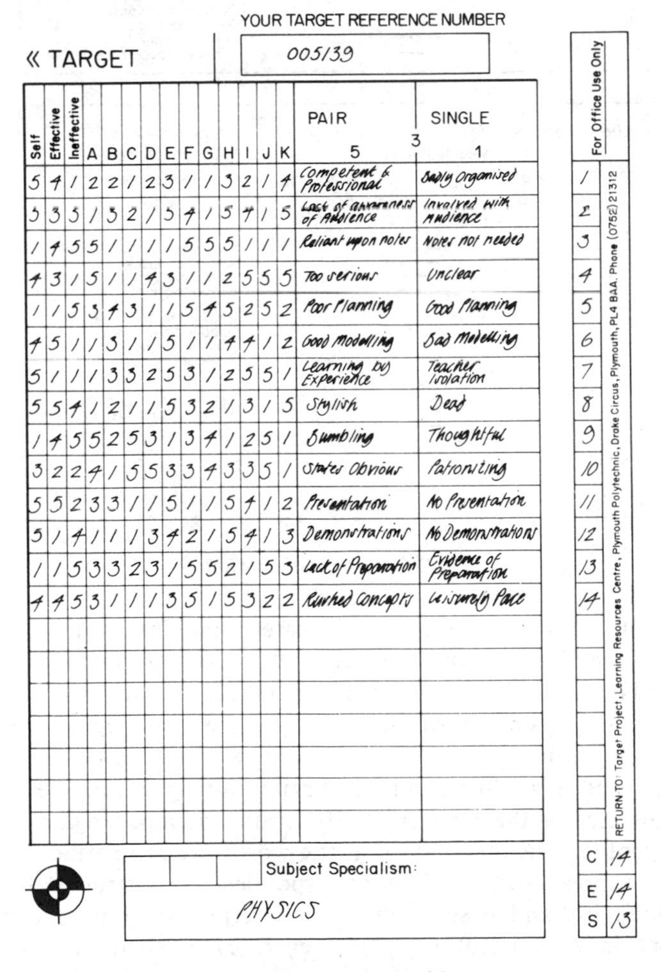

« TARGET

YOUR TARGET REFERENCE NUMBER: 005/139

Self	Effective	Ineffective	A	B	C	D	E	F	G	H	I	J	K	PAIR 5	3	SINGLE 1	For Office Use Only
5	4	/	2	2	/	2	3	/	/	3	2	/	4	Competent & Professional		Badly Organised	1
5	3	5	/	3	2	/	5	4	/	5	4	/	5	Lack of awareness of Audience		Involved with Audience	2
/	4	5	5	/	/	/	/	5	5	5	/	/	/	Reliant upon notes		Notes not needed	3
4	3	/	5	/	/	4	3	/	/	2	5	5	5	Too serious		Unclear	4
/	/	5	3	4	3	/	/	5	4	5	2	5	2	Poor Planning		Good Planning	5
4	5	/	/	3	/	/	5	/	/	4	4	/	2	Good Modelling		Bad Modelling	6
5	/	/	/	3	3	2	5	3	/	2	5	5	/	Learning by Experience		Teacher Isolation	7
5	5	4	/	2	/	/	5	3	2	/	3	/	5	Stylish		Dead	8
/	4	5	5	2	5	3	/	3	4	/	2	5	/	Bumbling		Thoughtful	9
3	2	2	4	/	5	5	3	3	4	3	3	5	/	States Obvious		Patronizing	10
5	5	2	3	3	/	/	5	/	/	5	4	/	2	Presentation		No Presentation	11
5	/	4	/	/	/	3	4	2	/	5	4	/	3	Demonstrations		No Demonstrations	12
/	/	5	3	3	2	3	/	5	5	2	/	5	3	Lack of Preparation		Evidence of Preparation	13
4	4	5	3	/	/	/	3	5	/	5	3	2	2	Rushed Concepts		Leisurely Pace	14

Subject Specialism: PHYSICS

C 14
E 14
S 13

RETURN TO: Target Project, Learning Resources Centre, Plymouth Polytechnic, Drake Circus, Plymouth, PL4 8AA. Phone (0752) 21312

Fig. 23. A typical grid.

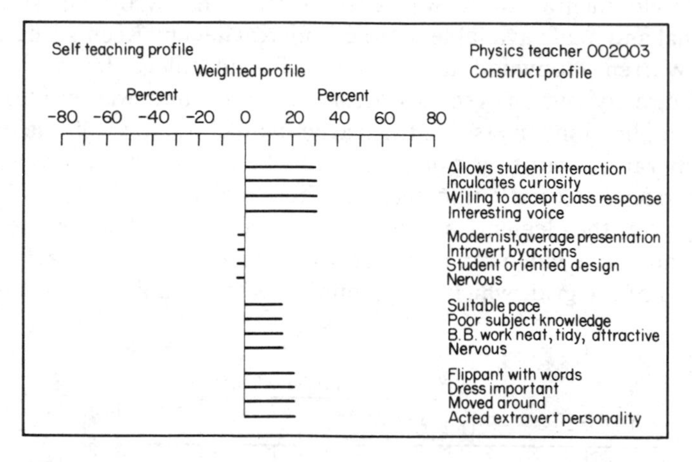

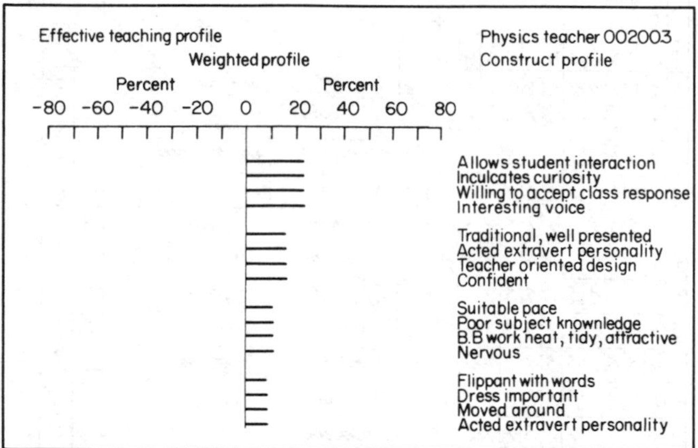

Fig. 24. A typical printout.

a member of the TARGET team, a sophisticated numerical analysis was undertaken based on Slater's INGRID package (1977). The production of a simply understood bar chart followed, from which the respondent could clearly see how his own perception of his performance matched his own ideal performance profile.

A typical grid (Fig. 23) and a typical printout (Fig. 24) enables the reader to see how clearly the teacher "self" profile mapped against his ideal effective profile. One must add that the words used to define each bar on the chart are those words used by the respondent as construct poles when he compiled the grid and as such cannot be interpreted by anyone except the respondent in any useful way. However, even when one ignores the verbal labels, in the example of Fig. 24, the powerful indication of one significant perceived defect is clearly evident.

The author administered the TARGET grid for two sets of respondents and provided bar chart feedback to half of the sample only. After two to four months a new set of grids were elicited from the same sample using common elements. In almost every case those teachers who had been deprived of feedback had not significantly altered their profile, but those for whom feedback had been given had all moved towards what they had defined as a more effective profile.

Critics of TARGET would argue that there is no guarantee that the respondent's idea of "effective" is really any nearer to some "true" effective style. This is of course true, however, the authors' stance, it will be recalled, was one which placed the teacher in the position of the "expert" or professional and one could argue that his criteria of effectiveness must necessarily be more relevant than some externally set, and often misunderstood criteria. It is for the reader to decide, but the authors have no doubt that the technique makes explicit those hidden facts, implicitly acceptable, but otherwise hidden from the external world of the observer.

The TARGET technique was later refined by Keen and modified as a management appraisal tool and has been used in a variety of management training programmes by a number of industrial and educational bodies.

STUDENT LEARNING

It is the last few years which have shown a change in emphasis from teaching to learning. During the same period, Drama has emerged as a "respectable" discipline, and been distinguished from what many laymen (including the authors) had formerly called "Theatre". It was to this area that Keen directed his attention in 1979 when he became an advisor to a research student investigating the effectiveness of learning in Drama (Keen and Abbott, in preparation). In this project a quite different use of the grid was developed.

A group of students studying Drama in a large secondary school were to be given a series of Drama sessions centred on relationships between themselves and their significant others (e.g. siblings, relatives, parents, peers, etc.). The researcher wanted to know to what extent the Drama experience affected these relationships. The usual experimental precautions were taken (e.g. control groups, etc.), and the experimental groups asked to complete a grid where the elements were "significant others". Conversational elicitation was used and no analysis or feedback was provided. After the Drama experience the experimental group were again asked to complete a grid from the same elements and constructs as before, but encouraged to expand the grid by elements and/or constructs. The analysis (this time a clustering technique was used, Shaw, 1978) was very revealing, and convincing changes had occurred in the individuals who had been exposed to the Drama experience which were not evident in the "control" group.

RAISING PERCEPTUAL AWARENESS

All work using personal construct psychology leads to the raising of perceptual awareness but the authors, in their attempt to illustrate three quite different approaches which have been used, chose this heading to describe the kind of activity, based in personal construct psychology, which can be adopted without using a grid and which does not require any statistical analysis. Such an approach is particularly useful in group training seminars when students or teachers need to focus their attention on a specific problem at great depth, and endeavour to see unusual or unique solutions in a more systematic way than could be achieved by such approaches as brainstorming. Keen has used this approach with secondary school and polytechnic students in learning to learn courses as well as in his role as "staff developer" attempting to improve its quality of teaching performance from his staff. The format of the approach is that of a game which is called "Misunderstood".

The Rationale for the Game

This game has been developed at Stantonbury Campus Resource Centre by Keen, from a research method used by Thomas and Mendoza at the Centre for the Study of Human Learning, Brunel University and used by Reid at Plymouth Polytechnic. Thomas and Mendoza were concerned with developing simple techniques by which misunderstandings and failures of communication between people might be highlighted in a way that enabled them to discuss and come to terms with their differences. The theory which forms the basis of the game is Personal Construct Psychology (Kelly, 1955; Bannister and Mair, 1968). This has been used by a number of researchers as a forcing technique in encouraging respondents to think more carefully about the way they construe the world around them. It also functions in such a way that it encourages people to invent and test out new ways of viewing what seem to be intractable problems.

In the version of the game developed by Reid at Plymouth Polytechnic, the object was to score as many points as possible with individuals competing against each other. This version of the game was called "Misconstrued". Points could be scored in two ways — by persuading and convincing other players to view a discussion topic as you do and by inventing ways of viewing the discussion topic that other players have not yet thought of. In the Keen version of the game called "Misunderstood", the competitive element is less important, although it is crucial that game participants endeavour to search out all possible ways of viewing the areas of difficulty, and utilize the game as a means of highlighting their perception awareness in terms of their understanding of other people's constructions of the problem.

Materials

In order to play the game, groups of three or four players are required. With less than three the range of constructs explored is somewhat limited, and with more than four, the length of time taken to play each round of the game is so long that the game cannot be completed in a realistic time period. Thus, if it is intended to play "Misunderstood" for large groups, it is essential that the group be broken up into small sub-groups of three or four persons. Each individual player requires one score sheet, a number of construct trays, depending on how long it is intended to let the game run for (two construct trays enables a game with four players to be completed in about one and a quarter hours), one pack of topic cards consisting of twelve cards of the same colour, and for each group, one pack of twelve differently coloured topic cards.

To Start

(1) Decide on a topic area. It is useful to choose a topic area relevant to the area of training being considered.

(2) Working as a group, name twelve examples of the chosen topic, making sure the examples are as varied as possible. The intention here is to get down as many as twelve different aspects of the topic chosen, some of which may be advantageous, some may be strengths or weaknesses, or difficulties associated with the topic area. Anything can be used, providing there can be some defensible connection explained between the choice of the topic and the item written on the cards. These twelve examples of the chosen topic are written on the twelve coloured cards for each team.

(3) Someone takes the twelve cards, having completed the writing of the twelve items on to them and shuffles them. The randomly sorted pack is

then numbered from 1–12. Each player then copies the twelve examples on to his separate personal topic cards, numbering them in exactly the same way as the original pack of topic cards. It is essential that all players number their topic cards in exactly the same way so that for each individual player, the twelve examples correspond to exactly the same number for each one of them. The numbers should appear on the reverse side to the chosen items.

(4) Each player, now working individually, takes a construct tray, writes his or her name in the appropriate space, and begins playing the game.

To Play the Game

(1) Each player, working individually, selects the first three topic cards numbered on the score sheet from his personal pack.

(2) Working entirely on his own, he thinks of some important and original way in which any two of the three topic examples seem to be alike and in contrast to the third.

(3) Once the players have made up their minds, they take a construct tray and write in the box provided a word or phrase that summarizes how the two topic cards he has chosen are alike. He then writes in the other box a word or phrase to summarize how the third topic card differs from the pair. It is crucial that at this stage of the game that each player continues to work individually.

(4) All twelve cards are now picked up by each individual player. He considers the cards one at a time and decides whether each is best described by the left-hand or right-hand definition on the construct tray. Having made that distinction, he places the card face down on the appropriate pack. Thus, at the end of the game, he has two packs of cards, one pack corresponding to each of the two descriptors he has written on the construct tray.

Sending and Receiving Constructs

(1) When all players have completed the steps above, toss a coin to decide who will send their construct first.

(2) The sender then describes his construct poles to the other players, without any reference to the sort of topic cards he has made. Whilst he is doing this, the receivers may interrogate him in any way they wish except by enquiring about the sender's allocation of his topic cards.

(3) The sender, once the receivers are satisfied that they have understood the sender's construct, then takes each card from the group pile of topic

cards (they are the ones that are coloured differently), and discusses with the rest of the group where he thinks it should go in relation to his own construct. Clearly, the receivers will have their own views as to which pile each particular topic card should be placed on, bearing in mind their understanding of the construct used by the sender. It is likely that some heated debate will ensue, and where it is impossible to come to some unanimous decision, a vote may have to be taken to determine where the card has ultimately to be placed. At the end of this part of the game there will be two piles of cards in addition to the two piles placed by the sender on his construct tray.

(4) When these packs are complete, the sender turns over his topic cards and compares his allocation with that agreed by discussion in the group.

(5) If the sender and receivers agree completely on the allocation of topic cards, the sender scores five points for every card which is placed in the same pile by the group as he placed the card in his original sort. For each of these cards, the receivers are not awarded any points.

(6) If sender and receivers differ in the allocation of topic cards, the receivers score five points for each difference and the sender receives no points. The system of scoring advantages the receiver because for every single mis-match there will be two cards that are not paired and therefore this score will be double that of the sender. Having completed this, each member writes down his personal score in the appropriate place on the score sheet.

(7) The coin is flipped again to determine the next sender and the steps above are repeated. When all players have sent and negotiated their constructs, the game is started again, but only after the total score for the round is entered on the appropriate space on the score sheet. The game is started again by each player taking a second construct tray, selecting the second set of three topic cards numbered on the score sheet and forming, sending and receiving a second, and different, construct.

The function of the game, as was indicated in the introduction, is to understand more clearly the way other people perceive problems and, we hope, to generate unique solutions to these problem areas. If, however, no unusual or unique solutions emerge, it is likely that all participants have learned to construe and understand the problem area in a much more complete way and have become able to look at difficult areas, not only from their own perspective, but from that of their colleagues.

This chapter has, we hope, already given the reader some indication of the range of application of personal construct psychology Keen has made in the last year or so. His current interests have been directed towards analytical techniques (with Bell) and the application of fuzzy set mathematics to grid analysis (with Roberts). This is particularly exciting work as it enables a grid to be elicited completely without numbers, using normal conversation. Returning to more traditional techniques, Keen and Bell considered the advantages of using microprocessors to elicit grids when developing their DYAD package.

DEVELOPMENT OF COMPUTER ANALYSIS AS A TOOL IN EDUCATIONAL ENQUIRY

A computer can be used in two ways to assist the researcher who is collecting and analysing repertory grid data. The first is to analyse the matrix of numbers obtained, so as to reveal the underlying structure of the constructs and their relationships amongst the elements. Sophisticated numerical analytical techniques are required for this aspect and a number of programmes have been written to achieve this end (Slater, 1977; Shaw and Thomas, 1976, *etc.*). Repertory grid usage has increased recently largely as a consequence of the increased availability of computers for this kind of analysis. The second way in which computers can be used by the researcher or clinician using repertory grids is to facilitate the elicitation of the grid itself. Shaw and Thomas (1978), and Shaw (1978) describe one such programme, PEGASUS, and Boxer (personal communication) has developed a similar kind of programme.

Shaw and Gaines (1979) noted the value of the absence of interpersonal interaction. "When constructs are being elicited by a computer program then one is more likely to accept that it is precisely and only oneself that is being portrayed." Bell and Keen have drawn attention to another advantage. If grids are monitored as they are elicited then statistical information may be used in decision making about such things as the termination of the elicitation procedure.

However, in the above mentioned procedures, the repertory grid technique is assumed to be fairly standard. Firstly, a set of relevant elements is fed into the computer which returns three of them (a triad), among which the respondent must group two to form the emergent pole of the first construct and identify the third with the implicit pole of the construct. The procedure is basically repeated with subsequent triads, although feedback may be employed with respect to constructs and/or elements as in PEGASUS.

This procedure has a number of advantages, although there has been surprisingly little research into actual elicitation procedures. Triadic elicitation tends towards the statement of unidimensional bipolar constructs, although it is arguable whether this necessarily extends to the rating of the elements on this construct, and thus analysis by clustering or principal components may proceed from reliable bases.

As has been indicated in Chapter 4, a person eliciting a grid in what may be termed traditional ways can choose from an enormous repertoire of techniques, many of which have been well documented in Fransella and Bannister (1977). The grid, as Kelly would probably have argued, is merely a means of communication by conversation and the techniques referred to above are a means to achieve that end. One feature of many such strategies is triadic elicitation and whilst this, as we have shown, exhibits a number of advantages, it does present difficulties when used by clients of low intellectual ability or with young children who find the technique difficult to grasp. Indeed, there have been a number of research projects which chose to use grids and later abandoned the method due to apparently insurmountable "administrator" difficulties (Cashdan and Philps, 1974). The terminology is often unavoidable and the notions, such as triad, may appear an unusual and perhaps somewhat unnatural way of thinking. The argument can be raised that computer elicitation of this kind does not actually do anything a human administrator could not (leaving aside interpretive aids) do.

Keen and Bell's present approach attempted to avoid these problems. They began by thinking about how people think and converse. Drawing on their own experience, talking with their wives about the works of Conan Doyle, Poe and James Joyce, not to mention Freud, they came to the conclusion that thinking reflectively and conversing is meandering and unsystematic. People "string thoughts together" and often "one thing leads to another". Whilst it is difficult for an administrator to systematize such thoughts into a form suitable for analysis, they reasoned that a small computer ought to be able to cope. Thus, DYAD emerged.

One Thing at a Time

The basis of DYAD is the consideration of one element at a time. A second element is chosen as being different in some way (this way being the construct) and a third element is also chosen as relating to this construct. This third element becomes the first element for the next construct and so on. The elicitation procedure is shown diagrammatically in Fig. 25.

In this way elements and constructs are elicited conjointly. We would argue that it is not possible to consider elements without constructs (witness Zen paradoxes) and that classical elicitation may leave the real constructs (as opposed to their verbal labels) unstated and the elicitation is a procedure of uncovering these. In DYAD an element cannot be included without an accompanying construct, and likewise the constructs cannot exist without elements. The reason for including the third element (somewhere on the

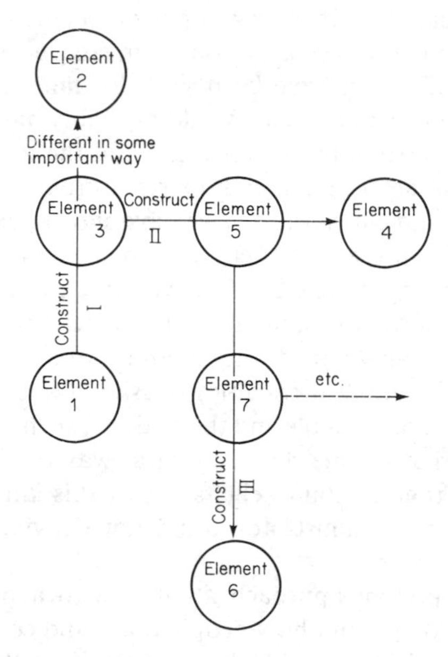

Fig. 25. DYAD elicitation of elements and constructs.

construct) is that we would argue that this element is introduced because it is important to the person (not in the way of the just elicited construct), and it would have been chosen as the second pole, but in a different way. Thus the subsequent construct emerges from the previous construct and element (see Fig. 25).

By looking again at the administration process and trying to identify an alternate approach in line with conversations and ideas generated by respondents, Keen and Bell decided that the natural way of conducting a "conversation" is incrementalist, i.e. one thing leads to another. Why not therefore start from a single theme and grow (element and construct) from there? This seemed to overcome some of the difficulties of administration and almost accidentally resulted in a dyadic approach which was unique in grid research, namely an elicitation procedure which could *only* be undertaken simply by a computer. They would not deny that there may be apparent weaknesses in this, not the least of which is the difficulty of ensuring bipolarity of constructs elicited in this way. Limited pilot schemes, however, have not shown this to be a major problem. Furthermore, the growing interest in developing fuzzy set mathematics (Shaw and Gaines, 1979) in relaton to grid elicitation could provide a mechanism for permitting degrees of membership of each pole and thus reduce any error which may emerge from this area. Keen, in an associated research project, has been considering the possibility of using probability estimates for every element in terms of being a full member of the set identified by each pole. Whilst this work is far from conclusion, due to enormous analytical problems, such a strategy might ultimately further strengthen the DYAD program. These associated developments are only seen as potentially useful if the reflective, simple language approach is further enhanced by their use. The authors contend that any complication of the simple task would weaken the instrument, even although statistical analyses might be demonstrably more robust.

In any evaluation of a "new" technique a potential user will weigh the "gains" (over alternative approaches) with the "losses", and the authors believe that there are some areas where the "balance" of such considerations is likely to make DYAD almost essential (see previous comments on the elicitation of grids from young children and mental defectives), whilst in other areas the "traditional" approach will clearly be seen to be "best". The one feature the authors would want to highlight is the simple way in which the "client" never sees a "grid" and yet is, nevertheless, completing a matrix, sometimes by column and sometimes by row, but always in the cognitive space uniquely defined by the interaction of both the element and the construct sample (see pp.60–63).

FUZZY SET MATHEMATICS AS APPLIED TO THE ANALYSIS AND INTERPRETATION OF REPERTORY GRID DATA

Kelly's original work on repertory grids was essentially bipolar in nature, and may be thought of as corresponding to the classical set theory, in which elements either are, or are not, members of a particular set. An extension of Kelly's repertory grid has been the use of multipoint rating scales in allocating elements to the poles of constructs, and these scales may be taken to define a "degree of membership" to the fuzzy sets defined by the construct poles. For example, in considering the fuzzy set of "pleasant music" and asking the question "What degree of membership does 'The Rite of Spring' have to this set?" Kelly's original work would imply that it must either belong, or not belong to that set. However, the use of multipoint rating scale would allow some graded set membership, i.e. the use of some form of fuzzy set theory.

There are several difficulties and questions concerning the use of numbers to allocate this degree of membership to the fuzzy set. In the above example, the question posed could be interpreted on a numeric scale of 1–5, say 2. If a second piece of music is then considered the response might be such that the most appropriate numeric score is once again 2. It may well be that the number 2 is being used to mean two entirely different things on each separate occasion.

A second problem with the use of numbers in grid elicitation is concerned with the allocation of a particular element to a certain number. This number must necessarily cover a wide range, and while it is possible to increase the number of scale points, there is still uncertainty as to whether an element can be allocated to a particular number or to one of its neighbours. Furthermore, there is evidence to suggest that respondents confronted with a scale upon which several fine increments exist find it difficult to determine the precise location of the element upon the scale. This uncertainty of allocation leads fairly naturally to the idea of using probability estimates for every element, in terms of it being a full member of the set identified by each pole.

There are then two main strands to this proposed research:

(1) The use of probabilities to classify elements in relation to sets identified by each pole.

(2) The use of a non-numeric language in eliciting the grid.

A major advantage in the use of a fuzzy set approach is that there already exists an associated linguistic semantic model in terms of Zadeh's fuzzy "hedges" and this may be incorporated to avoid the difficulties associated with the use of numerical scales while eliciting a grid.

COGNITIVE COMPLEXITY, OR ARE YOU SIMPLE MINDED?

The repertory grid technique has proved to be a useful tool in eliciting the constructs a person uses in relating the elements of his world. This usefulness, however, has perhaps only become apparent with the advent of computer analyses of grid data. A grid consists of a series of responses by the person, one for each element with respect of each construct. The aim of grid analysis is to show the relationships among constructs and elements which have resulted in the responses made, and as has already been mentioned, there have been two major approaches to this analysis. One has been the use of clustering algorithms (Shaw and Thomas, 1979); and the other, a singular-value decomposition or "principal components" approach epitomized in the work of Slater (1977) (see Chapters 4 and 5). While there has been some discussion of these different approaches (e.g. Fransella and Bannister, 1977), and indeed some empirical comparison (Rathod, 1981), is it not yet clear how the different analyses might produce methodological artifacts, or how the methods might react to abnormalities in the data. With respect to the last issue, namely data abnormalities, there has been little an investigator could do until recently, as these would only be detected, if at all, during the analysis which was conducted after the grid had been completely elicited.

Within the clustering approach, Shaw (1979) has described an interactive program PEGASUS, which is accessible to the investigator and which is simple enough to be programmed for a microcomputer. Shaw has now developed a microcomputer version of PEGASUS called PETRA. Keen and Bell have developed a simple technique (GRIDDLE) which relates to the alternative tradition of principal components, and has a ready interpretation in terms of repertory grid theory. The intraclass correlation among elements can be easily computed by a small computer, as each construct is elicited, and may be said to provide a measure of cognitive complexity at that stage of elicitation.

The notion of cognitive complexity may be said to have originated with Bieri (1955) who defined it in the following way:

> A system of constructs which differentiate highly among persons is said to be cognitively complex. A construct system which provides poor differentiation among persons is considered to be cognitively simple in structure.

Eleven years later Bieri (1966) redefined the concept as:

> Cognitive complexity may be defined as the tendency to construe social behaviour in a multi-dimensional way, such that a more cognitively complex individual has available a more versatile system for perceiving the behaviour of others than does a less cognitively complex person.

We can see here the element intraclass correlation operationalizing the earlier definition, in the broader sense of applying to any elements rather than just persons.

There has been substantial interest in this idea for some time and measures of intensity of construct relationship have been developed, e.g. Bannister (1960, 1962) and used in a number of studies, e.g. Warren (1966), and Mair (1964). Bannister considered that a high intensity score might indicate a high degree of organization in the area of the subject's component space being investigated, and thereby represent what Kelly termed "tight" construing. Low intensity, he hypothesized, might indicate a relative lack of clear-cut conceptual structure. Bonarius (1965), Adams-Webber (1969, 1970) and Landfield (1971) have all considered the concept of cognitive complexity, but a review of this literature provides a less than clear picture of what could be called a definition of the term, indeed measures purporting to be a "cognitive complexity" show amazing differences in nature. In an attempt to clarify the position, Vannoy (1965) produced evidence suggesting that the concept of cognitive complexity is in itself multidimensional, and that all the different indices measured different aspects of it.

Metcalfe (1974) has argued that Bieri's 1955 definition, and thus our measure, is a measure of "cognitive differentiation". However, we do not propose to engage in this semantic argument here, but rather we would claim that Keen and Bell's measure can be a useful summary index that can be used in decision-making during the elicitation of a grid. For example, in grid elicitation one needs to know when to stop eliciting constructs. Any researcher who has used a repertory-grid-based methodology will have experienced this dilemma at some stage. Respondents vary from those who seem to be able to provide an endless stream of constructs, all claimed to be independent (until subsequently proved otherwise in analysis) while others find extreme difficulty in progressing beyond nine or so.

Cognitive complexity, like other grid measures, depends on the constructs elicited. Not only the quality (range of convenience, etc.) of cognitive complexity but also the quantity depends on this. The cognitive complexity of a two-construct elicitation is likely to be less than the complexity of a twelve-construct elicitation.

Thus, we may look at the change in our measure of cognitive complexity as each construct is added to the system, and if normal grids provide element intraclass correlations which vary as the hypothetical curve in Fig. 26, then this index might be included in the information used to decide when to stop eliciting grids.

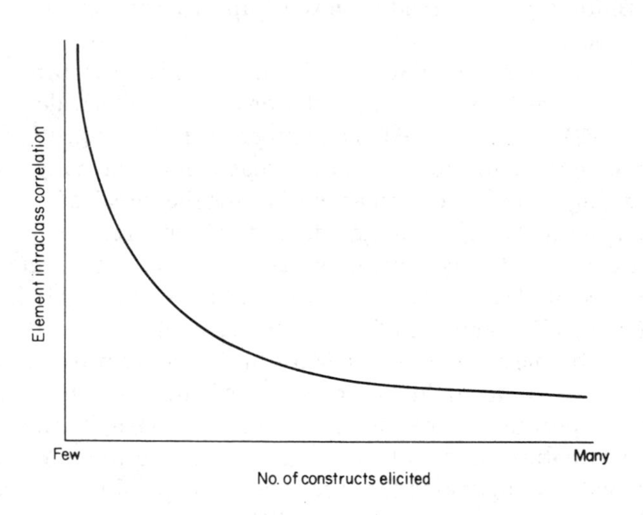

Fig. 26. Hypothetical relationship between number of constructs and element intraclass correlation in grid elicitation.

A Measure of Cognitive Complexity

The measure Keen and Bell propose relates to the general linear model proposed for grid data by Gower (1977):

$$\gamma_{ij} = \mu + \alpha_i + \beta_j + (\nu_i \nu'_j + \text{error}),$$

where γ_{ij} is the number assigned to element i (among m) for construct j (among n); μ is the grand mean effect; β is the vector of construct effects; α is the vector of element effects; and $\nu\nu'$ is the matrix of interaction effects.

With some assumptions (namely that each vector sums to zero) least squares estimates may be made of the element and construct effects, thus:

$$\begin{aligned} a_i &= y_{i\cdot} - y_{\cdot\cdot} \\ b_j &= y_{\cdot j} - y_{\cdot\cdot} \\ \text{and } z_{ij} &= y_{ij} - y_{i\cdot} - y_{\cdot j} + y_{\cdot\cdot} \end{aligned}$$

This is in fact a simple two-way ANOVA grid. The matrix containing z_{ij} (the remainder in ANOVA terms) is amenable to decomposition into multiplicative terms (see Gower, 1977) where each term corresponds to a latent root of the matrix $Z'Z$. Associated with the sum of squares $a_{i.}$, $b_{.j}$, and z_{ij}, are degrees of freedom, and thus we may compute ordinary mean squares. From these mean squares (or variance estimates) it is possible to compute an intraclass correlation, R_{ic}:

$$\text{where } R_{ic} = \frac{MS_c - MS_r}{MS_c + (m-1)MS_r},$$

where MS_c is the mean squares between constructs,

and MS_r is the remainder mean squares.

This intraclass correlation is in fact equivalent to the average intercorrelation among the elements. If a high correlation results, then the elements are similar (according to the constructs elicited) and if a low correlation is obtained then the elements are differentiated by the constructs.

As mentioned earlier, this index relates to the principal components approach, and in fact the remainder mean squares (MS_r) is equivalent to the latent roots of a principal components analysis. The size of the first latent root has often been taken as an index of cognitive complexity,

No. of Constructs

Subject	2	3	4	5	6	7	8	9	10	11	12	13	14	15	16	17	18	19	20
3027	021	010	016	003	014	026	041	034	028	030	025	022	033	035	038	039	032	040	045
3026	-045	-006	004	-011	020	015	022	017	014	013	004								
3024	-029	-032	-036	-038	-032	-043	-043	-047	-041	-037	-001								
3023	-071	-056	-059	-061	-038	-031	-037	-012	-002										
3021	099	053	027	048	026	033	071	057	057	061	060								
2009	-062	-055	-035	-030	-034	022	011	004	-001	-003	007	008	002	000	-003				
2010	-017	-027	067	053	044	049	045	026	031	025	013								
2010	348	266	268	234	219	207	180	246	230	219	205	194	212	247	246	255	251	253	248
2011	284	195	120	088	079	086	062	091	094	089	099	094	085						
2013	148	151	113	076	067	073	064	073	065	062	055								
2006	459	376	296	261	196	204	192	166	162	157	130								
2008	548	111	096	074	050	048	078	074	068	066	059								
2015	328	014	037	018	088	094	113	121	102	150	133								
2012	229	146	122	091	083	066	060	077	068	154	137								
2018	076	084	100	041	039	037	026	032	075	078	123	120	115	111	107	109	107	118	112
2019	-037	-010	-018	-026	-032	-034	-028	-031	-037	155	140	127	118						
2020	-075	-033	122	161	193	194	156	145	126	108	112								
3022	000	071	063	351	318	304	267	228	219	200	198								
2007	040	011	009	008	152	127	108	099	115	106	086								
2016	016	097	049	104	070	057	105	103	081	071	074								

Fig. 27. Table of interclass correlations for elements of a grid as each successive construct is added.

although this will depend in part on the removal of element and construct effects.

The ideas postulated here were tested on a random sample of data selected from some two hundred grids elicited by one of the authors (Keen, 1979). Twenty grids were selected thus with a common element sample. Figure 27 lists the grid reference numbers and the element intraclass correlations.

The respondents could be seen to fall into four categories. Consistent values for element intraclass correlation were obtained for 40% and for those respondents the authors would feel that the original elicitation procedures had not continued for long enough, or in other terms the elicitation of further constructs would have been a worthwhile exercise. Figure 28 gives a graphical representation of a typical response from this category (the solid line).

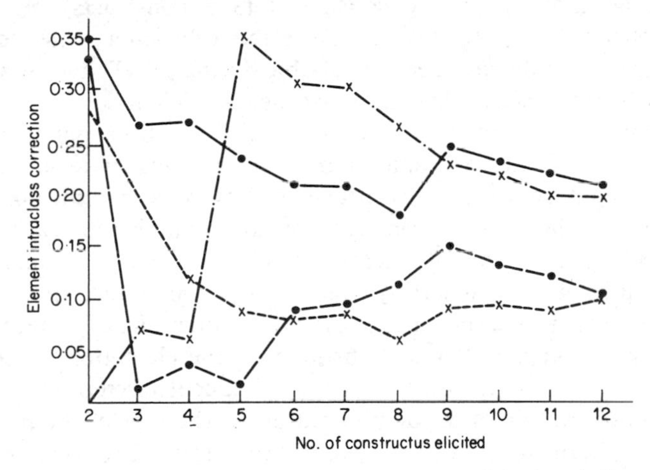

Fig. 28. Relationships between number of constructs elicited and element interclass correlation for a selection of grids.

20% of the sample followed the hypothesized curve and it is suggested that elicitation of further constructs would have produced no additional information, and indeed the elicitation could well have ceased earlier (say after construct eight in the example of Fig. 27) with no real difference emerging from the re-analysis of the grid. The dotted line of Fig. 28 is typical of this set of respondents. It is the remaining two categories which, accounting for 40% of all the respondents, provide interesting, and perhaps, surprising, results. The first of these two categories we call "High–low–High". The dashed line in Fig. 28 is typical and a decline akin to that hypothesized is followed by a "second breath" type of rise. We would hesitate to suggest causes, but are confident that ceasing elicitation of constructs at a time when the element intraclass correlation is rising is almost certainly depriving those involved of additional worthwhile data, even although the client might be adamant that he has exhausted his repertoire of constructs. While one is hesitant to make generalizations from such a small data-producing sample, there is no evidence from our data to suggest that a resurgent rise in element intraclass correlation will occur after the eighth or ninth construct has been elicited. Thus it might be possible to cease elicitation when three successive element intraclass correlations do not change significantly, if and only if a minimum of eight constructs had been elicited at that time.

The final category, represented by the dot-dashed line of Fig. 28 has been termed the "Low–high–Low" group. Here the hypothesized curve is followed only after an initial rise from zero, suggesting that some time was spent eliciting undiscriminating constructs (3–5 constructs) before the constructs elicited began to differentiate effectively among the elements. Data such as this would have been invaluable during the elicitation process, to enable the researcher to guide and assist the respondent.

The enormous range of uses to which grids have been put in the last decade has resulted in the evolution of a wide range of techniques for elicitation. The advent of the microprocessor has facilitated the analysis in order to provide immediate feedback for the administrator and client. Notwithstanding these developments, there have been a number of problems which have been largely ignored and the proper time to stop eliciting constructs is one such area. Some techniques allow the respondent to add constructs and/or elements throughout the elicitation process but even for such techniques the finishing time is frequently determined only by some casual observation of the administrator or when the client appears to have "dried up", or run out of his expressed repertoire of constructs.

Keen and Bell, in their attempt to develop a new interactive computer program, wished to relieve the client of the decision of when to stop, or, at the very least, build into the program the kinds of "prompts" regarding ceasing elicitation which an experienced clinician familiar with grid elicitation procedures might use. Element intraclass correlation looks promising as an indicator or when elicitation of further constructs might not yield worthwhile additional data.

Having looked at the results with respect to the original analysis, it is clear that the final conclusions drawn from a grid analysis will not be significantly different if construct elicitation is ceased when three successive values of the element intraclass correlation do not change. This is likely to be true for grids analysed by Slater's INGRID (1977), FOCUS (Shaw, 1978) and a new package being developed by Keen and Bell. Thus a microprocessor to hand during an elicitation, and into which the growing grid is fed, enables a practitioner to know what is happening with respect to the cognitive complexity of the respondent, and to assist him or her in managing the elicitation as well as giving advance warning of the time when further construct elicitation is unlikely to be of additional value.

Thus, in concluding this chapter, the authors would stress that this is merely an overall description of some of the applications of personal construct psychology in general, and repertory grid methodology in particular, used by one of the authors. Chapter 8 describes some of the approaches Pope has used and Chapter 9 will highlight significant developments elsewhere.

8

Awareness and Negotiation in Teaching and Learning

As a researcher, a lecturer (involved in staff development, student counselling and the teaching of psychology in education), and as a consultant to several management education projects, Pope has used a variety of repertory grid techniques. This chapter concentrates on some of these applications. Most of these involve the use of grid technique as a reflective device to raise self-awareness and to encourage understanding of another's perspective. She would argue that whilst the repertory grid techniques suggested have proved useful in many contexts one should not lose sight of the underlying philosophy of personal construct psychology, which perhaps poses the greatest challenge and opens up potential areas for innovation in both research and teaching methodology (see Chapters 3 and 4).

TEACHER AS LEARNER — A PERSONAL CONSTRUCT PSYCHOLOGY APPROACH TO TEACHER TRAINING

Reviews of teacher education have pointed to the close parallel that exists between the history of teacher education and that of the history of schools and the societies in which they function (Wragg, 1974; Dent, 1971). The different viewpoints on "the nature of man", knowledge, learning and instructional methods, outlined in Chapter 1, have had their impact on the education of teachers as well as the education of pupils in schools. Similarly, the various arguments regarding the appropriateness of research methods for evaluating aspects of school education, which were discussed in Chapter 2, also have relevance for research into teacher education. It is apparent that there exists a diversity of views on the objectives, means of attaining objectives and the evaluation of outcomes in education. Conflict often arises where there is inconsistency between aims, means and evaluation of outcome. For example, if one is judging the "success of a school" solely from the criteria of "A" level results, one does not tap what may be other equally important aims of a particular school, for example the fostering of emotional growth in each individual pupil or the production of a league-winning football team. Similar diversity exists within teacher education. Storm (1971) notes that

> Everyone knows exactly what is wrong with the teacher training course. And that is the problem. (p.91)

Willey and Maddison (1971) also emphasizes the diversity of viewpoints on teacher training. Thus they comment

> Teacher training has never proved a subject conducive to agreement. The training of teachers cannot be divorced from the aims and purposes of Education, and definitions of those aims and purposes are legion. (p.8)

However, Willey and Maddison proceed to suggest that the Department of Education and Science and the Local Education Authorities have "emphasised the quantitative demands of the service, at the expense of the qualitative nature of much of the training" (p.14). They suggest that there has been too much stress on quasi-educational issues such as the number of students to be trained. They also point out that such reports as the James' Committee Report will not provide a final solution since

> The problems are continuous, and in future teacher training must be open to constant adjustment and change . . . . (p.100)

Whilst there is a lack of consensus on many issues relating to teacher education, there seems to be a growing agreement that more and varied research in this area is needed. Much educational research has been devoted to the performance of pupils under a variety of teaching methods or organizational structures within schools; rather less emphasis has been placed on the behaviour and attitudes of teachers. Traditional research on teachers tended to concentrate on the development of inventories for selecting persons who would make "good" teachers. Critical reappraisal within the whole framework of education has led to an increase in the scope of research into teacher training. Morrison and McIntyre (1969) summarize research findings on teachers and teaching within this extended framework. Wragg (1974) provides a useful summary of studies of student teachers and points out the paucity of research in this area.

Research that has been carried out in order to tap student teachers' views about their training seems to highlight a considerable degree of dissatisfaction with many aspects of their courses. However, one of the general findings in many student attitude surveys is the recognition of the importance of teaching practice (Bourne, 1971). In the main students report that teaching practice is a valuable learning experience which has significant impact. It is during teaching practice that student teachers can test out the adequacies of the theories presented in their college courses.

Sorenson (1967) suggested that in a great many cases the anxiety provoked during teaching practice was frequently excessive and detrimental and noted the perceived gap between the content of professional courses and the activities of student teaching. Many educationalists now argue that we should focus on what student teachers learn about teaching practice, and attempts should be made to reconcile what seems to be a gap between theory and practice. Any evaluation of what is learned during teaching practice should include the student's perspective on his own learning.

Wragg (1974) makes the following comment which we feel is of the utmost importance when we consider the difficulty of establishing general criteria (Poppleton, 1968) and the considerable anxiety which may occur if there is a wide gulf between students and supervisors' perspective on what is learned during teaching practice (Sorenson, 1967):

> After long periods of history when there was not a great deal of conflict about the nature of good teaching, we have relatively little harmony. This suggests that students must be pressed more in the direction of self-evaluation and self-determined behaviour modification. (p.65)

Students themselves recognize the importance of teaching practice and it would seem that more emphasis could be given to negotiation of criteria of assessment between student and supervisor. In this way the apparent ambiguity of teaching practice assessments, which is felt by many students, could be overcome. Of course the criteria established by the student will be a reflection of his underlying assumptions or attitudes about what teaching involves, and will be the standard against which he makes assessments of both his own and pupils' actions. Fuller (1969) suggested that the concerns of student teachers change throughout the course. At first they are concerned with self in terms of such factors as the ability to keep control in class. Later the concerns switch their focus to those of pupil progress and professional development. More recently Taylor (1975) has studied the concerns of students on a postgraduate certificate in education course, and the findings support the view of Fuller, that concerns change throughout the course.

On the basis of this work Taylor suggested that, "The early part of the Education Course must acknowledge and work with the 'personal' quality of the students' early concerns, and give them an early opportunity for reality testing in as threat-free and as supportive a context as possible" (p.158) thus emphasizing the importance of incorporating information about the concerns of students into the framework of the course itself. It is clear that recognition is now given to the importance of students' viewpoints. However, researchers continue to base their research on questionnaire techniques which may mask the more idiosyncratic viewpoints of student teachers, which nevertheless are part of a particular student's frame of reference *vis à vis* teaching. Whilst there are few researchers prepared to investigate the "personal" viewpoints of student teachers, even fewer concern themselves with developing the means whereby these personal viewpoints can be integrated to the "personal development" aspect of a college of education course.

The element on teacher training courses usually labelled "Personal Education" has been critically analysed of late. Renshaw (1971) notes that this concern with "Personal Education" or "Personal Development" has been closely tied up with the academic study of a "main subject". As Renshaw points out, it might be appropriate to consider that "Personal Development" can be an integral part of other areas of the curriculum. Renshaw suggests that

> Central to the idea of a person is man's capacity to reflect on himself as a person and to grasp the relationship between himself and the world. In other words, a person is a centre of consciousness whose awareness gradually develops into a deeper understanding of the different modes of thought and feeling that constitute the basis of our civilisation. The notion "Personal Development" partly implies that man's simplistic view of the world is refined and widens as he builds up elaborate conceptual structures . . . the concept "Personal Development" embraces a range of qualities that cannot be realised through the academic study of a main subject alone. Some, in fact, could not be developed through the curriculum at all, as they are more likely to be the result of social and emotional experience outside college or within the student-staff community. (pp.54, 55)

The development of a personal model of teaching is an integral part of the teacher training enterprise. The formal concepts presented in the college courses need to be transformed and assimilated into the particular frame of reference held by the student teacher. The student teacher as learner should become aware of his frame of reference from the outset and continue to explore his developing assumptions which will underlie his teaching behaviour. Postman and Weingartner (1971) have also suggested that in the training of teachers innovations similar to those they propose for the education of pupils in schools should hold. Theoretical recognition is given to the importance of finding out what is relevant for the pupil, giving him freedom to explore and test out various strategies of learning, and emphasize the process of personal development which is as fundamental a part of education as the inculcation of literacy and numeracy. As Postman and Weingartner (1971) comment

> Following the medium is the message or you learn what you do theme, it is obvious that teacher education must have prospective teachers do as students what they as teachers must help their students, in turn, to do. How might such

> a teacher–education programme operate? In general, something like this: it would shift the prospective teacher into the role of the inventor of viable new teaching strategies. It would confront him with problems specifically intended to evoke from him questions about what he's doing, why he's doing it, what it's suppose to be good for and how he can tell. (p.138)

Micro-teaching evokes the question "What is he doing?", but although it is a valuable addition to teacher training programmes it has some limitations. Often the emphasis is solely on the student teacher's performance and no attempt is made to link this with his underlying assumptions. Whilst providing the trainee teacher with a vehicle which aids reflection on his performance as a teacher, micro-teaching is less useful as an aid to reflection regarding the continuing process of attitudinal change. If one acknowledges the importance of the student teacher's "frame of reference", it would seem that attention should be given to the development of methods which will allow the student teacher to explore this aspect of his personal development.

It is apparent that in an increasingly complex society there is a growing need for individuals, students and teachers alike, to be adaptive, personally viable and self-directive. Such self-direction or self-organization can only come about if the individual makes an effort to explore his viewpoints, purposes, means for obtaining ends and keeps these under constant review. Postman and Weingartner (1971) suggest that honest self-examination by teachers is a necessary step. They suggest that the question "Why am I a teacher, anyway?" may produce an answer such as "I can tyrannize people". We might be confronted with a view of ourselves which we find surprising or disconcerting. As Postman and Weingartner (1971) point out, however,

> The teacher who recognises that he is interested, say, in exercising tyrannical control over others is taking a first step toward subverting that interest. (p.193)

Personal construct psychology provides a framework within which such exploration can take place; rather than impose a monolithic view on education a Kellian framework can embrace the diversity of viewpoints held by those involved in teaching. The diversity can be seen to result from the differing models which individuals have erected in order to impose meaning on the events they experience. It is suggested that the repertory grid techniques, which have their basis in the theoretical assumptions of George Kelly (see Chapter 3), may be a useful adjunct to teacher training programmes, especially in the areas outlined above.

A major tenet of the discussion so far has been the importance of the "frame of reference" of the individual student which he or she brings to bear on any learning event. Theoretical recognition has been given to the influence these viewpoints may have on the outcome of any learning situation and the need for the tutor/teacher/researcher to be responsive to the variety of personally relevant issues held by the student. Since the "frame of reference" of the student teacher may be an important factor in his teaching behaviour this would seem to be an aspect that needs to be monitored. The student teacher would also benefit from reflecting on the way he or she construes teaching. With this in view Pope (1978) carried out a study aimed at monitoring the viewpoints of students during a period prior to, during, and shortly after, a major teaching practice. A major aim of the project was an evaluation of the repertory grid as a means of monitoring changes in students perspectives, and as a vehicle for feedback to the student teacher, which could provide an opportunity for reflection on changes in relation to experiences during teaching practice.

Some brief details of the main project may be necessary at this stage. Volunteer subjects within two teacher training establishments were obtained and then randomly assigned to one of three groups:

Group 1: Subjects interviewed before and after teaching practice.

Group 2: Subjects interviewed before and after teaching practice plus completion of 3 grids, one before teaching practice, one during teaching practice and the third on return to college.

Group 3: Subjects completed the same schedule as Group 2 with the addition of feedback sessions during which the analysis of their previous grid was discussed.

Each person in Group 2 and Group 3 provided their own elements and constructs. Since a major purpose of the study was to determine what the individual student thought was relevant to his or her teaching, the elements were those things which the person thought of when he or she had "teaching" in mind. Tape recordings of interviews and feedback discussions were made. The grids were analysed using the FOCUS program devised by L. F. Thomas and M. L. Shaw (1976b).

The grids provided a useful basis for developing an insight into the students' frameworks. At one level of analysis one was able to categorize the types of constructs generated by the groups of students. We would suggest that this approach may well throw light on issues such as school ethos or organizational climate. One should, however, be aware of the difficulties which arise when one attempts to construe someone else's construing, and one should acknowledge the limitations of the content analysis approach, i.e. the meaning one attributes to a particular construct item may not be the meaning intended by the person giving the item. Having acknowledged this, it seemed that the students' constructs did fall into broad categories and that differences between students could be highlighted in terms of the emphasis they placed upon particular categories of constructs. The most common type of construct elicited reflected a concern for or an awareness of external constraints in teaching, for example *Governmentally controlled/No Government control*. Another common construct indicated a concern for pupils, e.g. *To do with the broadening of children/less to do with*.

Discussion with students about their constructs and the elements which they felt represented their views about teaching raised issues about their personal philosophy of education and their aims. The two sets of elements given in Fig. 29 indicate a divergence in ideas about teaching held by two of the students in Pope's study. During conversations with student No. 19, this

Student No. 8	*Student No. 19*
Children	To broaden a child's knowledge
Books	Widen child's interests
Chalk	Build a bridge between home and school
Headmaster	Work in an atmosphere of fun
Classroom	Try to get on with the rest of staff
School	Relationship with the head
Ability	Plenty of space
Board	Trying to adapt method to suit child
Pens	Be where the child is at
Exams	Happy relationship with children
Worry	Understanding each child
Sense of achievement	Making allowances for individual problems
Film	
Attitudes	

Fig. 29.

student teacher emphasized the need to have an atmosphere of fun within the classroom and to establish good relationships with each pupil. However, student No. 8 never made specific reference to classroom atmosphere or relationships with the pupils: her emphasis was on achievement and reference was made to "the state their homework is in" and "whether they give it in on time".

Figure 30 shows the hierarchical element "tree" or cluster diagram for a subject belonging to Group 3. At the outset Pope was immediately struck by the fact that despite many conversations with student teachers before this study she would not have provided *Needing adult company* as an element. This, however, proved to be a very important element as far as this student teacher was concerned. It was one of the reasons behind her decision to enter teacher training. *Family commitments* were also important, as these could affect her performance as a teacher. This particular subject was divorced, with a young child.

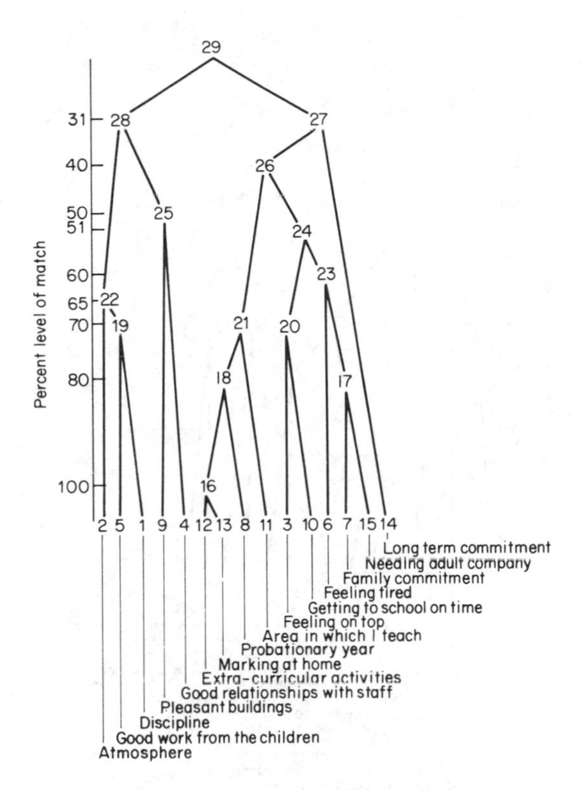

Fig. 30. Element tree for grid completed prior to teaching practice.

The "tree" diagram (Fig. 30) was shown to the subject during the feedback session and she was asked to comment. Individual groupings, for example *Marking at home*, *Extra curricular activities*, *Probationary year* and *Area in which I teach*, were discussed. The emphasis was on the subject providing the labelling or rationale for the cluster rather than the researcher naming the factor, which is often the case in other studies. As Pope was interested in monitoring possible changes due to experience and reconstruction during teaching practice, the subject was given her original list of elements and constructs, was allowed to add any elements or constructs and was then asked to rate the elements on the constructs again. Thus one had a base comparison between original elements and constructs on each occasion plus a monitoring of any additions. Figure 31 is from the same subject's second grid, completed in the middle of her teaching practice. She decided to add *Relationships with the children* to her element list, as she now realized this was an important factor in teaching. One can see that there was a tight cluster, consisting of *Feeling tired*, *Family commitments*, *Needing*

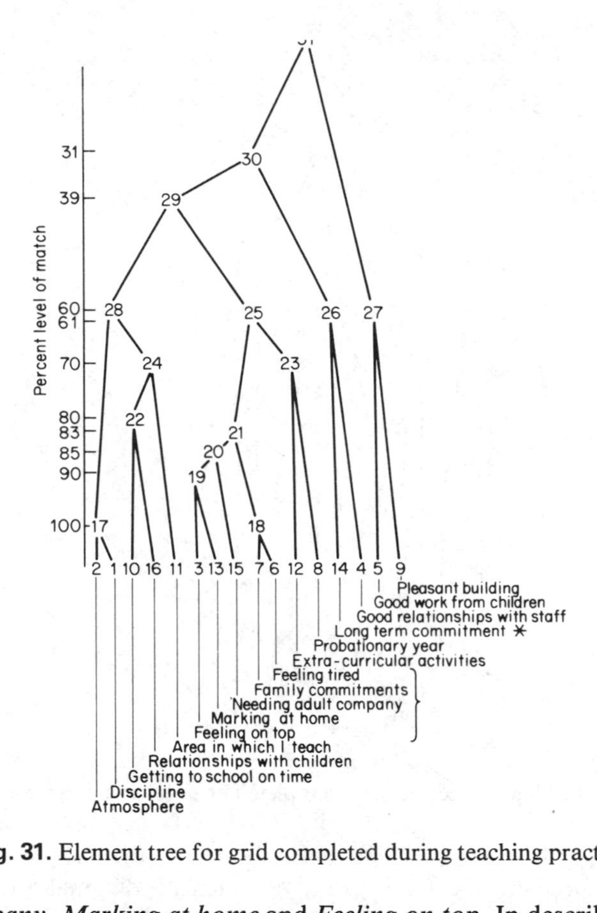

Fig. 31. Element tree for grid completed during teaching practice.

adult company, *Marking at home* and *Feeling on top*. In describing this the subject explained that she was very pressurized during teaching practice and found it difficult to cope with both family and school work. She now realized how important the *Atmosphere* in the classroom was for the general *Discipline* of the children. She commented on the fact that *Good work from children* and *Pleasant building* seemed to be linked — she was not surprised by this and felt it represented her feelings and experience during teaching practice, as the following extract from her tape recording indicates:

> It was a Victorian school with very high ceilings, and very little display space, and it was very difficult to organise the classroom so that it looked attractive. The vast ceilings, and you had to stick things on the wall with sellotape and it looked messy. There weren't any nice display boards. You felt you wanted to — it would be more incentive to get the classroom looking nice and get the

children producing stuff if you could in fact have displayed it nicely, but it was very difficult.

Her comments on the new link between *Good relationships with staff* and *Long term commitment* were also revealing:

When I was at the school that I was on Teaching Practice at I found that staff . . . well I just was not compatible with them at all and I just couldn't imagine teaching for a long time in that situation with that kind of company. I would really find it very off-putting unless there was staff there that I felt I fitted in well with. I don't think you can isolate yourself in the classroom all day, I think you need to have some kind of feedback from the staff which I just didn't have at that school . . . . I really do think I need to be, feel inspired. You know I just found the staff exceptionally dull, exceptionally unimaginative and I just felt completely an outcast. You know they weren't antagonistic towards me, I just had absolutely nothing in common with them at all which is quite horrifying. I couldn't possibly consider doing a job if I felt like that about people.

In addition to using the clusters and changes in clustering as a basis for generating further discussion, the changes in ratings for each element on the two occasions were explored. As indicated in Chapter 5, if one keeps the constructs constant and enters the ratings for the elements on two occasions in the same raw grid, one can compare the ratings for each element. By putting the ratings in in this way one can obtain a matching score matrix for elements. Figure 32 is a portion of a 30 × 30 element matrix which highlights the different matching scores obtained for each element with itself for the subject in this case study. Whilst there was not a great deal of change in the elements, three were somewhat different, namely *Atmosphere*, *Long term commitment* and *Area in which I teach*. Again, the verbatim report on the subject was of interest:

And the *Area in which I teach*, I did change my mind about that actually, because I was thinking more of travelling, and yet when I was teaching in this suburban area I started thinking of the areas in terms of social class, which I certainly wasn't thinking of to begin with. I would be far happier to teach in an area where I felt comfortable, where I felt I was achieving something, than to teach in a school which was very dull close by.

This case study illustrates that using grid analysis as a base one can gain a great deal of insight into how the person feels about teaching in *his or her own terms*. We would suggest that these extracts tap issues of personal importance to the student teacher which will have significant bearing on both her performance as a teacher and her own career choice. The discussion of such learning experiences could be a valuable addition to tutorials or counselling sessions and would draw on the experiences during teaching practice which students value but feel that their tutors neglect.

Having had some subjects complete grids without feedback Pope was

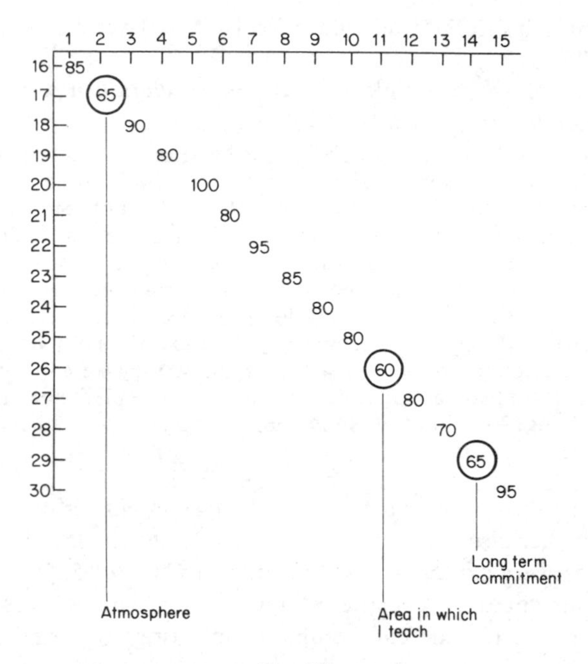

Fig. 32.

able to assess how useful she felt both methods were. The majority of subjects in Groups 2 and 3 enjoyed reflecting on their thoughts about teaching — many reported that it was probably the first time that they had sat back and reflected on their personal approach. The following quotes indicate the advantage of such an exercise from the students' viewpoint:

> I think initially it made you think about what was likely to go on and the sorts of factors you were likely to come across. It gave you an idea about the things you would be wanting to aim for. (Student No. 1)

> There is a fun element in it. I think it was useful in terms of trying to identify elements. It is not the sort of thing people ask you to do, except in a research project of this sort. To be actually asked to put down the elements which you think of as being important in relation to the education system, I think is a good thing in itself. Then you realise things like *Physical layout of the school* are important things as far as you're concerned and you've probably never written it down before, although it's perhaps been in the back of your head. (Student No. 2)

> Because it caused me to think about what I was here for. What I expected to do. What was relevant to teaching. That, and what I hoped to do. It is good that I thought about it because you tend just to drift along, otherwise. (Student No. 7)

I find it quite interesting, the whole idea of compiling the questionnaire yourself. Just the fact that you have made it up yourself and you are questioning yourself on things that you think about, and not someone else's questions. (Student No. 15)

It made you think about your attitudes and things that are important to you. (Student No. 23)

However, Pope felt that Group 3 subjects gained more from the exercise, as they had sessions where the analysis of their grids were discussed. Apart from the additional benefit to the subject, we feel that the researcher gains enormously by adopting the strategy of discussing the analysis with the subject. In this way the interpretation can be as the subject sees it rather than that of the researcher "with his hat on".

In this project each student was asked to give a "self description", i.e. what the grid data conveyed to him. Adopting an approach whereby the "subject" was involved in the interpretation and description of the data allowed both the student teacher and the researcher to explore the personal ideas about teaching and the areas of concern for each student. One student was concerned with his feelings of antipathy towards the Headmaster's examinations and any form of social pressure. Another felt that her grids reflected an early concern for material aspects of teaching and that she now realized the importance of relationships. One student saw teaching as a role which a person adopts — "One puts one's coat on in the morning and takes it off again at 4 o'clock" whereas another saw teaching as a "caring situation". One young divorcée with a child, felt pressurized by her family commitments and her need for adult company and thus has reservations about her ability to cope as a teacher. One student who had a teaching practice school within an education priority area had experiences on teaching practice which were reflected in the items on her grid. *We suggest that all of these personally relevant issues are of paramount importance to the teacher concerned and will most certainly affect their teaching behaviour.* If a college course does not provide an opportunity for personal exploration of these issues and the necessary support and guidance, it is perhaps not surprising that some students, especially those in a college advocating child-centred approaches to education, perceive a gulf between theory and practice in relation to their own learning. *Grid methodology should facilitate the exploration, reflection and discussion of these issues within a tutorial framework.*

Whilst the major aim of the project was to gain some insight into the representational models of the individual student teachers, the data obtained raised some other interesting points. Given that there was a common set of elements and constructs on the three occasions that subjects completed "grids", it was possible to obtain, for each subject, a crude numeric for the amount of change between any two occasions by the summation of the differences between ratings on the two occasions for each cell of the grid and expressing this as a percentage of the theoretical possible difference between the pair of grids. In this way it was possible to explore when the largest amount of change occurs. Results indicated that the greatest change occurred between the occasions "prior" to and "during" teaching practice since the difference between grids 2 and 3 for many subjects was less than the difference between grids 1 and 2. Many investigations into teacher training have emphasized the importance of teaching practice for the student teacher. It would appear to be a time of considerable reconstruction for the individual. Indeed the subject of the case study given earlier emphasized that, although she had been made aware of sociological factors involved in teaching from lectures on sociology, it was experiences during teaching practice that had turned these "sociological facts" into personally relevant issues. This represents a shift from public to personal knowledge (Polanyi, 1958).

We have stated that it is important to consider the learner's perspective when evaluating a learning event. This is not to say that the tutor's appraisal is irrelevant. It is relevant to the tutor and is often relevant to the student. In Pope's study it was found that the trend was for those within the "grids with feedback group" to obtain higher teaching practice assessments than those who completed grids, and that those who completed grids had higher assessments than those who were interviewed without completing grids. Given that there was no contact between the researcher and the college staff as to who volunteered to take part in the study and that the staff were unaware of the full details of the project, these results are encouraging.

These findings, albeit with a small sample, may well indicate that the raising of student teachers' personal awareness has implications for the external criteria applied by the tutors. We feel that such results suggest that the methodology allows one to attack the qualitative aspects of teacher training. It provides a framework within which the "person" can emerge and their attitudes can be examined in their own terms. Changing viewpoints throughout the course of training are significant aspects of the student teacher's learning and should be of interest to those responsible for guiding their learning. Feedback on academic performance is usually given as a matter of course. We would suggest that reflection on their change of ideas about teaching is also of importance to the student teacher and knowledge and an understanding of these personal perspectives is critical if the tutor–student dialogue is to be useful.

NEGOTIATION OF PERSPECTIVES

What is relevant to the person is important, because for education to be a joint venture between teacher and learner, it is essential that each has some awareness of the other's personal constructs. The perspective of the student as well as that of the teacher must be considered although traditionally learning has been defined mainly from the latter's perspective. Jahoda and Thomas (1965) outlined four different perspectives from which the learning experience can be viewed (see Fig. 33).

Purpose	Learner	Teacher
Prospective	1	2
Retrospective	3	4

Fig. 33. Perspectives on learning.

Each of the 4 quadrants in Fig. 33 represents a different and valid point of view: quadrant 1 represent the learner's anticipation of the event, quadrant 2 represents the teacher's objectives, whereas quadrants 3 and 4 denote a retrospective view of the experience from the perspective of the learner and the teacher respectively. Kelly (1969b) maintained that

> humanistic psychology needs a technology through which to express its humane intentions. Humanity needs to be implemented not merely characterised and eulogised (p.135)

Humanistic psychologists and educators must develop technologies appropriate to their orientation, i.e. tools which help in the articulation of personal perspectives. We would suggest that PEGASUS, DYAD, and SOCIOGRIDS represent tools which meet this purpose.

Recently Pope has been involved in a number of projects with individuals and groups who have been concerned to review their ideas on a variety of topic areas. These have included managers reviewing their criteria for appraisal of subordinates, identification of training needs, evaluation of training programmes, identification of criteria for graduate recruitment and staff development of teachers in primary and secondary schools. In many of these PEGASUS and SOCIOGRID packages were used.

One advantage of the PEGASUS program is that it provides continuous feedback which enables the learner to examine and bring into awareness his own conceptual system with respect to an area under investigation. It offers the learner a choice of continuing reflection by adding new elements or constructs and the ability to push themselves into further differentiation between elements or constructs which have proved to be highly matched (see Chapter 5). By providing an analysis of the results immediately on completion the computer acts as a cognitive mirror in which the user sees himself. The student is free either to reflect personally on the outcome or to discuss the printout and the experience with a tutor or fellow student. Pope has used the PEGASUS program with school children, university students, lecturers and managers, who have all used the program to construe a variety of elements related to a wide variety of purposes. Examples of these have been significant learning events, subordinates at work, school subjects, training techniques, mathematical concepts, books, teaching methods and prospective careers. Students have reported that they found the opportunity to reflect on prospective careers particularly useful and the program encouraged them to explore and focus systematically on the choice criteria which would be important to them when deciding on their future jobs.

There are of course many occasions when the learner must relate his construction of personally relevant meanings to bodies of established knowledge and traditional constructions within educational disciplines. PEGASUS–BANK is a development of PEGASUS which allows the user to complete a grid on a topic area and get continuous feedback on the relationships between his constructs and those of "an expert" or the consensually validated definitions which represent public knowledge in the area (Shaw, 1980). If a tutor and student complete grids on the same topic area this provides a basis for discussion. Externalizing areas of similarity and dissimilarity between a tutor's grid and that of the student gives a framework for negotiation of differences between the tutor's and the student's perspectives. This leads to a greater awareness and understanding of the other's point of view. If the technique of grid elicitation together with grid feedback is used in a "learning centred" way a person's models can be brought into awareness, revised and refined.

The SOCIOGRIDS program was devised in order to explore the similarity and differences in construing between members of a group (Shaw, 1978). This technique is based on an assumption rooted in Kelly's commonality corollary that there may be areas of shared meaning among any group of individuals. Starting with the negotiation of a common set of elements by the group concerned, this program analyses the set of repertory grids elicited from the group. Each person is free to use his or her own personal constructs. Similarity between constructs is not based upon literal similarity but upon an operational definition of similarity in terms of the ordering of the element set (McKnight and Shaw, 1976).

Using the SOCIOGRIDS technique each individual in the group can have feedback on his own mapping of the area from a FOCUS-ed grid (as in Fig.

18, Chapter 5). In addition, a "mode" grid of the most commonly used constructs by all the members of the group is extracted and focused, exhibiting the content of the shared construing in the group. Each construct in the mode grid has been obtained from an individual in the group and is in no way changed when used in the mode. This grid is not then a consensus grid which averages out the individualities to produce a pale imitation of the group, but is strongly weighted towards the commonality of construing within the group. Due to this the constructs tend to be highly clustered in a mode grid, and generally these clusters display a high degree of both literal and conceptual similarity in the construct labels.

Figure 34 illustrates a mode grid from a group of trainers who were concerned with identifying their ideas about tools for evaluating performance at work. Thus, the elements were a common set of "tools" chosen by the group and the constructs reflected their ideas in relation to the tools. One can see that there is a high degree of emphasis on constructs of the type *Quantitative/Qualitative*. One can also see that, for some people, slightly different meanings may be attributed to the same words, e.g. constructs 11, 15 and 1, whilst for others different words may be used to express the same underlying meaning. Reflection on such results facilitates negotiation of personal meaning and a deeper understanding of alternative perspectives.

The program also produces a sequence of "socionets" from the matrix of similarity measures between pairs of individual grids. The highest related pair in a group can be extracted as a sub-group where the most commonality of construing occurs, and subsequent individuals can be defined by their position in the rank ordering of the similarity measures. Thus, this set of socionets exposes those members of the group who have most in common and those with strongly individualistic viewpoints.

Figure 35 illustrates a socionet diagram from a study carried out into subjective standards in the inspection of knitwear (Pope *et al.*, 1977). The purposes of the study were to help each member of a group concerned with quality control to become more aware of his or her own personal dimensions for judging faults in garments and to explore the patterns of judgements within the group in order to discuss the similarities and differences that existed between individuals. The points of interest to note from this diagram are:

(1) Three inspectors and trainee production technologist shared similar views of faults.

(2) One of the inspectors seemed to differ from this group.

(3) The supervisory and management group shared similar views of faults although the similarity is less strong and it differs from that of the inspectors.

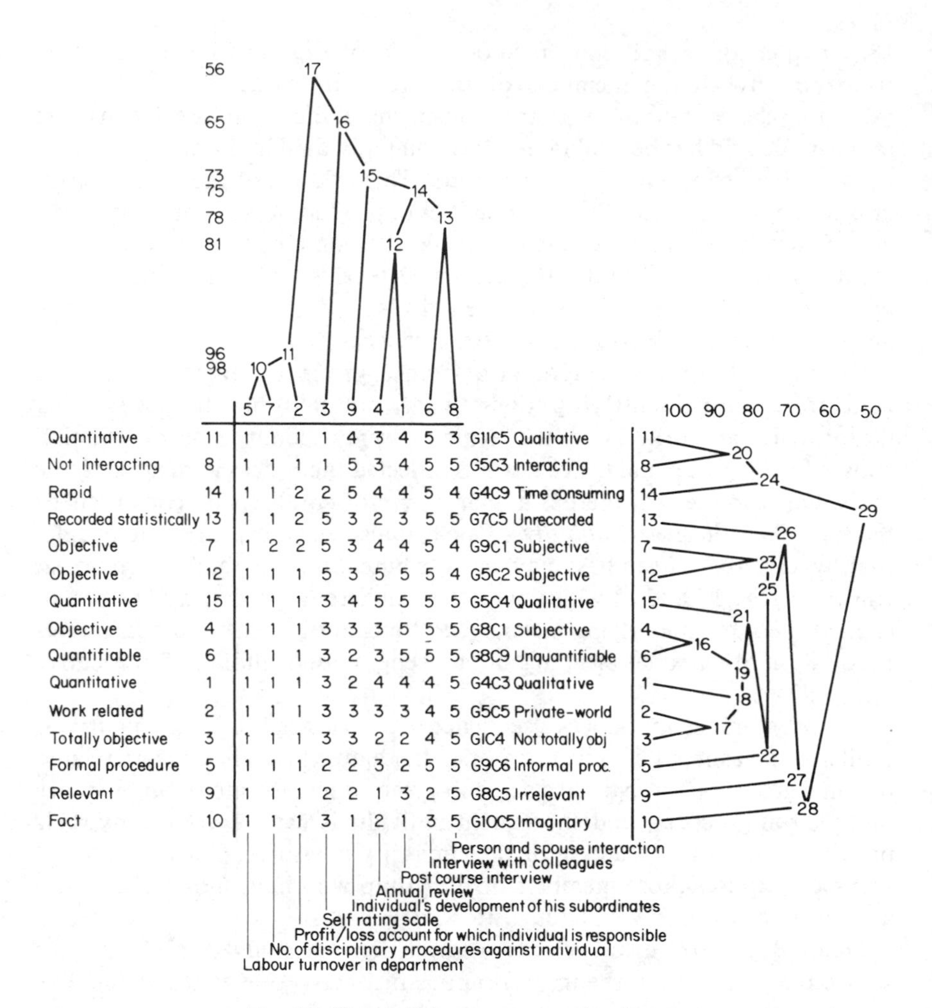

Fig. 34. "Mode" from a group of trainers.

(4) The patterns of reciprocal similarities, i.e. amongst inspector and trainee, between supervisor and production manager and divisional manager.

(5) Each of the supervisory/management group related to inspector A.

These results highlighted the fact that different roles within the company incorporated different viewpoints of quality, and provided a foundation for the negotiation and exchange of meaning. Having had feedback using the "mode" grid and the socionets, the individual can refer to his own set of constructs and discuss these with other members of the group.

It may seem that this industrial example is totally removed from

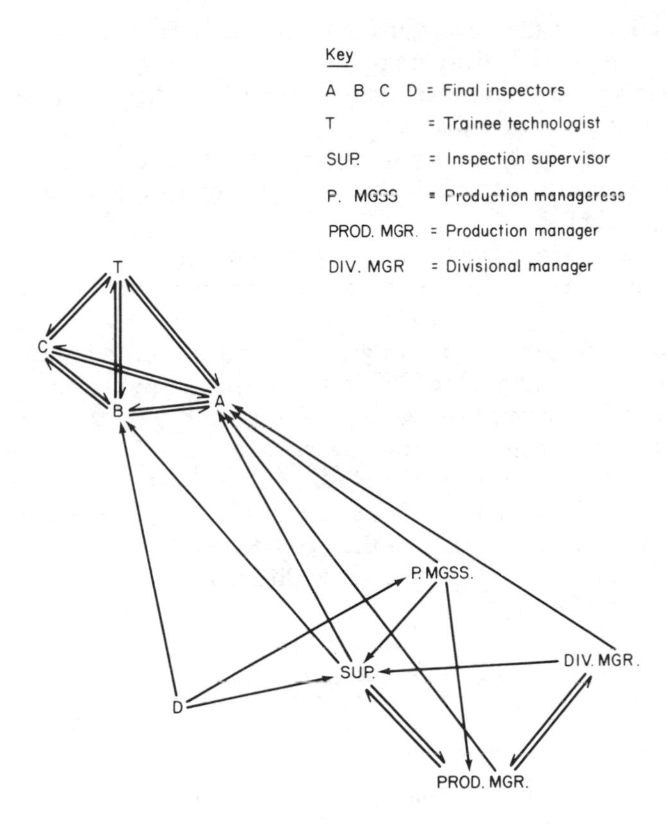

Fig. 35. Diagram showing the systems of connections between participants (expressed as the three grids which were most like each person's own grid).

educational practice. However, the techniques developed through such action research are useful resources for the education researcher and teachers and students in the classroom.

Whilst teaching on an in-service teacher training course, Pope used SOCIOGRID techniques to encourage her students to reflect on what teaching meant to them as individuals (Pope, 1978). Many possible items were suggested by the students and written on the board and the group discussed them with a view to arriving at a consensus list. In our experience the negotiation of such a common set of elements is in itself a worthwhile teaching activity. Students benefit from the brainstorming exercise and they find other students suggest items which they had not come up with, and the discussion of what these items mean to them has added advantage. The consensus list developed into the set of elements and each teacher completed a repertory grid using their own personal constructs. These grids were then analysed using the SOCIOGRID program.

During feedback sessions the teachers were able to reflect on the analysis of their own focused grids and noted:

(1) High relationships between pairs or groups of elements.

(2) Personal reasons why particular pairs or groups within the total set were alike or dissimilar.

(3) High relationships between pairs or groups of constructs.

(4) Construct clusters in order to ascertain possible superordinate constructs.

Having considered his or her own grid each teacher was referred to Fig. 36 which gives the "grid-mix" of similarity measures between any pairs of grids for one of the groups of teachers. The numbers along the top and down the side of this matrix refer to the teacher number. Thus one can see, for example, that the grids of teahers Nos 2 and 6 are matched at 70% level, whereas the match between teachers 4 and 7 is only 45%. The teachers were able to explore this grid matrix and then go back to their original grids in order to compare the terms in which they differed or were similar to any other member of the group.

Gridmix matrix of similarity measures using maximum values

	1	2	3	4	5	6	7
1		59	60	45	63	56	67
2	59		54	53	63	(70)	64
3	60	54		58	50	54	62
4	45	53	58		50	48	(45)
5	63	63	50	50		47	50
6	56	70	54	48	47		69
7	67	64	62	45	50	69	

Fig. 36. Gridmix matrix of similarity measures using maximum values.

Given that elements are the same for each teacher, the individual teacher was able to explore the similarity and differences in clustering on his or her own element tree and those from the rest of the group. Each teacher was encouraged to consider whether any particular different ordering of the elements could "make sense" to him or her. This sharing of element trees and discussion of constructs is an important activity and one that usually provokes personal involvement and a frank interchange.

Having explored the relationship between his or her own grid and that of any other member, teachers were then shown the inter-linkages within the

1	2	3	4	5	6	7	Link count	New link	Max value
	2				6		1	2 > 6	70.37
	2				6	7	2	6 > 7	69.13
1	2				6	7	3	1 > 7	67.9
1	2				6	7	4	2 > 7	64.81
1	2			5	6	7	5	5 > 1	63.88
1	2			5	6	7	6	2 > 5	63.58
1	2	3		5	6	7	7	3 > 7	62.96
1	2	3		5	6	7	8	1 > 3	60.18
1	2	3		5	6	7	9	2 > 1	59.72
1	2	3	4	5	6	7	10	4 > 3	58.33
1	2	3	4	5	6	7	11	6 > 1	56.94
1	2	3	4	5	6	7	12	2 > 3	54.62
1	2	3	4	5	6	7	13	3 > 6	54.62
1	2	3	4	5	6	7	14	4 > 2	53.08
1	2	3	4	5	6	7	15	5 > 3	50.92
1	2	3	4	5	6	7	16	7 > 5	50.61
1	2	3	4	5	6	7	17	5 > 4	50
1	2	3	4	5	6	7	18	4 > 6	48.14
1	2	3	4	5	6	7	19	5 > 6	47.22
1	2	3	4	5	6	7	20	4 > 1	45.83
1	2	3	4	5	6	7	21	4 > 7	45.67

Fig. 37.

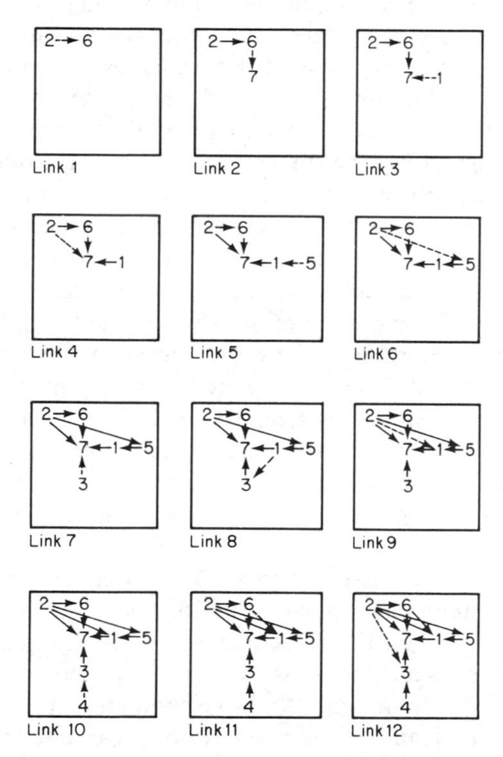

Fig. 38. Socionet diagrams — denotes latest linkage.

group. Figure 37 gives the rank ordering of similarity between all pairs of individuals. Figure 38 shows the socionet diagrams derived from this table. Reference to these allowed the teachers to note:

(a) The most highly matched pair, i.e. teachers 2 and 6.

(b) The order in which individual members were drawn into the socionet.

(c) Where each individual was placed within his or her overall pattern.

(d) Which individual or individuals were least like other members, i.e. teachers 3 and 4.

(e) Which individuals had early linkages with many other members, i.e. teachers 2 and 7.

It was noted by the group of teachers that:

(1) Teachers 2 and 6 taught the same subject.

(2) Teachers, 2, 6, 7 and 1 taught subjects which could be defined as practical, e.g. motor vehicle studies and office studies.

(3) Teachers 3, 4 and 5 taught more "academic" subjects — nutrition, library studies and social work theory.

The SOCIOGRIDS method represents a technological advance which allows the learner to reflect on his personal model while offering each member of the group the facility to become aware of the inter-relationships between ideas within the group. They are powerful techniques appropriate for inter-dependent learning situations (Pope and Shaw, 1980). It has been our experience that learners become very involved in the process of reviewing similarities and negotiating the differences within the group and find it a relevant learning experience. In some cases it has been the first time the person has dwelt upon the notion of relativity in constructions of reality.

We would argue that it is important for the persons who completed the grids to take the lead in analysing the interconnections between group members and suggesting any explanations of the results as did the group of teachers in the above exercise. If the group has already established a degree of mutual trust both with fellow group members and any person acting as a consultant the discussions arising from the analysis of SOCIOGRID data can be very illuminating. However, on some occasions the consultant/investigator must proceed with caution and not identify the names of each group member within the socionet until the group members suggest that they themselves wish this.

Pope has recently been assisting in staff development projects in which repertory grid techniques have played a major role. Examples of these are:

(1) A group of primary school teachers who wished to examine and refine their ideas on the social and moral aspects of the curriculum.

(2) A mathematics department of a large comprehensive school who were concerned to negotiate and define a set of objectives and to construe these in terms of what behaviours are required from the teacher to meet such objectives.

In both of these projects the repertory grid technique proved a useful catalyst in the discussion.

PEGASUS, DYAD, SOCIOGRIDS and paper and pencil grids offer teachers and learners a resource which encourages the individual to reflect on his conceptualizations of his world and an opportunity to explore differing conceptions. Active involvement with his own and others' ideas may encourage the learner to see himself as a more potent force in the determination of his own learning and in the development of new knowledge.

9

Current Educational Applications of Personal Construct Psychology

The International Congress on Personal Construct Psychology has now met three times. After an encouraging start at the first conference, the venue was set for a gathering of all the workers in the field within the cloistered surroundings of Christ Church, Oxford, in 1977. Whilst it cannot be denied that the very existence of such a congress must be accredited to a few dedicated researchers (such as Bannister, Mair, Fransella, etc.), it was this second congress at Oxford which established personal construct psychology as a creditable and powerful branch of modern psychology. The congress is memorable not so much for its academic content, which was undoubtedly good, but for the air of enthusiasm and comradeship between some 200 practitioners throughout the world. Many of these folk established close working relationships and by 1979, when the third congress met at Castle Nijenrode, Utrecht, a great deal of exciting work had emerged from both these informal teams and individuals.

The authors have only reviewed some of the work more relevant to the theme of this book in this chapter but there is no doubt that personal construct psychology has come to a period of consolidation and we anticipate that the fourth congress in Toronto in 1981 will reflect this view. In reading this chapter, the reader must appreciate that the nature of the treatment we have given to the work is little more than a listing of interest areas, and that a chapter (albeit one of the last chapters to actually be written) will be dated by the time the book appears on the library shelves. Our objective is not to describe all that is happening, but rather to give an indication of the research in action and suggest people to contact should the reader desire more detailed information. We have deliberately not given a précis of each study as we feel the interested reader would find such an approach less rewarding than following up more thorough treatments in the original publications.

May we start with a further word of warning? In compiling this chapter, we not only reviewed all the papers in our possession, the lists of papers at major relevant conferences and our general knowledge of the field, but also commissioned a full computer search in the UK and the USA. To our amazement nothing appeared in the search which we had no knowledge of, but more important, and more worrying, is that only 34 citations appeared in total. This represented a very small, and not very representative proportion of the total field.

We have, in reviewing the current personal construct psychology research, only considered those projects which we consider relevant to our specific theme, namely education (no matter how loosely defined). This consideration enables the work we have identified to fall into five distinct areas:

(1) The use of the repertory grid and general applications in education.
(2) Management education.
(3) Vocational guidance and training.
(4) Teacher and teaching assessment.
(5) The general theme of curriculum development, and in particular a few "one-off" projects tenuously linked to the theme, which have particularly excited us.

We deal with each area in turn:

THE USE OF THE REPERTORY GRID AND GENERAL APPLICATIONS IN EDUCATION

A "traditional" (if one can have tradition in such a new branch of psychology) approach is taken by Don Bannister and Phillida Salmon (1975) in a journal article which reports on "A personal construct view of education". The authors are, in this article, devoted to the interpretation and elaboration of Kelly's psychology of personal constructs. Kelly's theory and applications for education and psychotherapy are described and they purport to describe how the theory explains total human behaviour in terms of the related contexts in which people expect events to occur.

On a similar tack Hall (1978), at the University of Nottingham, has produced the "Rediguide" entitled "Using Personal Constructs". This elaborates on the basic concepts and theory as well as considering methods of use and application.

Moving away from this theoretical treatment, some novel techniques are being considered. We must remember that there is no such thing as "the grid", and personal construct psychology can prove valuable to the practitioner in many guises. The relationship between the degree to which people see others as like themselves (assimilative projection) and the frequency with which they use positive adjectives to describe people is examined in the context of changing role perspectives by Benjafield and Adams-Webber (1975), whilst Elizabeth Rix (1979) considers the semantic case by asking the question, "Do people know they mean what you say they said, and does it matter anyway?" We make no comment on her conclusions because we know you would believe you understood what you think we said, but we are not at all sure that you would realize that what you interpret from what you read is not necessarily what we meant! However, Rix is trying to say how different people mean different things by the same words. This has a great deal of significance in education which relies so heavily on verbal instruction and communication.

Mildred Shaw and Brian Gaines started the "Barbican Grid Group" in 1979. We have been members of that group since its inception and have found the work conducted interesting. All the members have, like ourselves, their own research interests, but as a whole the group has been looking at non-verbal ways to elicit grids. Colours, music and other quite revolutionary techniques have been examined. Progress is slow in such a difficult area, but we are confident that efforts will be rewarded by the increased value of grid-based methodologies. As an interim measure, Roberts, one of Keen's Ph.D. research students, is working on the possibility of utilizing either fuzzy set theory or probability estimating to reduce anxiety felt by a respondent when using words he can't fully comprehend or numbers about which he is uncertain. Gaines and Shaw have already worked in this field and such futuristic techniques as using the "Apple" voice recognition unit to enable a grid to be elicited by *talking* to a computer are being seriously considered by several people, including the authors.

To conclude this section, it would be a serious omission not to note the excellent "occasional publications" which have emerged from the Centre for the Study of Human Learning at Brunel University. Directed by Laurie Thomas, many excellent researchers have contributed to these papers, including Fraser Reid, Cliff McKnight, Nick Pope, Sheila Harri-Augstein and Ranulf Glanville. These papers cover many areas of personal construct psychology in education. Indeed, it is our view that the work of Laurie Thomas at Brunel may have been the single most important contribution to personal construct psychology in the 1970s. Many of these papers are listed in the references, but a full list is available from the Centre for the Study of Human Learning, Brunel University, Uxbridge, Middlesex, England.

MANAGEMENT-RELATED FIELDS

There is a great need in industry for any technique which can improve management effectiveness. Both the authors have been heavily committed to developing such uses, Keen using the IMAGE (Individual Management Appraisal by Grid Elicitation) system, and Pope in industrial consultancy.

Historically consultants have used techniques from psychology, e.g. Transactional Analysis (TA) and the system has fallen into disrepute because the consultant, who is often untrained, has drawn unrealistic conclusions from the data, and failed to appreciate what the technique can, or more often, cannot do. We hope this problem will not arise with application of personal construct psychology. In our opinion some of the practitioners who are leading a thoroughly professional approach to this area are those we have cited here, although there are, of course, many others.

This section attempts to do no more than list the major workers whom the authors believe have made particularly valuable contributions. Their work is not described in any detail, but this book is not the place for a detailed management services manual.

(1) Boot and Boxer (1980). These authors have considered relating learning activities to personal goals and management decision making.

(2) Stewart and Stewart (1976). The Stewarts have considered management effectiveness, design of performance appraisal techniques, the identification of management potential, and training needs analysis.

(3) Thomas (various dates, see references). Thomas has studied subjective judgment in quality control, and personal criteria used in appraisal and selection and management development. There have also been many associated projects, some unpublished. As we have already indicated, we feel that Thomas may have been responsible, through the Centre for the Study of Human Learning, for much of the development of personal construct psychology in management and education throughout the 1970s.

(4) Fairbairns (1978). Manpower Services Commission. Fairbairns has considered women's perception of work, the work environment and the work role.

(5) Easterby-Smith (1980). Easterby-Smith, of Lancaster University, has been considering the design and evaluation of training in industry and his monograph *How to use Repertory Grids in H.R.D.* is specific to the needs of managers.

(6) Honey (1979). An independent consultant, Honey has produced a series of papers for managers and in common with Easterby-Smith has been largely responsible for the dissemination of information relating to personal construct psychology in management education.

(7) Brown (1979). Brown has been working with the intention of discovering and developing decisions people make about people, especially in relation to educational administration. He therefore merits special mention in this section, although we feel he has also made a valuable contribution in personal construct psychology generally.

The interested reader will find all the researchers above willing to provide further information on their work while the reference list in this book might direct such a reader to some useful additional material. It is our view that the use of methodologies based on personal construct psychology, in the appraisal and education of managers, will greatly expand in the early 1980s and much scope exists for developmental work in this aspect of personal construct psychology.

VOCATIONAL GUIDANCE AND TRAINING

Bryan Tully (1976) attempts, and, we think, succeeds, to summarize personal construct theory and what is often called its most developed experimental investigating technique, the role construct repertory grid. Issues in professional training in adjacent professions are examined for relevant parallels to social work. The specific notion of emotion as change in the mode of information processing is introduced through the neuro-psychological model proposed by Pribram and Melges (personal communication). Personal construct theory is seen as congruent with that model for dealing with uncertainty, and as particularly suitable for examining personal change in social work training. Studies comparing the personal construct systems of social work students in training with professionally qualified social workers are reviewed. They conclude that the processes involved in social work education are, because of the nature of their characteristics, capable of leading a person to develop either desirable, sensitive, articulate, and imaginative ways of construing people and personal problems, or to develop over-simplified, rigid, impersonal and incompetent modes of construing. Suggestions are made as to how personal construct theory can help social workers involved in training to deal with problems.

Smith *et al.* (1978) direct their attention to the guidance given to a 20-year-old university leaver. They employ repertory grid technique in the course of vocational guidance by eliciting the elements of the grid (the occupations on the student's cognitive map), eliciting the constructs (qualities used to differentiate between the elements), constructing and administering the grid, analysing the grid by computer, and interpreting the results. This work is unusual in that it focuses on the university leaver whilst the majority of work relates to university entrance.

David Tiedeman (1967) in *Thought, Choice and Action* considered work in career development research at Harvard University. The purpose of his papers was to review, clarify, and offer a critical commentary on several issues crucial to current research, and to emphasize a point of view from which important resources of conceptual analysis can be brought to bear on the issues. Section I in his book, on Developmental Context, and Section II, called Stock Taking include the following chapters: (1) The Harvard Studies in Career Development: Retrospect and Prospect; (2) Decision and Vocational Development: a Paradigm and its Implications; (3) The Self-Concept: A Critical Analysis; (4) Self as Process; (5) The Self-Concept: A Construct in Transition; (6) From Self-Concept to Personal Determination in Career Development; (7) Occupational Psychology and Guidance in Education; Foundations for a Language in Career Development; (8) Personally Determined Career and Entrepreneurial Behaviour: Annotated Texts and Contexts; (9) Current Findings: Precursors of New Directions; and (10) Creativity and Career.

Reid and Holley (1972) conducted a two-stage investigation of applicants' choice of university, using group versions of tests based on a repertory grid technique. In the first stage, nine major constructs were elicited from 32 students, which were used in a second stage test completed by 70 students. Data were also collected on personal and educational backgrounds, and analyses were carried out on possible relationships between university choices and assessment of universities as indicated on the constructs and background data. It is concluded that these analyses provide important insights into the determinants of the choices which applicants make, and indicate that repertory grids may profitably be used on a group basis to investigate choice situations of this type.

Reid (1972) and Reid and Holley (1972) use repertory grid based methodologies to identify the components of the images held by sixth formers of university. They go on to suggest that some aspects of the image which is held of a particular university help to decide whether or not it is chosen by applicants.

On another aspect of vocational guidance, Judith Brook (1979) considers the school leaver who is not a potential university entrant. She endeavoured to determine the perceptions held by secondary school students of people who gave them vocational counselling. Findings showed that subjects made their discriminations between people on two major construct dimensions, an intimacy and a potency factor, and that vocational counsellors appeared in two generalized figure clusters.

TEACHER AND TEACHING ASSESSMENT

In this section we deliberately ignore our own work which is fully reported elsewhere in this volume. The other work we have considered falls into two groups:

(1) Teacher appraisal by students, peers or others.

(2) Student appraisal by teachers.

We do not see these as distinct but as closely related aspects of a common problem. Teacher appraisal has become one of the more seriously researched areas due to an increasing demand on "education" to become more efficient and effective. Indeed in some cases this is related to the "accountability" issue. In the USA appraisal of teaching competence is commonplace for decisions on tenure or promotion, whereas in Great Britain most academic "teachers" react against the mere thought of formal assessment for such things! If we can look into the future, we see this as a likely development on a wider scale, and it therefore becomes of paramount importance to develop assessment procedures which are acceptable to all and yet clearly achieve their objectives.

A digression may be made to consider the Formative v. Summative debate. One is often asked if an assessment instrument is summative or formative. Our philosophy demands that one should lead to the other thus leading to increased teacher autonomy, which enables the individual teacher to take over control of his own "development", at the same time achieving an increased effectiveness in the profession in total. Thus summative assessment intended to determine performance for tenure and promotion must, in our view, provide a raising of self-awareness which in a formative sense improves the teaching strategies of the subject.

"Repgrid" type instruments already exist and there are clear indications that they have made a distinct and significant step forward. Some, like the Tuckman Teacher Feedback Form (1976), whilst claiming to be grid-based, are in fact not so: behavioural elements of pedagogy are identified and then "applied" in a manner more akin to semantic differential. However, it does, even so, represent a more valid attempt to identify the appropriate elements of effective teaching than the many behavioural systems currently in circulation.

The Tuckman Teacher Feedback Form (TTFF) is claimed to be appropriate for determining teacher behaviour. The propositions are:

(1) The teacher relates to the environment by means of personal

constructs used for processing incoming information.

(2) These constructs mediate between information the teacher receives and behaviour that he emits.

(3) Types of personal constructs the teacher uses to construe his environment will also be the ones used by an observer to construe the teacher–classroom behaviour.

(4) Constructs are organized into more stable and meaningful systems of clusters of constructs.

(5) The relative predominance of construct systems will reflect the characteristics of the situation, the disposition of the teacher, and the previous history of the teacher.

The TTFF is a series of 28 paired adjectives, each paired with its approximate opposite. Each pair presents a personal construct that can be used to construe teacher behaviour. It can be used by supervisor, trained observer, peer, or student to describe teacher behaviour over approximately a 45 min span of time.

Olson (1980) is concerned with curriculum change, and reports an interesting study in which he used repertory grid techniques to investigate teachers' constructs about their work, in an attempt to illuminate how innovative ideas are often translated into a "Pale reflection of the original as they are implemented in the classroom". Olson's work indicates that teachers seem to construe forms of teaching along a dimension of high to low teacher influence. Low influence teaching involved such activities as acting as a discussion leader organizing a student seminar and setting essays on social issues. Teachers found it difficult to comment on the intellectual goals of low influence teaching and to construe significant roles for themselves within this form of teaching. This was in contrast to forms of teaching where they were in charge and able to act in familiar ways. Olson argues that innovative ideas require methods which add to the role diffuseness of the teacher and they may be construed as having low influence. High influence teaching is used by teachers to obtain "a sense that something is being accomplished". Innovations which add to role diffuseness and which teachers construe as not giving *them* a sense of accomplishment, may thus have little impact.

McConnell and Hodgson (1977, 1979) used repgrids to develop student-generated Lecture Feedback Questionnaires. Generally speaking, such questionnaires do not help lecturers improve their teaching because the terms used in them, e.g. "Clarity and Rapport" are too vague to be of use to lecturers in improving their teaching. McConnell and Hodgson set out to break down these vague teaching variables into the specific teaching behaviours, of which they consist, as perceived by students. Students were asked to compare and contrast university lecturers whom they liked and disliked (according to certain criteria), and a set of eight detailed questionnaires were compiled from the students' construct, each dealing with a general teaching variable which had been broken down into its specific teaching behaviours. Lecturers have found these detailed feedback questionnaires of great benefit in the improvement of their teaching.

Gonzalez (1979) used repgrids as one of her methods when studying the nature of students' interactions in individualized learning classrooms. She was interested in how students perceive each other and their behaviours under such arrangements. In addition, she was interested in the observations of teachers using different approaches to individualized learning, in order to gain insight into teachers' views of such new activities, and to find out how teachers draw distinctions between different words used in relation to individualized learning. Having used repgrids in conjunction with observation and interview, Gonzalez concluded

> In my experience the repgrid provides an opportunity to study the aspect of the classroom from both teacher and student viewpoint. As such, it was a powerful tool to be used in conjunction with observations and interviews. (p.57)

Nash (1973) used Kelly's model as a basis for looking at how primary school teachers typify their pupils, i.e. what were the common constructs which they tended to use. He found three such common constructs: *Hard-working/Lazy*, *Mature/Immature*, and *Well behaved/Poorly behaved* and in addition noted that individual teachers also employed a range of idiosyncratic constructs. Subsequently, Nash (1976) investigated the constructs used by pupils to typify their teachers and found that these could be grouped into six major types of constructs, e.g. *Interesting/Boring*, *Explains/Doesn't explain*, and *Keeps order/Unable to keep order*.

The work of the researchers outlined above has some links with Francis Wardle's (1978) PACER model.

The PACER model outlines the skills and qualities that an elementary school teacher operating in an alternative open framework should possess. These criteria are based on the PACER model of 30 students, aged 4–12, learning in an ungraded, unstructured environment. (The PACER model adheres to the idea that all experiences and all learning situations are of equal importance.) Some of the skills and characteristics emphasized here are: ability to continually change and adapt to the environment; love of children; ability to counsel students; pleasure in physical activities; ability to teach basic subjects; ability to construct and play games; the ability to work well with other adults; possession of an even temper and ego; adequate knowledge of psychology and learning theories; and an ability to make creative decisions. Having reviewed teacher assessment, the authors moved on to consider the teachers' assessment of students, an area where we were surprised that more effort had not been expended. There is clearly much improvement to be made and yet little "pressure" exists to encourage research in the field.

Wood and Napthali (1975) explored the idea that teachers look for different behaviours to reward when making assessments of students' achievement. Using a repertory grid technique, 16 secondary school teachers of geography and mathematics were asked to name the attributes they look for and to rank them in order of importance; data were collected on 355 students. Cognitive attributes were generally predominant but there was a class of attributes, termed "motivational" which appeared to exert considerable moderating effects. It was in their response to sets of behaviours like "industry" and "perseverance" that teachers showed greatest individual differences in rating performance. Suggestions are made for bringing greater systematization into assessments although it is recognized that there is likely to be a limit to what it is possible to do. Their results support the findings of Keen in his Ph.D. thesis relating to physics students.

These studies indicate the importance of the personal criteria of teachers and students in relation to the subject of teacher assessment. Nash shows clearly that teachers have personal constructs and perceptions of students that they themselves may be unaware they are holding, or using. Considering the recent emphasis on the process of typification in classroom interaction (Hargreaves, 1977) we feel that personal construct psychology has much to offer, and that this is certainly an area worthy of further work.

CURRICULUM DEVELOPMENT AND "ONE-OFF" PROJECTS OF SPECIAL INTEREST

In this section we have exercised "poetic licence", in that we have included one project, initiated by a colleague of ours from Australia (Simon Hasleton) which is only tenuously linked to "education". Our justification is that education must be a life-long experience and any technique affecting life must therefore be educative! We refer to marriage "guidance" techniques. It has been said that marriage guidance is a club, run by untrained volunteers who often have marital problems themselves. We disagree with this sentiment, but there is in fact a need for formal professional aids for the counsellors. Simon Hasleton has developed such a grid-based technique in Australia and the authors are currently considering a means of using this system in England. In this country Jill Norfolk (1979) looked at how counsellors "see" their clients with a view to incorporating this in professional training for marriage guidance counsellors.

Frank Richardson and Richard Weigal (1969) have described an integrative theoretical framework for the conceptualization of the marriage relationship, in terms of Kelly's psychology of personal constructs. They argue that personal construct theory offers a productive model which can account for research findings related to most of the variables found to be relevant to marital success. Personal construct theory is shown to be useful in providing an integrative model for the assimilation of the various research findings into a significant overall context. The theoretical model is further discussed in terms of its implications for the generation of testable hypotheses regarding the marriage relationship.

These approaches offer, we feel, the possibility of personal construct psychology making a real contribution in a new area in the 1980s, particularly as "education" will increasingly become more a part of living rather than a preparation for life. We have already introduced this idea in Chapter 1 with our comments on de-schooling and are convinced that the 1980s will see an extension of this notion of education.

Returning to the main theme of this section, namely curriculum development, there is a great deal to report. In general terms there are works which look at the relationship between modes of instruction and education (Shaw and Thomas, 1979). Here the repertory grid is analysed by new methods of computer analysis and is used as a sensitive instrument allowing individuals to model any topic in terms of personal constructs. On the same topic Thomas and Harri-Augstein (1976) illustrate how the Kelly repertory grid and the Thomas focusing technique can be used to help teachers and learners become aware of learners' purposes for reading, and how these purposes can be used in a program for improving competencies in reading for learning. The grid elicitation and focusing techniques are briefly described by the authors. Four focused grids elicited from students in a college of education are used to show how differently the same universe of discourse (purposes for reading) can be interpreted. A consensus grid illustrates how nine students differentiated between those purposes related to educational activities, pleasure and real learning. These grids were used as a starting point for learning conversations, in which students reviewed and changed their repertoire of purposes. Improvement in reading skills resulting from the learning conversations is reviewed, as well as results from a follow-up consensus grid.

James Ewing (1977), also considering reading, has said that historically less emphasis has been put on the importance of attitude factors than on the skills of reading. When defining attitudes as a person's views, interests, expectations, and so on, attitude toward reading is a combination of all the components that contribute to a person's underlying disposition to reading including expectations, interest, appeal of material and personal satisfaction.

One way to group these components is to consider the characteristics of the reader (internal) and the characteristics of the situation (external). If both components can be independently positive or negative then it would be possible to consider the effects of internal or external factors on the reader's skills. Four techniques are available for measuring attitudes: attitude scales, self-reports and interviews, the semantic differential, and the repertory grid. Ewing claims that planning of a reading curriculum can be aided by the use of attitude analysis to learn what should be emphasized in a particular group or among readers generally. This might be especially important if it can be shown, for instance, that readers who have negative attitudes toward internal components and positive attitudes toward external components are poorer readers than those with opposite attitude scores.

Turning to another aspect of the curriculum, the grid has been used to monitor attitudes towards the introduction of new technology into a traditional craft-based industry. In a further study the attitude, toward their school subjects, of 600 second-year and fifth-year grammar school pupils, was investigated using a repertory grid developed specifically for this purpose (Duckworth and Entwistle, 1974).

Whilst these researchers were interested in curriculum generally, there are many discipline-specific studies. The two disciplines of Journalism and Drama have been selected to illustrate this here as we have some experience of working in both areas.

Hugh Culbertson and Byron Scott (1978) developed two exercises that can be used with journalism students to help them clarify and think through the editorial process. These are the repertory grid and the co-orientation model. The repertory grid asks students to rank ten or twelve authors on criteria such as social acceptability, professional effectiveness, and liberalism–conservatism. The student then decides which authors are closest and which are farthest from his or her "ideal self" and "actual self". The follow-up discussion clarifies the issues involved in defining oneself. The second exercise, the co-orientation model, requires students to rank or rate story titles or leads according to interest or probable readership for themselves and for a clearly defined audience. These ratings are then compared with hypothetical play in editing a publication or with actual survey results of audience ratings. Effective use of these two techniques involves consistent discussion and evaluation on the individual level along with statistical analyses.

Our Drama examples are less well-known and have not (at the time of writing) been published. Tony Arnott, a deputy head of a residential approved school (and a member of the Barbican Grid Group), has conducted some work with adolescent boys, whilst Gill Abbott (1980) is developing grid-based techniques to measure the effectiveness of a Drama course.

Rosie (1979) presents a critique of psychometric social order paradigms in relation to investigating the interpersonal relations between teachers and children in the classroom. He suggests that personal construct theory is a fresh alternative which recognizes the importance of the views of children and teachers as active meaning makers in the classroom. Adopting such a perspective, he has described a study which highlights differences between "the school's official constructs" and the "personal version of the official construct", as held by the individual children. For example, *Learning to work on your own* (school's official construct) v. *Discovering that teachers don't know everything* (child's personal version).

Rosie's work is a welcome addition to the growing body of interest in personal construct psychology in education.

In concluding this chapter we hope we have succeeded in giving a flavour of the kind of personal construct psychology work which is being conducted. It cannot, and does not pretend to be, a comprehensive survey, but it does intend to suggest areas where researchers might themselves become involved in active research, and give some indication of the potential for new work.

10

Spectres, Spirit and a Crystal Ball?

In the preceding chapters we have endeavoured to sketch some of the more pervasive streams of thought in philosophy, sociology, psychology and educational theory which have had an impact on conceptions of the learning process, and we have suggested that personal construct psychology provides an important alternative approach which has yet to be fully explored in terms of its implications for education. In this final chapter we will try to review some of the issues which have already been touched upon, and to raise further points which may help interested readers in their own exploration of such implications.

In our opinion the strengths of personal construct psychology, which have considerable relevance for those involved in education, are as follows. Firstly, its emphasis on the relativistic nature of knowledge, which allows one to view the various theories outlined in Chapter 1 from a perspective other than that of notions of absolute truth. *Theories or models of man can be seen as alternative constructions which are reliant on the particular vantage point of the theory builder.* At any particular moment in history a theorist puts forward a model which he or she hopes will offer a better prediction of events than a preceding framework. This model will be influenced by personally selected aspects of knowledge from other theories and statements of position which have become public knowledge, i.e. disseminated via textbooks, conference reports and other media. Intuition and implicit ideas on the nature of man and the approach to be adopted in education combined with the life space of interests, attitudes, social contacts and previous experience which surround the individual, will all have a bearing on the model which is offered. The order of influence of each of these will of course vary from individual to individual.

Each of the streams of thought in relation to education outlined in Chapter 1 represents a set of ideas from individuals which have evolved and become consensus positions at particular points in time. The student teacher will be subjected to many of these viewpoints in the course of his training, but, as we pointed in Chapter 8, student teachers might value more opportunities to reflect on their personal positions regarding teaching. Olson's work (1980), which was mentioned in Chapter 9, highlights the importance of the way practising teachers view their jobs, in relation to how particular theories and suggested methods of teaching are implemented in their classrooms.

A Kellian perspective would value the personal reconstruction of publicly accepted models, and would recognize this as an inevitable consequence of teachers forming their personally-viable positions, which they operate within. However, these personal positions should not be seen as fixed, as these theories too will be developed and modified as their predictions are played out in application. This notion should also, as Kelly suggested, be applied to his own theory. The models of personal construct psychology have been erected by humans and emphasize the mobility inherent in all humans and hence, as a consequence, these should be constantly open to change. We would argue that in all educational endeavours participants might benefit from making explicit and keeping under review their personal approaches, whether as a learner, student teacher, teacher or researcher within the system.

We believe that the negation by the personal construct scientist of the traditional subject/experimenter distinction is another strength of this approach. The "naive subject" as a passive object facing an active experimenter would seem to be a caricature whose demise is nigh. Any investigation involving people, whether it be an experiment, tutorial or just a chat, involves an interaction of two meaning systems. Those involved in investigations in education should reflect on their personal models of the learning process. It should be acknowledged that the method of investigation usually mirrors the implicit philosophy of science of the investigator. We would argue that researcher should be more self-conscious of their assumptions and make their views explicit, since the nature of the method used is a factor in determining the type of data acquired and potential interpretations. Personal construct psychology would lend theoretical support to any investigator who recognized the importance of incorporating all those involved in the particular educational issue with which he is concerned. The "triangulation method" used by Elliot and Adelman (1973) bears witness to the fruitfulness of involving the teacher, the pupil and the researcher in an analysis of classroom behaviour.

Following on from the pioneering work of the Centre for Applied Research in Education, at the University of East Anglia, there is a growing number of researchers in education who are working in very close contact with teachers and pupils in an attempt to get an insider's view of affairs rather than coming in as a stranger who remains at a distance. Indeed, a number of teachers have begun to research the processes which are going on in their own classrooms (Enright, 1979).

Teachers adopting a personal construct psychology approach would be interested in the different perspectives of learners in relation to specific tasks. This awareness of the different positions of the learner would be obtained through conversational approaches rather than traditional test procedures. Their aim would be an increased understanding of the learning process, rather than an attempt to define students according to some rank ordering of performance. Through a process of interchange, the learner's model could be compared with that of other learners, with that of the teacher or a source such as a body of knowledge in a textbook. Any attempt to monitor changes in the learner's view of a task would be evaluated in the learner's terms as well as those of the teacher.

In the preceding chapters we have suggested that the repertory grid technique would be a fruitful device for use in educational settings. The following are areas where we have found the repertory grid to be a useful tool and we suggest that others may find them such within the classroom:

(1) Repertory grid technique is a fruitful device for monitoring such changes which may occur in the "frames of reference" or in "personal constructions" of students as they undergo a course of study/training.

(2) The grid provides a mirror which allows the trainee the opportunity to reflect on these changes in relation to his or her experiences.

(3) The trainer or tutor can have a firmer base upon which to counsel a student and provide pointers to area of personal development which the student may not have considered.

(4) Mismatch between the expert/tutor/trainers' view and that of the novice/student/trainee can be exposed and the ensuing conversations can be beneficial to both participants.

(5) Producing a series of grids from the start of a course through to its close will be a more useful indication of the progress and evaluation of the course, than the usual before and after measures evolved by the tutor.

(6) With recent developments in computer programs, e.g. PEGASUS, SOCIOGRIDS, PEGBANK (Shaw, 1980) it is possible to store grids so that:

(a) the trainee can match his or her views with those of the expert;

(b) the trainee can match his or her views with those of any other trainee.

Using the repertory grid as a vehicle the student can see the development in his learning in his own terms and can evaluate the success or otherwise of his actions throughout the course. Exposure to differing views helps to overcome ideas of absolute truth and static knowledge. Even when matching one's viewpoint with that of the "expert", the provisional nature of the "expert's" view should be stressed. Development of knowledge or ways of proceeding is rarely enriched by strict adherence to the established viewpoint.

Whilst we have put forward personal construct psychology and repertory grids as a possible source of ideas and methods, it is not intended that this should pre-empt the use of other approaches. It is possible and perhaps desirable in many cases to implement a personal construct psychology approach to learning and teaching without incorporating repertory grid techniques. For example, Warner (1971) suggested the use of a "journal of introspection" as a means of encouraging student teachers to reflect on their changing ideas and attitudes as they proceeded through their course of study. The emphasis Warner placed on personal reflection seems to fit entirely with a personal construct psychology framework. Similarly, Enright (1979), a practising teacher, kept a diary in which each night after school she wrote down all that she could remember from the classroom work that day and in addition taped some of the lessons and recorded conversations with pupils about the work they had been doing. Using this approach Enright found that she became more attentive to what pupils actually said, and she maintains that the pupils changed their perception of her role, and in consequence discipline problems occurred less frequently.

A colleague, Gilbert (see Gilbert and Osborne, 1980) has developed a series of cards showing drawings of aspects of science, depicted in various ways. Using this approach he has studied the pupils' conceptualization of concepts such as force and energy. Gilbert uses the cards as an initial stimulus to generate a conversation about, for example, the concept of force, and records in the pupil's own language their descriptions of the cards. In this way Gilbert has been able to point out that pupils often have alternative frameworks or misconceptions which the teacher should be aware of, otherwise they may run counter to the formal concepts of science which the teacher is trying to develop. Gilbert calls this approach Interview About Instances (IAI) and although his work was initially influenced by a Piagetian framework he now recognizes personal construct psychology as offering an alternative set of ideas. This is perhaps not surprising as other researchers have pointed out some parallels between the developmental model of Piaget and Kelly's ideas on the development of a personal construct system (Adams-Webber, 1970).

The Illuminative Incident Analysis used by Cortazzi and Roote (1975) is another interesting approach which we feel has parallels with the aims and philosophy of personal construct psychology. The object of their approach is to gain insight into areas which are centrally important to an individual by having the individual describe important events. Pope has recently been to a symposium on The Lecture Method during which a variant of this approach was used to raise a group discussion. Each member of the symposium was asked to draw a picture which represented their conclusions about what they had learnt during the previous two days. This picture was drawn on overhead transparency sheets and, after some discussion in pairs, volunteer members placed their overhead transparencies on the projector and these acted as stimulus for further discussion and review of personal learning which had taken place.

Ference Marton (1980) and his group at the University of Göteborg in Sweden have been investigating student learning using an approach which aims to provide qualitative description of the process used when a particular learner is going about a specific learning task. This group places considerable emphasis on the contextual nature of learning, and do not draw generalizations from the phenomena observed to the population at large. Marton's approach involves interviews with students who describe how they go about completing specific tasks, and subsequent analysis of transcripts has led Marton to describe several qualitatively different types of processing in relation to learning tasks. Thus he describes "surface level processing" where the individual is picking up isolated facts, as opposed to "deep level processing" where the individual is relating these facts to each other and to other ideas and thoughts which he holds. In his paper "Studying conceptions of reality" Marton (1980) stresses that "there are qualitatively different ways of seeing aspects of the world, in a sense we live in different realities". He goes on to point out that thinking in terms of multiple realities is an alternative philosophical standpoint to that of naive realism. We would suggest that these notions are inherent in Kelly's (1955) ideas on individuality and his philosophy of constructive alternativism. Marton suggests that the approach

> (which deals with the different ways of thinking about specific aspects of reality) though being complimentary to psychology (which deals with thinking in general) seems at least as relevant to educational practice as psychology is. (p.10)

We would argue that it is possible to see this domain within the framework of psychology as opposed to being complementary to it. This, however, represents our different way of thinking about a specific aspect of reality. In the same paper Marton suggests that since teaching is about "facilitating ways of thinking about certain aspects of the world" it might be useful if the teacher who is dealing with for example, the aspect of "power" to know something of the "possible ways in which their students think about power". Similarly, in relation to the concept of correlation he suggests it might be useful to know about "the different ways in which people spontaneously reason about statistical relationships". These suggestions are totally in accord with the view taken by Gilbert in his work on alternative frameworks and misconceptions in science, and indeed as personal construct psychologists we would take a similar position. Although Marton does not make reference to Kelly's work we feel that there is much in common between his phenomenological approach and the philosophy of personal construct psychology.

Boot and Boxer (1980) working within a personal construct psychology approach have developed a computer program package called NIPPER, which elicits and analyses repertory grid and allows for comparison between grids stored on file. They have also used a variety of other techniques to encourage reflective learning. Boxer (personal communication) described one sequence of techniques which he has found has brought about significant self-awareness in the individuals whom he has counselled. The learner/manager is encouraged to map out the main context of the area which is to be considered and to identify which aspects are to be explored further. The NIPPER interchange is used to provide feedback on constructs and inter-relationships between elements. In addition Boxer asks for life stories highlighting good and bad points, encourages the learner to plan a course of action and to review his own progress judiciously. A final stage is to write an obituary. These counselling sessions are aimed at encouraging the learner to look at aspects of his life and to review emotional blocks which may be impeding progress so that he can become more self-directed. The obituary may be seen as a way of reviewing whether or not one is satisfied with how one is proceeding, and highlighting other areas which the learner may want to work through further.

It seems to us that, whatever approach one adopts, it is desirable that one should retain a high degree of flexibility and recognize that, given a variety of perspectives on the nature of man, whether physiological, sociological, mystical or psychological, the problem usually becomes one of extracting a theory or methodology which one feels is appropriate to the particular issue at hand. If the reader should at this stage find personal construct psychology and/or repertory grid technique of interest, we would stress the importance of becoming familiar with the basic assumptions of the theory. If one should choose to implement repertory grid techniques there will be a need to adapt the general methodology to suit the specific purpose as one cannot pull down a repertory grid off the shelf so to speak. There will always be a need to explore and extract pertinent aspects of personal construct theory and repertory grid methods to suit particular needs. Unless one is sensitive to the assumptions behind the technique and the practical considerations which we have discussed in Part Two of this book the reader may well get into difficulties, draw unwarranted conclusions from grid data, and have unrealistic expectations as to what the grid can or cannot do. At this stage it might be useful to summarize some of the main assumptions of Kelly's theory:

A person's processes are psychologically channelised by the ways in which he anticipates events.

This is the fundamental postulate of personal construct theory, and it implies that what one does in the present is determined by the way one anticipates what will happen in the future. People are seen as oriented towards the future rather than shaped by their past. In presenting his view of the individual as a "scientist", Kelly argued that a person will be continually exploring the world around them by putting forward hypotheses about the way events may turn out and the way people may react, and will be constantly checking out the validity or otherwise of the meaning which the individual ascribes to the world around him. The repertory grid can be seen as a tool which might allow someone to gain some awareness of the world view of another (extractive mode). However, we argue that it is best used as a psychological "mirror" which should help the individual, rather than the investigator, to understand his world (reflective mode). This latter purpose was the central issue for Kelly, in that his clinical use of the grid was to encourage his client to reflect on the way he or she was viewing events and significant people.

In considering the grid as a means of providing a reflection of a person's construct system we feel we should drawn the reader's attention to at least two points. Firstly, the grid is at best only a mirror and like all reflections it does not provide something which is identical with the particular sub-system of constructs which is the focus of attention. We would argue that it provides the learner, tutor or researcher with some insight into this system but it does not capture and fully describe it. In addition, mirrors can distort depending on the characteristics of the mirror itself. In this connection one should be aware that the particular mathematical analysis chosen to analyse repertory grid data does affect the projected image. This point does not concern us unduly since we do not see ourselves in the business of producing absolute statements about the nature of construing, rather we see personal construct psychology and repertory grid methods as useful catalysts to help in coming to some understanding of any individual's ideas. Personal construct psychology and methods such as the grid would not be happy bedfellows for the naive realist.

A second point about interpretation of grids may be apt at this point. The primary aim of the grid is to gain an insight into how an individual sees some aspects of reality, rather than to describe reality. We would argue that it is important, if at all possible, to encourage the individual to help in the elaboration and interpretation of constructs and other information contained in a grid conversation. We have found that occasionally, especially in relation to management education, a person will be most surprised at being asked to draw interpretation from his own data. All too often the expectation is that the "expert" will give the answer and, especially when faced with computer printout, the person may feel the absolute answer is contained within the numerical analysis. In addition, we have found that some managers who have, for example, construed their subordinates in order to reflect on the types of constructs they use in appraisal, have looked at data and seen that certain subordinates fall into one group and other subordinates fall into another group, and an immediate reaction has been "ah, yes, those are the good guys" or "they are the deadweight". We feel it is necessary at this stage to remind anybody who makes such a statement that the data seem to be indicating that they see those particular individuals in that light and it represents their view of the subordinates, rather than describing the subordinates in any more absolute sense. This message usually comes over very clearly when a number of managers construe the same set of subordinates and compare their viewpoints.

This brings us to another key assumption of Kelly's personal construct theory, i.e. his individuality corollary:

Persons differ from each other in their construction of events.

The implications of this for education may be apparent. Each person will have a particular perspective on learning and teaching and individuals will differ as to their aims, aspirations, expectations and ways of operating in relation to how they construe education. Emphasis on individuality can be seen in the learner-centred approach and independent or individualized learning methods. This corollary has influenced a number of folk interested in self-development. They argue, for example, that if one is offering a course on self-development it seems reasonable to start with some idea of how each individual sees himself, how he might want to be, and some indication of an individual's priority in terms of the areas in which he sees self-development as necessary.

The Air Transport Travel Industry Training Board's Management Development Group have taken this approach with a recent course on self-development. Prior to the course each individual completed a repertory grid and in the ensuing conversations with a tutor from the course each individual indicated the areas which he felt needed to be improved, and these conversations helped the tutor to structure the course in relation to the needs of the learners and, within the course, develop a form of learning contract with each manager.

In education we are often faced with syllabi, and external examination constraints, which are given as reasons why it is not possible to allow each learner to follow his or her own path. This may be the case, but those who take Kelly's individuality corollary seriously will want to offer each individual as much freedom as is possible given such constraints and, indeed, some would wish to operate outside the structure of an externally-imposed framework.

Returning again to repertory grid methodology one should draw attention here to attempts to combine data from different individuals who have completed repertory grids. We have mentioned such techniques as SOCIOGRIDS and the game of "misunderstood", which we have found to be useful in highlighting similarities and differences amongst individuals in a group. However, it should be realized that in essence any individual's grid is unique, and whilst one may combine data if, for example, an agreed common set of elements has been negotiated, one should stress the provisional nature of any interpretations one can draw from such combinations and one should see the fruitfulness of this approach as catalytic and not descriptive.

Despite Kelly's emphasis on individuality he did raise the possibility of shared areas of personal meaning and this is explicit in his commonality corollary:

> to the extent that one person employs a construction of experience which is similar to that employed by another, his processes are psychologically similar to those of the other person.

Sharing of a common view of experience can often be noted on training courses. If one has a set of trainees there may be some who come from the same organization, and it is not unusual for these trainees to share a common language and put forward similar constructs about a topic area such as "management effectiveness", which differs from that of other trainees. Thus the "construing past" is an important issue. Trainees on particular training courses may erect similar constructs with respect to the issues considered on the course, and similarly students within particular colleges may have viewpoints which are, at least in part, very similar to each other. This may relate to what is referred to as "educational ethos" or "classroom climate" and, as we have suggested, techniques such as repertory grids might be used to explore such aspects of education.

As we noted in Chapter 3 Kelly's assumption about communication embodied in his sociality corollary "to the extent that one person construes the construction processes of another, he may play a role in a social process involving the other person" has important implications for education.

One should stress here that Kelly is not suggesting that people have to have the same ideas or constructs as each other in order to communicate, but he did suggest that to interact effectively people do have to have some knowledge and understanding of another's viewpoint. Some of the applications discussed in Chapters 7 and 8, e.g. SOCIOGRID and MISUNDERSTOOD are aimed at helping to create such a situation within group settings. Apparently, within management education, there is interest in team building exercises and we have been involved in a number of situations where grids have been used, constructs exchanged and discussed, and attempts made by one individual to either use another's construct or to predict how the other would have used the construct. This has been the basis of discussions, the aim of which was to improve communication between group members and allow various people within an organizational setting to explore similarities and differences in their construing of tasks, objectives, strategies etc., with which they are faced.

When applied within the educational context of a school or college this aim and the implications of the sociality corollary are equally important. In the course of discussion one of the students in the Pope (1978) study commented that she felt sure that every student would have supplied the element PUPILS when asked to give aspects which they felt were important in relation to teaching. One student in particular did not make reference to pupils or relationships with pupils within her first grid, and if these two students had had an opportunity to compare and exchange their ideas about teaching using the repertory grid exercise as a base we suggest that a fruitful exchange of ideas about teaching would have taken place. If a tutor and student complete grids on the same topic area this also provides a basis for discussion, and externalizing areas of similarity and difference between a tutor's grid and that of a student provides a framework for understanding each other's point of view. A greater awareness and understanding of another's point of view should, we hope, lead to improved communication and democracy in education.

Returning to management education, the importance of the "organization view" is relevant here. Whilst reflecting on his or her own view a manager may have to come to terms with a divergence between that view and the one commonly held by other individuals within his organization. In addition, this "commonly held view" may not be as common as people within the organization think.

In Chapter 8 we attached importance to encouraging student teachers to review the relationships between the formal concepts presented on their course, with the personal experiences gained during teaching practice and argued that, unless the formal concepts are assimilated as personally significant viewpoints they will become a fragmented part of the student's construct system which will remain unrelated with other concepts, and may not be utilized. Pope (1978) suggested this as an underlying reason why, for example, the students in Shipman's (1967) study jettisoned the attitude which they had professed whilst on the course after leaving college. In industrial training the transitory nature of "training course constructs" is notorious, especially if the views of the people in the trainee's organization diverge radically from those considered on the course. Trainees may be eager to implement ideas acquired during a training course but on return to their organization may find some difficulty in doing so. This will give rise to different reactions — some may undergo a change in constructs, abandon their training course constructs, and comply with the company view, while others will face frustration, conflict and possible withdrawal from the organization. Much depends on the extent to which the ideas presented on the course are related to the trainee's personal view at the outset and the amount of reconstruction that has taken place during the course. Constructs which have become only loosely "welded" on to the trainee's initial viewpoint may prove too fragmented to be a potent force behind subsequent behaviour.

We feel that these assumptions have important implications for education, and since they underlie grid techniques we suggest that the reader must reflect on the extent to which these assumptions fit with their own view and decide whether the repertory grid, as described here, is an appropriate technique to use. It is quite possible to use the technique without any knowledge or reference to the assumptions underlying it, though we feel that this is not advisable as it often leads to inappropriate applications, unwarranted interpretations and inferences, and disillusionment with the technique as opposed to how the technique has been applied.

In common with all methods of sensitive enquiry there is a need for the investigator/tutor and learner to create a rapport in which trust and empathy are established. Without feelings of mutual trust any explorations may be tentative and constrained. We must also recognize the importance of the wider social environment and learning experience to data of the learner. Adherence to personal construct psychology with its emphasis on individuality often leads one to neglect the importance of such issues. It is not necessary to take a social deterministic view of social environment, e.g. that the social class of the learner will affect his or her educational aspirations. However, one should recognize, as Kelly did, that people build their construct system in part through their interactions with others, the most significant others in the early stages being the immediate family and thereafter social contacts as school, work, etc. The particular social environments and experience to date of any learner will place some limit on the "universe of discourse" which the learner can enter. For example, a person who has very little contact with classical music could perhaps construe a particular piece of classical music as being different from two pieces of popular music, but may have more difficulty in articulating the similarities and differences between various pieces of classical music. Thus, while it is important to enter the "here and now" construing of the learner, one should be aware of the importance of previous learning experiences and of the influence of the current co-sociates. There may be occasions when it is necessary to enter a "life conversation" (Thomas and Harri-Augstein, 1976) with learners in order to make them reflect on such influences. Thomas and Harri-Augstein place considerable emphasis on discussion of aspects of a learner's life which may have a bearing on a particular learning problem and they encourage learners to become aware of the inter-relationship between "personal issues" and aspects of content, and the strategies which they employ as learners. These authors, through their work at the Centre for the Study of Human Learning at Brunel University, have based their approach on the assumptions of Kelly's work and in drawing implications from it have made a considerable impact on the development of ideas on learning to learn, self-organization in learning and learner-based methods of teaching.

We started this chapter by expressing what we thought were some of the strengths of personal construct psychology, and have drawn attention to the potential danger of implementing grid techniques without due recognition of the underlying assumptions. We now turn to what we feel may be a weakness with respect to how personal construct psychology has been implemented within educational and industrial contexts. Emphasis has, quite rightly in our opinion, been placed on how people feel and think about their lives, their learning, their jobs, etc. However, we feel that the tendency has been to neglect any attempt to systematically collect information about what people actually do in their lives. We are not suggesting a return to a behaviourist approach, nor do we assume what seems to the observer to be the same behaviour is construed in similar terms by the actors. (We have drawn attention to the problems inherent in classroom observation and have suggested that Elliot and Adelman (1975) have made a useful contribution to the dilemmas encountered in such observations.) We would rather seek a return to the emphasis Kelly himself placed upon behaviour.

Kelly saw behaviour as an expression of a person's constructs and suggested that, although behaviour may have been intended as "the embodiment of a conclusive answer", a person's actions will inevitably give rise to further questions, i.e. "the actor finds that he has launched another experiment". In other words Kelly saw behaviour itself as an embodiment of an experiment. In his fixed role therapy, Kelly would negotiate with a client a commitment to test out by action as well as thought and feeling a mode of operation tangentially different from a mode with which the client is experiencing some problem of living. We would suggest, therefore, that a monitoring of what learners and teachers do, as well as what they think and how they feel, is of importance if we wish to fully acquaint ourselves with and come to some understanding of their perspectives.

Watching what learners do and discussing with them what they think they do in relation to specific tasks may highlight some of the strategies they employ in relation to their learning. Reviewing their strategies and perhaps trying out an alternative strategy, i.e. performing a new experiment instead of repeating habitual strategies, may help the learner to increase his potential ways of operating. The approach taken by Gibbs (1977) in relation to developing students' study skills develops this notion, and the work of Thomas and Harri-Augstein lays a similar stress on the learner reviewing the purpose, the strategies to be employed, the outcome of their experimentation with strategies and being continually aware of what one is doing as well as what one is thinking and feeling about learning. Boxer (personal communication), in his counselling sessions with learners, does seem to follow some of Kelly's ideas on the importance of action. We regard the constant interplay between thought and action, and the movement of a learner from an initial definition of personal interests through to a learning contract in which self-conscious action is an essential ingredient, and the keeping under review of one's initial definition of interests and success of one's actions, as important elements in the learning process. We suggest that such an approach is clearly implied in the assumptions of personal construct psychology and is perhaps an area which is stressed somewhat less frequently than the personal ways in which a learner describes his thoughts and feelings through the medium of the written or spoken word.

Kelly stressed that one should not equate the verbal labels used by a person to convey his personal meanings with constructs themselves. For Kelly, a construct embodied emotional and intellectual aspects and in many instances a person may not be able to articulate, using words, some of his or her constructs. Thomas and members of the Centre for the Study of Human Learning have for a number of years been concerned with the exploration of non-verbal constructs. We feel this is an area where new applications of personal construct psychology are likely to develop. Following the adage "actions speak louder than words" we would suggest that looking at what people do alongside what they say about their thoughts and feelings will enrich our understanding of their construing.

Susan Leese (personal communication) has recently embarked on a study of the theoretical links between Rudolf Laban and George Kelly. Laban has had considerable influence on Dance Education and he lays stress on non-verbal communication via movement and on the bi-polar nature of such movement. Leese is using personal construct psychology and Laban's theories in an attempt to gain insight into the needs of dance students in higher education as seen from the student's perspective, and to draw implications from this work which have a bearing on curriculum design. This work not only represents an interesting new application of personal construct psychology, but also indicates a concern for an area of human activity which is often neglected within education. In Chapter 3 we argued that Kelly's notions on individuality and the development of such potential seemed to us to be in sympathy with theorists such as Joyce, who argued for a pluralistic as opposed to a monolithic curriculum. Leese's work on dance and Abbott's work on drama studies mentioned in the last chapter follow this spirit.

In this book we have tried to relate some aspects of Kelly's original theory which we feel have relevance for education, to give the reader some appreciation of techniques which have evolved, and to discuss areas in which research and development have taken place. It is important at this stage to stress that this represents a very personal selection on the part of ourselves and does not cover the many other implications which may be seen in personal construct psychology for education. Indeed, we hope that having reflected on something within this book the reader may be tempted to suggest further implications and develop other applications relevant to his or her specific educational setting. In one sense, we hope too that this chapter will not be "the end" in that we hope that some of you may want to get in touch with us and tell us of your own experiments. We look forward to such conversations! However, an end this book must have and so let us return to the cryptic title of this chapter, which we feel encapsulates the message which we would like to wind up with.

From time to time we have drawn the reader's attention to some of the issues which must be considered when applying repertory grid techniques. We have included, especially in Chapter 6, discussions on the numerical analysis of repertory grid. However, as we have indicated elsewhere, over-reliance on numerical analysis of grids and the drawing of unwarranted assumptions and interpretations based upon such analyses are potential hazards if the reader ignores our words of caution. We hope that such spectres will be laid to rest and that it will be the spirit of Kelly's work, with or without the application of repertory grid techniques, which will survive and provide an impetus for new approaches in education.

Recently a postgraduate student we know commented that things would be better if he was able to pick particular bits of a theory rather than take on board all the tenets of the particular theory he was referring to. A student operating a Kellian framework would not have such a problem. Indeed, the spirit of Kelly's approach is that it invites each of us to review his theory and take away from it those aspects which we find useful in our own explorations. A growing number of people have taken up this challenge, and in keeping with this spirit of exploration are going beyond Kelly's original notions and techniques and are developing new ideas and techniques and are drawing on aspects of other theoretical approaches which they find relevant to their work. In the same spirit we hope that you will do the same with our contribution.

In the first chapters we described some notions about educational practice and research, but what then of the future? We do not feel tempted to look into a crystal ball to answer this question. However, we do suggest that in one sense the future of education is contained in the present: each of us who is involved in education plays a part in structuring its future. Our beliefs and assumptions influence how we operate within the system and this behaviour will help shape the immediate educational environment in which we work. We feel that this is an important point to recognize and much of our own work has centred on encouraging individuals and groups of learners and teachers to become more aware of their thoughts and the ways in which they operate in an educational context. We agree with Postman and Weingartner (1971) who stated:

> There can be no significant innovation in education that does not have at its centre the attitudes of teachers and it is an illusion to think otherwise. The beliefs, feelings and assumptions of teachers are the air of a learning environment; they determine the quality of life within it. (p.43)

However, we do not see the quality of the learning environment as being solely shaped by the teacher's view, since we feel that these interact with those of the students, parents, other teachers and administrators. One has to acknowledge the effect of economic and political constraints, but these decisions too are made by people who will be construing education from their particular vantage point.

It is clear that there are a diversity of viewpoints about what education is and should be, and while some will follow closely the positions we outlined in the early chapters, others will be more idiosyncratic. It is our own belief that individuals and groups working in an educational setting will have evolved a particular construction of education within which they operate and that many different views on what education is and should be can and do co-exist. It seems to us that problems arise when an individual or group operates with one set of assumptions, and tries to impose or communicate these assumptions to others without any acknowledgement or understanding of an alternative framework or set of assumptions which the other values.

We would suggest that each of us must, from time to time, review how we are construing education and the extent to which we understand the position of others with whom we interact. This seems to us to be a central message of Kelly's work and one which we feel is relevant to those who wish for an effective and democratic educational process. The responsibility for the future lies therefore, not in a crystal ball, but in the attempts each and every one of us are making to reflect upon on our "personal constructs", and to negotiate with others who may hold alternative perspectives towards the construction of education.

Appendix

LISTING OF DYAD

```
1 REM-PROGRAM FOR DYADIC ELICITATION
2 REM-OF A GRID
5 PRINT§2, ''THIS PROGRAM FOR DYADIC ELICITATION OF A GRID HAS BEEN WRITTEN BY DR TERENCE
   R. KEEN AND MR RICHARD BELL AT STANTONBURY CAMPUS RESOURCE CENTRE''
6 PRINT§2, ''THE PROGRAMME IS AVAILABLE WITHOUT CHARGE PROVIDING USERS ACKNOWLEDGE
   ITS SOURCE IN ANY PUBLICATION OR APPLICATIONS IN WHICH IT IS USED''
30 CLEAR 25000
40 DIM C$ (2,20), E$(20), GRID (20,20)
50 PRINT:PRINT''LET'S LOOK AT THE WAY YOU THINK ABOUT THINGS.''
60 PRINT:PRINT:PRINT
70 PRINT''INPUT THE NAME OF THE KIND OF THING (MAN,BOOK,DOG,ETC) YOU WISH TO CONSIDER''
80 EN = 0
90 CN=0
100 INPUT POP$
110 PRINT:PRINT:PRINT
120 PRINT''INPUT THE NAME OF A '';POP$;'' WHAT YOU WOULD LIKE TO CONSIDER''
130 EN=EN+1
140 INPUT E$(EN)
150 PRINT''INPUT THE NAME OF A'' ;POP$; ''WHICH IS DIFFERENT IN SOME IMPORTANT WAY FOR
   YOU''
160 EN=EN+1
170 IF EN<20 THEN 490
180 INPUT E$(EN)
190 PRINT:PRINT:PRINT
200 PRINT ''WHAT IS THIS CHARACTERISTIC AS IT APPLIES TO '';E$(EN-1)
210 CN=CN+1
220 IF CN>20 THEN 490
230 INPUT C$(1,CN)
240 PRINT:PRINT:PRINT ''WHAT IS THE OPPOSING TRAIT OF'' ;E$(EN)
250 INPUT C$(2,CN)
260 PRINT:PRINT:PRINT ''GIVE ANOTHER'' ;POP$; ''THAT''
270 PRINT C$(1,CN); ''/'';C$(2,CN); ''ALSO APPLIES TO''
280 EN = EN + 1
```

```
290 IF EN>20 THEN 490
300 INPUT E$(EN)
310 PRINT:PRINT:PRINT
320 PRINT"IF YOU WERE RATING THESE THINGS ON A SCALE OF 1 TO 5 (WHERE 1 MEANS MORE
  LIKE ";C$(1,CN);", and 5 MEANS MORE LIKE ";C$(2,CN);")"
330 PRINT"IF THE DESCRIPTION"C$(1,CN);"/";C$(2,CN);" DOES NOT APPLY AT ALL, ENTER
  ZERO (0)"
340 PRINT"HOW WOULD YOU RATE THEM?"
350 FOR 1=1 TO EN
360 PRINT"RATING FOR";E$(I)
370 INPUT GRID (CN,I)
380 NEXT I
390 PRINT:PRINT:PRINT
400 PRINT"DO YOU WANT TO ADD ANOTHER";POP$" ?ANSWER 'YES' OR 'NO'."
410 INPUT ANS$
420 IF ANS$="NO" THEN 490
430 PRINT:PRINT:PRINT
440 PRINT"INPUT THE NAME OF A";POP$;" WHICH IS DIFFERENT IN ANOTHER IMPORTANT WAY
  FROM";E$(EN)
450 EN=EN+1
460 IF EN 20 THEN 490
470 INPUT E$(EN)
480 GOTO 190
490 PRINT:PRINT:PRINT
500 PRINT"YOU HAVE AN INTERESTING";POP$;" GROUP. YOU MAY HAVE REALIZED THAT THE
  LATER ELEMENTS ADDED HAVE NOT BEEN RATED ON EARLIER TRAITS."
510 PRINT"WOULD YOU LIKE TO GO BACK AND 'FILL THESE IN'? ANSWER 'YES' OR 'NO'"
520 INPUT ANS$
530 IF ANS$="NO" THEN 1000
540 PRINT:PRINT:PRINT
550 PRINT"OKAY. REMEMBER TO RATE AS BEFORE WHERE 1 MEANS MORE LIKE THE LEFT-HAND
  TRAIT, AND 5 MEANS MORE LIKE THE RIGHT-HAND ONE"
560 PRINT "IF THE DESCRIPTION DOES NOT APPLY AT ALL, ENTER ZERO (0)"
570 LET K=0
580 FOR J=4 TO EN
590 PRINT"FOR";E$(J)
600 LJ=INT(J/2)
610 KJ=LJ*2
620 IF KJ <> J THEN 640
630 K = K + 1
640 FOR 1 = 1 TO K
650 IF I < CN THEN 700
670 PRINT"RATING FOR"; C$(1,I);"/";C$(2,I)
680 INPUT GRID (I,J)
690 NEXT I
700 NEXT J
710 PRINT:PRINT
720 PRINT"YOU HAVE CONSIDERED THESE ELEMENTS—"
730 FOR J=1 TO FN
740 PRINT E$(J)
```

```
750 NEXT J
760 PRINT:PRINT"IN THESE WAYS—"
770 FOR I = 1 to CN
780 PRINT C$(1,I);"/";C$(2,I)
790 NEXT I
800 PRINT:PRINT:PRINT
810 PRINT"CAN YOU THINK OF ANY OTHER WAYS YOU SOMETIMES DISTINGUISH BETWEEN THEM?
    ANSWER 'YES' OR 'NO'"
820 INPUT ANS$
830 IF ANS$ = "NO" THEN 1000
840 CN = CN + 1
850 IF CN > 20 THEN 1000
860 PRINT"OKAY. ENTER ONE END OF THE NEW CONSTRUCT"
870 INPUT C$(1,CN)
880 PRINT "NOW THE OTHER"
890 INPUT C$(2,CN)
900 PRINT:PRINT:PRINT "NOW RATE THEM AS BEFORE. 1 MEANS MORE LIKE";C$(1,CN);", 5
    MEANS MORE LIKE",C$(2,CN)
910 PRINT"IF THE DESCRIPTION";C$(1,CN);"/";C$(2,CN);"DOES NOT APPLY AT ALL, ENTER
    ZERO (0)"
920 FOR J = 1 TO EN
930 PRINT"RATING FOR";E$(J)
940 INPUT GRID (CN,J)
950 NEXT J
960 PRINT:PRINT:PRINT"CAN YOU THINK OF ANOTHER SOURCE OF DIFFERENCES? ANSWER 'YES' OR
    'NO'"
970 INPUT ANS$
980 IF ANS$ = "NO" THEN 1000
990 GOTO 840
1000 PRINT"THANK YOU FOR YOUR INTEREST. I HOPE YOU ENJOYED THINKING ABOUT THE WAY YOU
    THINK ABOUT THINGS"
1010 PRINT:PRINT:PRINT:PRINT
1020 PRINT §2, "YOUR AREA OF INTEREST WAS:";POP$
1030 PRINT §2, PRINT §2, "IN WHICH YOU CONSIDERED THE FOLLOWING ELEMENTS—"
1040 PRINT §2
1050 FOR J = 1 TO EN
1060 PRINT §2, J;SPC(3);E$(J)
1070 PRINT §2,: NEXT J
1080 PRINT §2,: PRINT §2, "AND YOU THOUGHT ABOUT THEM IN THESE WAYS—"
1090 PRINT §2
1100 FOR I = 1 TO CN
1110 PRINT §2, I;SPC(3);C$(1,I);"/";C$(2,I)
1120 PRINT §2,:NEXT I
1130 PRINT §2,:PRINT §2,:PRINT §2,"YOU RATED EACH ELEMENT ON EACH CONSTRUCT (WITH 1
    MEANING MORE LIKE THE LEFT POLE OF THE CONSTRUCT, AND 5 MORE LIKE THE RIGHT) IN THE
    FOLLOWING WAY, THE COLUMNS REPRESENT THE ELEMENTS AND THE ROWS THE CONSTRUCTS."
1140 PRINT §2,:PRINT §2,
1150 FOR I-1 TO CN
1160 PRINT §2,
1170 FOR J = 1 to EN
```

```
1180 PRINT §2, GRID (I,J);
1190 NEXT J
1200 PRINT §2,
1210 NEXT I
1220 END
```

Note: on some machines replace "§" by "#" and on others replace "PRINT §2" by "LPRINT" (e.g. Tandy TRS80).

Bibliography

Abbott, G. (1980). The effectiveness of a dramatic experience. M.A.dissertation. (In preparation.)
Abercrombie, J. M. L. (1960). "The Anatomy of Judgement." Hutchinson, London.
Adams-Webber, J. R. (1969). Cognitive complexity and sociality. *Br. J. Soc. Clin. Psychol.* **8**, 211–216.
Adams-Webber, J. R. (1970). Elicited versus provided constructs in repertory grid technique: a review. *Br. J. Med. Psychol.* **43**, 349–353.
Adelman, C. and Walker, R. (1975). Developing pictures for other frames; action research and case study. *In* "Frontiers of Classroom Research". (G. Chanan and S. Delamont, eds). N.F.E.R., Slough.
Allport, G. W. (1955). "Becoming." Yale University Press, New Haven.
American Educational Research Association (1952). Report of Committee on Criteria of Teacher Education. *Rev. Educ. Ref.* **22**, 238–263.
Annett, J. (1969). "Feedback and Human Behaviour." Penguin Books, London.
Ashley, B., Cohen, H., McIntyre, D., and Slatter, R. (1970). A sociological analysis of students' reasons for becoming teachers. *Soc. Rev.* **18**, 53–59.
Bakan, D. (1967). "On Method — Towards a Reconstruction of Psychological Investigation." Jossey-Bass Inc., San Francisco.
Bannister, D. (1959). An application of personal construct theory (Kelly) to schizoid thinking. Ph.D. thesis, London University.
Bannister, D. (1960). Conceptual structure. Thought disordered schizophrenics. *J. Mental Science*, **106**, 1230–1249.
Bannister, D. (1962). Personal construct theory: a summary and experimental paradigm. *Acta Psychologica*, **20**, 104–120.
Bannister, D. (1970). "Perspectives in Personal Construct Theory." Academic Press, London and New York.
Bannister, D. (1977). "New Perspectives in Personal Construct Theory." Academic Press, London and New York.
Bannister, D. and Fransella, F. (1971). "Inquiring Man." Penguin Books, London.
Bannister, D. and Mair, J. M. M. (1968) "The Evaluation of Personal Constructs." Academic Press, London and New York.
Bannister, D. and Salmon, P. (1975). A personal construct view of education. *NY Univ. Educ. Quart.* **6**, 4, 28–31.
Barker-Lunn, J. C. (1970). "Streaming in the Primary School." N.F.E.R., Slough.

Barnes, D., Britton, J. and Rosen, H. (1969). "Language, the Learner and the School". Penguin Books, London.

Barr, A. S. *et al.* (1961). Wisconsin studies of the measurement and prediction of teacher effectiveness: a summary of investigations. *J. Experimental Educ.* **30**, 5–159.

Bateson, G. (1972). "Steps to an Ecology of Mind: Collected essays in Anthropology; Psychiatry, Evolution and Epistemology." Chandler Pub. Co., San Francisco.

Bell, R. C. and Keen, T. R. (1980). A statistical aid for the grid administrator. *Int. J. Man-Machine Studies*, **13**, 145–150.

Benjafield, J., and Adams-Webber, J. (1975). Assimilative Projection and construct balance in the repertory grid. *Br. J. Psych.* **66**, 2, 169–173.

Berger, P. L. and Luckmann, T. (1967). "The Social Construction of Reality." Allen Lane, London.

Berman, L. M. and Roderick, J. A. (1973). The relationship between curriculum development and research methodology. *J. Res. Devel. Educ.* **6**, (3), 3–13.

Bieri, J. (1955). Cognitive complexity — simplicity in predictive behaviour. *J. Ab. Soc. Psych.* **51**, 263-268.

Bieri, J. (1966). "Clinical and Social Judgement: the Discrimination of Behavioural Information." John Wiley, New York.

Biggs, J. B. (1976). Educology! The theory of educational practice. *Contemp. Educ. Psych.* **1**, 274–284.

Biles, B. (1976). IDEA. Internal Memoranda, Kansas State University.

Biles, B., Biles, L., Keen, T., and Hopwood, W. (1976). Traditional Methods of Teacher Appraisal: TARGET and IDEA. Proceedings of the Third International Conference on Improving University Teaching, Vol. IV. D468.

Blumer, H. (1966). Sociological implications of the thought of George Herbert Mead. *Am. J. Soc.* **71**, 535–548.

Bonarius, J. C. J. (1965). Research in the personal construct theory of George A. Kelly: role construct repertory test and basic theory. *In* "Progress in Experimental Personality Research" (B. A. Maher, ed.) Vol. 2, pp.2–46. Academic Press, New York and London.

Bonarius, J. C. J. (1970). "Personal Construct Psychology and Extreme Response Style." Swets and Zeitlinger, Amsterdam.

Boot, R. and Boxer, P. (1980). Reflective learning. *In* "Advances in Management Development." (J. Beck and C. Cox, eds). John Wiley, New York.

Bourne, R. (1971). "Fit to Teach" (B. Kemble, ed.). Hutchinson Educational, London.

Boxer, P. (1979). Reflective analysis. *Int. J. Man-Machine Studies* **11**, 547–584.

Britton, J. (1976). Bread and water. *J. Educ. Thought* **10**, 3–4.

Brook, J. (1979). A repertory grid analysis of perceptions of vocational counselling roles. *J. Voc. Behaviour* **15**, 1, 25–35.

Brookes, B. (1971). What is education. *In* "Teachers for Tomorrow — Diverse and Radical Views about Teacher Education." (K. Calthrop and G. Owens, eds.) Heinemann Educational, London.

Brown, A. (1979). Discovering and developing decisions people make about people. Paper presented to the Third International Congress on Personal Construct Psychology, Utrecht, 1979.

Bruner, J. S. (1956). You are your constructs. *Contemp. Psychol.* **1**, 355–357.

Bruner, J. S. (1966). "Towards a Theory of Instruction." Norton, New York.

Buber, M. (1965). "Between Man and Man." Macmillan, New York and London.

Cashdan, A. and Philps, J. (1974). Report of a study conducted at the Open University Faculty of Education.

Cashdan, A. and Philps, J. (1975). "Teaching Styles in Nursery Education." Open University.

Chanan, G. and Delamont, S. (1975). "Frontiers of Classroom Research." N.F.E.R., Slough.

Chapman, L. (1974). An exploration of a mathematical command system. Ph.D. thesis, Brunel University.

Cooley, C. H. (1964). "Human Nature and the Social Order." Schoken, New York.

Coombs, C. H. (1953). Theory and methods of social measurement. *In* "Research Methods in Behavioural Sciences." (L. Festinger and D. Katz, eds.). Dryden, New York.

Cope, E. (1971). "School Experience in Teacher Education." Bristol University.

Cortazzi, D. and Roote, S. (1975). "Illuminative Incident Analysis." McGraw-Hill, New York.

Cox, C. B. and Dyson, A. E. (1969). The fight for education, and The crisis in education. Black Papers 1 and 2, Critical Quarterly Society.

Cromwell, R. L. and Caldwell, D. F. (1962). A comparison of ratings based on personal constructs of self and others. *J. Clin. Psychol.* **18**, 43–46.

Culbertson, H. and Scott, B. T. (1978). Some editorial games for the magazine editing or writing class. Paper presented at the Annual Meeting of the Association for Education in Journalism, Seattle, Washington.

Dent, H. C. (1971). An historical perspective. *In* "The Training of Teachers." (S. Hewett, ed.) University of London Press, London.

Dewey, J. (1910). "How We Think." Heath, Boston.

Dewey, J. (1916). "Democracy and Education; an Introduction to the Philosophy of Education." Free Press, New York.

Dewey, J. (1938). "Experience and Education". Macmillan, New York.

Dewey, J. (1951). "Experience and Education." Macmillan, New York and London.

Dewey, J. and Dewey, E. (1915). "Schools of Tomorrow." Dutton and Co., New York.

Dewey, J. and McLellan (1895). *In* "Early Works 1882–98", Vol. 5. Carbondale, S. Illinois; University Press, London; Schaffer and Simon, New York (1972).

Duck, S. W. (1973). "Personal Relationships and Personal Constructs: a Study of Friendship Formation". John Wiley, New York.

Duckworth, D. and Entwistle, N. J. (1974). Attitudes to School Subjects: A repertory grid technique. *Br. J. Educ. Psych.* **44**, 1, 76–83.

Easterby-Smith, M. (1980). How to use repertory grids in H.R.D. *Leadership and Organisation Development Journal*, **1**, 1.

Elliott, J. and Adelman, C. (1973). Reflecting where the action is: the design of the Ford Teaching Project. *Educ. Teach.* **92**, 8–20.

Enright, L. (1979). Learning in my classroom. *Forum* **21** (3), 78–81.

Entwistle, N. J. (1976). The verb "to learn" takes the accusative. *Br. J. Educ. Psych.* **46**, 1–3.

Entwistle, N. J. and Nisbet, J. D. (1972). "Educational Research in Action." University of London Press, London.

Epting, F. R., Suchman, D. I., and Nickeson, K. J. (1971). An evaluation of elicitation procedures for personal constructs. *Brit. J. Psych.* **62**, 513–517.

Esland, G. M. (1971). Teaching and learning as the organisation of knowledge. *In* "Knowledge and Control" (M. F. D. Young, ed.). Collier Macmillan, London.
Ewing, J. M. (1977). Attitude of pupils to reading — and others. Paper presented at the Annual Meeting of the Reading Association of Ireland, Dublin.
Eysenck, J. H. (1970). "The Structure of Human Personality." Methuen, London.
Fairbairns, J. (1978). Evaluation of Wider Opportunities for Women. Paper presented to the Brunel Institute of Organisation and Social Studies Conference on Applications of the Repertory Grid.
Finlayson, D. S. and Cohen, L. (1967). The teacher's role: A comparative study of the conceptions of college of education students and head teachers. *Br. J. Educ. Psych.* **37**, 22–31.
Fjeld, S. P. and Landfield, A. W. (1961). Personal construct consistency. *Psych. Rep.* **8**, 127–129.
Flanders, N. A. (1970). "Analyzing Teaching Behaviour." Addison-Wesley, New York.
Fransella, F. and Bannister, D. (1977). "A Manual for Repertory Grid Technique." Academic Press, London and New York.
Freud, S. (1913). The claims of psycho-analysis to the scientific interest — the education interest. *In* "The Complete Psychological Works of Sigmund Freud, Vol. 13" (J. Strachey, ed.). Hogarth Press (1953), London.
Fuller, F. F. (1969). Concerns of teachers: A developmental conceptualization. *Am. Ed. Res. J.* **6** (2), 207–225.
Fuller, F. F. and Manning, B. A. (1973). Self confrontation reviewed: A conceptualization for video playback in teacher education. *Rev. Educ. Res.* **43**, 4, 469–528.
Gage, N. L. (1965). "Handbook of Research on Teaching." Rand McNally & Co., Chicago.
Gardner, A. (1978). Task Analysis: Can the grid help? Paper presented at conference on Repertory Grid techniques, Brunel University, May 1978.
Gibbs, G. (1977). "Learning to Study". Institute of Educational Technology. Open University Press, Milton Keynes.
Gilbert, J. K. (1979). "An Approach to Student Understanding of Basic Concepts in Science. I.E.T., Surrey.
Gilbert, J. K. and Osborne, R. J. (1980). A method for the investigation of concept understanding in Science. *Eur. J. Sci. Educ.* (In press.)
Gonzalez, G. (1979). The individualized learning of physics in secondary school classroom. Ph.D. Thesis, University of Surrey.
Goodlad, J. I. (1960). Cited in "Grouping in Education." (A. Yates, ed.). John Wiley, New York.
Goodman, P. (1972). "Compulsory Miseducation." Penguin Books, London.
Gower, J. C. (1977). The analysis of three way grids. *In* "Dimensions of Intrapersonal Space." (Slater, P., ed) Vol. 2. John Wiley, New York.
Groves, R. and Hancock, J. (1975). A search for the person in educational practice: A psychological viewpoint. *J. Human. Sci. Tech.* **6**, 32–38.
Hall, E. (1978). "Using Personal Constructs." Rediguide 9. University of Nottingham School of Education.
Hamilton, D. and Delamont, S. (1974). Classroom research: a cautionary tale. *Res. Educ.* **11**, 1–15.
Hargreaves, D. H. (1972). "Interpersonal Relations and Education." Routledge and Kegan Paul, London.

Hargreaves, D. H. (1977). The process of typification in classroom interaction: models and methods. *Br. J. Educ. Psych.* **47**, 274–284.
Hayes, C. (1978). Groundwork for a flexible future. *Personnel Management* March, 27–29.
Holland, R. (1970). George Kelly: Constructive innocent and reluctant existentialist. *In* "Perspectives in Personal Construct Theory." (D. Bannister, ed.) Academic Press, London and New York.
Holt, J. (1966). "How Children Fail." Pitman, London.
Honey, P. (1979). Series of articles on using repertory grids, Industrial and Commercial Training, Sept.–Nov. 1979. John Wellans Publication.
Hopwood, W. and Keen, T. (1978). TARGET: a new approach to the appraisal of teaching. *Plet* **15**, 3.
Hudson, L. (1967). "Contrary Imaginations." Penguin Books, London.
Hudson, L. (1968). "Frames of Mind." Methuen, London.
Hull, C. (1943). "Principles of Behaviour". Appleton Century Croft, New York.
Humphreys, P. (1973). A review of some statistical properties of the repertory grid (and their cognitive implications). Paper presented to British Psychological Society, Mathematical and Statistical Section. Bedford College, London.
Hutchins, R. M. (1936). "The Higher Learning in America." Yale University Press, New Haven, Conn.
Illich, I. (1971). "De-Schooling Society." Harper and Rowe, New York.
Isaacson, G. S. and Landfield, A. W. (1965). Meaningfulness of personal versus common constructs. *J. Indiv. Psych.* **21**, 160–166.
Jackson, B. (1964). "Streaming; An Education System in Miniature." Routledge and Kegan Paul, London.
Jahoda, M. and Thomas, L. F. (1965). Search for optimal conditions of learning intellectually complex subject matter. Centre for the Study of Human Learning, Brunel University.
James, Lord (Chairman) (1972). Teaching education and training. H.M.S.O., London.
Jordan, D. C. (1973). ANISA: a new comprehensive early education model for developing human potential. *J. Res. Dev. Educ.* **6**(3), 83–93.
Joyce, B. (1972). Curriculum and humanistic education. *In* "Humanistic Foundations of Education." (C. Weinberg, ed.) Prentice Hall, Inc., New Jersey.
Keen, T. R. (1976). Repertory Grids used to facilitate the improvement of medical training. Paper presented at a day conference of nurse teachers. Devon General Hospital Post Postgraduate Medical Centre.
Keen, T. R. (1977). Cognitivist systems of teaching appraisal. *In* "Personal Construct Theory". Academic Press, London and New York (1978).
Keen, T. R. (1978a). Developing students' learning skills. *Teaching News*, **5**, 19, (University of Birmingham).
Keen, T. R. (1978b). Repertory grid techniques for teaching appraisal. *In* "Staff Development in Higher Education." S.R.H.E., Guildford.
Keen, T. R. (1979a). Pedagogic styles in physics education: an attitude scaling and repertory grid study. Ph.D. thesis, Open University, Milton Keynes.
Keen, T. R. (1979b). TARGET: Two years on! Paper presented at the Third International Conference on Personal Construct Theory, Utrecht July 1979.
Keen, T. R. (1980). Microprocessor applications to assist in the elicitation and termination of Repertory Grids. Paper presented to the International Congress on applied systems and cybernetics. Acapulco, Mexico 1980.

Keen, T. R. and Bell, R. (1980). One thing leads to another: A new approach to elicitation in the repertory grid technique. *Int. J. Man-Machine Studies*. Special edition Sept. 1980.

Keen, T. R. and Hopwood, W. H. (1978). What kind of teacher do you think you are? *Impetus Co-ordinating Committee for the training of University Teachers* **8**, 20.

Kelly, G. A. (1955). "The Psychology of Personal Constructs" Vols. 1, 2. W. W. Norton & Co. Inc., New York.

Kelly, G. A. (1966). Fixed role therapy. M.S. prepared as a chapter *In* "Handbook of Direct and Behaviour Therapies", (M. Jurjevich, ed.).

Kelly, G. A. (1969a). Ontological acceleration. *In* "Clinical Psychology and Personality: the selected papers of George Kelly." (B. Maher, ed.) John Wiley, New York.

Kelly, G. A. (1969b). The strategy of psychological research. *In* "Clinical Psychology and Personality: the collected papers of George Kelly." (B. Maher, ed.) John Wiley, New York.

Kelly, G. A. (1970a). A brief introduction to personal construct theory. *In* "Perspectives in Personal Construct Theory." (D. Bannister, ed.) Academic Press, London and New York.

Kelly, G. A. (1970b). Behaviour as an experiment. *In* "Perspectives in Personal Construct Theory". (D. Bannister, ed.) Academic Press, London and New York.

Kemble, B. (1971). "Fit to Teach." Hutchinson Educational, London.

Korzybski, A. (1941). "Science and Sanity." Science Press, New York.

Kuhn, T. S. (1962). "The Structure of Scientific Revolutions." University of Chicago Press, Chicago.

Kuhn, T. S. (1970). Logic of discovery or psychology of research. *In* "Criticism and the Growth of Knowledge". (I. Laketos and I. Musgrave, eds.). Cambridge University Press, Cambridge.

Laing, R. D. (1967). "The Politics of Experience" and "The Bird of Paradise". Penguin Books, London.

Laurillard, D. M. (1979). Research methods in student learning. Paper presented at the third Congress of EARDHE, Klagenfurt, Austria, January 1979.

Lambert, R., Bullock, R. and Spencer, M. (1973). The informal social system. *In* "Knowledge, Education and Cultural Change", (R. Brown, ed.). Tavistock, London.

Landfield, A. W. (1965). Meaningfulness of self, ideal and other as related to own versus therapists' personal construct dimensions. *Psychol. Rep.* **16**, 506–608.

Landfield, A. W. (1971). "Personal Construct System in Psychotherapy." Rand McNally, Chicago.

Lippitt, R. and White, R. K. (1958). An experimental study of leadership and group life. *In* "Readings, in Social Psychology", 3rd ed. (E. E . Maccoby, T. M. Newcombe and E. L. Hartley, eds). Holt, Rinehart and Winston, New York.

Logan, D. (1971). The student teacher. *In* "Teachers for Tomorrow — Diverse and Radical Views about Teacher Education", (K. Calthrop and G. Owens, eds) Heinemann Educational, London.

McConnell, D. and Hodgson, V. (1977). Lecture Feedback Package. Institute for Educational Technology, University of Surrey, Guildford, Surrey, England.

McConnell, D. and Hodgson, V. (1979). Feedback on teaching. Paper presented at Conference on Feedback in Teaching. Trent Polytechnic, England, May 1979.

McGrath, J. H. (1970). "Research Methods and Designs for Education." International Textbook Company, Scranton.

McKnight, C. (1977). Purposive preferences for multi-attributed alternatives; a study of choice behaviour using personal construct theory in conjunction with decision theory. Ph.D. thesis, Brunel University.

McLeish, J. (1970). "Students' Attitudes and College Environments." Cambridge Institute of Education.

McQuitty, L. L. (1966). Similarity analysis of reciprocal pairs for discrete and continuous data. *Educ. Psych. Meas.* **26**, 825–831.

Magee, B. (1973). "Popper." Fontana/Collins, London.

Mair, J. M. M. (1964). The deviation, reliability and validity of grid measures, some problems and suggestions. *Br. Psych. Soc. Bull.* **17**, 55.

Mair, J. M. M. (1970). Psychologists are human too. *In* "Perspectives in Personal Construct Theory" (D. Bannister, ed.) Academic Press, London and New York.

Marklund, S. (1962). *In* "Grouping in Education." (A. Yates, ed.) John Wiley, New York (1966).

Marton, F. (1980). Studying Conceptions of Reality. Paper presented to American Education Research Association, Boston, Massachusetts.

Mead, G. H. (1934). "Mind, Self and Society." University of Chicago Press, Chicago.

Meredith, G. P. (1972). The origins and aims of epistemics. *Instruc. Sci.* **1**, 1.

Merleau-Ponty, M. (1962). "The Phenomenology of Perception." Routledge & Kegan Paul, London.

Metcalfe, R. J. A. (1974). Own vs. provided constructs in a reptest measure of cognitive complexity. *Psych. Rep.* **35**, 1305–1306.

Midwinter, E. (1971). Children from another world. *In* "Fit to Teach", (B. Kemble, ed.) Hutchinson Educational, London.

Miller, G. A., Galanter, E. and Pribram, K. H. (1960). "Plans and the Structure of Behaviour." Holt, Rinehart and Winston, New York.

Morris, B. (1972). "Objectives and Perspectives in Education: Studies in Educational Theory 1955-70." Routledge & Kegan Paul, London.

Morris, J. B. (1977). The prediction and measurement of change in a psychotherapy group using the repertory grid. *In* "A Manual for Repertory Grid Techniques." F. Fransella and D. Bannister, eds.) Academic Press, London and New York.

Morrison, A. and McIntyre, D. (1973). "Teachers and Teaching." Penguin Books, London.

Nash, R. (1973). "Classroom Observed." Routledge & Kegan Paul, London.

Nash, R. (1976). Pupils' expectations of their teachers. *In* "Exploration in Classroom Observation". (M. Stubbs, and S. Delamont, eds). John Wiley, New York.

National Union of Teachers (1970). "Teacher Education — The Way Ahead." NUT, London.

Neill, A. S. (1937). "That Dreadful School." Jenkins, London.

Neill, A. S. (1964). "Summerhill: A Radical Approach to Child-rearing." Holt, Rinehart and Winston, New York.

Norfolk, J. (1979). A Personal Construct Approach to Counselling. B.Sc. Thesis, Brunel University.

O'Donovan, D. (1965). Rating extremity: pathology or meaningfulness. *Psych. Rev.* **72**, 358–372.

Olson, J. (1980). Teacher constructs and curriculum change: Innovative doctrines and practical dilemmas. Paper presented to annual meeting of American Education Research Association, April 1980. Boston, Massachusetts.

Osgood, C. E., Suci, G. J. and Tannenbaum, P. H. (1957). "The Measurement of Meaning." University of Illinois Press, Urbana, Ill.
Otty, N. (1972). "Learner Teacher." Penguin Books, London.
Parkhurst, H. (1922). Education of the Dalton plan. *In* "Resources for Learning", (L. Taylor, ed.) Penguin Books, London.
Passow, A. H. (1966). The Maze of the research on ability grouping. *In* "Grouping in Education", (A. Yates, ed.) John Wiley, New York.
Peters, R. S. (1958). "The Concept of Motivation." Humanities Press, New York.
Piaget, J. (1954). "The Construction of Reality in Children." (M. Cook, trans.) Basic Books, New York.
Polanyi, M. (1958). "Personal Knowledge." University of Chicago Press, Chicago.
Polanyi, M. (1966). "The Tacit Dimension." Routledge & Kegan Paul, London.
Pope, M. L. (1978). Constructive Alternatives in Education. Ph.D. Thesis, Brunel University.
Pope, M. L. and Shaw, M. L. G. (1981). Negotiation in learning. *In* "Personal Construct Psychology" (H. Bonarius, R. Holland and F. Rosenberg, eds). Macmillan, London. (In press.)
Pope, M. L., Shaw, M. L., and Thomas, L. F. (1977). A report on the use of the repertory grid techniques in final inspection. Centre for the Study of Human Learning publication, Brunel University.
Popper, K. (1963). "Conjectures and Refutations: the Growth of Scientific Knowledge." Routledge and Kegan Paul, London.
Popper, K. (1970). Normal science and its dangers. *In* "Criticism and the Growth of Knowledge." (I. Laketos and I. Musgrave, eds) Cambridge University Press, Cambridge.
Poppleton, P. K. (1968). Assessment of teaching practice: What criteria do we use? *Educ. Teach.* **75**, 59–64.
Postman, N. and Weingartner, L. (1971). "Teaching as a Subversive Activity." Penguin Books, London.
Rathod, P. (1981). Methods for the analysis of rep. grid data. *In* "Personal Construct Psychology: Recent Advances in its Theory and Practice" (H. Bonarius, R. Holland and S. Rosenberg, eds). Macmillan, London and New York.
Reid, W. A. (1972). Applicants' images of universities. *Educ. Rev.* **26**, 1, 16–29.
Reid, W. A. and Holley, B. J. (1972). An application of repertory grid techniques to the study of choice of university. *Br. J. Educ. Psych.* **42**, 52–59.
Reidford, P. (1972). Educational research. *In* "Humanistic Foundations of Education", (C. Weinberg, ed.) Prentice Hall, Inc., N. Jersey.
Reimer, E. (1971). "School is Dead." Penguin Books, London.
Renshaw, P. (1971). The objectives and structure of the college curriculum. *In* "The Future of Teacher Education", (J. W. Tibble, ed.). Routledge & Kegan Paul, London.
Richardson, F. and Weigel, R. G. (1969). Personal Construct Theory Applied to The Marriage Relationship. Paper presented at the Rocky Mountain Psychological Association Convention, Albuquerque, New Mexico, May 1969.
Rix, E. A. H. (1979). Interviewing Rep. Testees: How do they mean what you say they said, or, does it matter? Paper presented to 3rd. International Congress on Personal Construct Psychology, Utrecht.
Roberts, J. (1980). Fuzzy Semantics as an aid to repertory grid elicitation and evaluation. Ph.D. Thesis, Open University. (In preparation.)

Rogers, C. R. (1961). "On Becoming a Person." Constable and Co., London.
Rogers, C. R. (1969). "Freedom to Learn: A View of What Education might become." Merrill, Columbus, Ohio.
Rosenthal, R. (1966). "Experimenter Effects in Behavioural Research." Appleton-Century-Crofts, New York.
Rosenthal, R. and Jacobson, J. (1968). "Pygmalion in the Classroom." Holt, Rinehart and Winston, New York.
Rosie, A. J. (1979). Teachers and children: interpersonal relations and the classroom. *In* "Constructs and Individuality" (P. Stringer and D. Bannister, eds). Academic Press, London and New York.
Runkel, P. J. (1965). A brief model for pupil–teacher interaction. *In* (Gage, N. L., 1965), pp.126–127. Rand McNally, Chicago.
Runkel, P. J. and Damrin, D. E. (1961). Effect of training and anxiety upon teachers' preference for information about students. *J. Educ. Psych.* **52**, 354-361.
Salmon, P. and Bannister, D. (1974). Education in the light of Personal Construct Theory. A.T.C.D.E. Education for Teaching Journal.
Sartre, J. P. (1947). "Existentialism." Philosophica Library, New York.
Schroder, H. M., Karlins, M. and Phares, J. (1973). "Education for Freedom." John Wiley, New York.
Schutz, A. (1953). Commonsense and scientific interpretation of human action. *Phil. Phenomenol. Ref.* XIV, I.
Schutz, A. (1967). "The Phenomenology of the Social World." North Western University Press, Evanston.
Shaw, M. L. G. (1978). Interactive computer programs for eliciting personal models of the world. *In* "Personal Construct Psychology" (F. Fransella and D. Bannister, eds). Academic Press, London and New York.
Shaw, M. L. G. (1980). "On Becoming a Personal Scientist". Academic Press, London and New York.
Shaw, M. L. G. and Gaines, B. R. (1979). Externalizing the personal world: computer aids to epistemology. Paper presented to the Society for General Systems Research, Silver Anniversary Meeting, London.
Shaw, M. L. G. and Thomas, L. F. (1978). FOCUS on education — an interactive computer system for the development and analysis of repertory grids. *Int. J. Man-Machine Studies* **10**, 138–173.
Shaw, M. L. G. and Thomas, L. F. (1979). Extracting an Education from a Course of Instruction. *Br. J. Ed. Tech.* **10**, 1, 5–17.
Sheldrake, P. and Berry, S. (1975). Looking at Innovation two approaches to educational research. N.F.E.R., Slough.
Shipman, M. D. (1966). The assessment of teaching practice. *Ed. Teach.* **70**, 28–31.
Shipman, M. D. (1967). Theory and practice in the education of teachers. *Ed. Res.* **9**, 208-212.
Silberman, . (1971). "Crisis in the Classroom: Remaking of American Education". Vintage, New York.
Skinner, B. F. (1968). "The Technology of Teaching." Appleton Century Crofts, New York.
Skinner, B. F. (1971). "Beyond Freedom and Dignity." Jonathan Cape, London.
Slater, P. (1964). "The Principal Components of a Repertory Grid." Vincent Andrew, London.
Slater, P. (1977). "Dimensions of Intrapersonal space", Vol. 2. John Wiley, New York.

Smith, M., Hartley, J. and Stewart, B. (1978). A case of repertory grids used in vocational guidance. *J. Occupation. Psych.* **51**(1), 97–104.

Snow, R. E. (1974). Representative and quasi-representative designs for research on teaching. *Rev. Educ. Res.* **44**, 265–291.

Sorenson, G. (1967). What is learned in practice teaching? *J. Teach. Educ.* **18**, 2, 173–178.

Stewart, A. and Stewart, V. (1976). "Tomorrow's Men Today." Institute of Personnel Management, Institute of Manpower Studies.

Stones, E. and Morris, S. (1972a). The assessment of practical teaching. *Ed. Res.* **14**, 110–119.

Stones, E. and Morris, S. (1972b). "Teaching Practice — Problems and Perspectives." Methuen, London.

Storm, M. (1971). What is wrong with the three year course? *In* "Fit to Teach" (B. Kemble, ed.). Hutchinson Educational, London.

Sullivan, H. S. (1953). "The Interpersonal Theory of Psychiatry." (H. S. Perry and M. L. Gawel, eds). Norton, New York.

Sutherland, N. S. (1964). Visual discrimination in animals. *Brit. Med. Bull.* **20**, 54–59.

Taylor, L. C. (1971). "Resources for Learning." Penguin Books, London.

Taylor, P. H. (1975). A study of the concerns of students on a postgraduate Certificate in Education course. *Br. J. Teach. Educ.* **1**, 2, 151–161.

Thelen, H. (1967). "Classroom Grouping for Teachability." John Wiley, New York.

Thomas, L. F. (1971). Interactive method of eliciting Kelly repertory grids; real-time data processing. Paper read at the Annual Conference to the Occupational Section of the B.P.S. York University.

Thomas, L. F. (1977). A personal construct approach to learning in education, training and therapy. Paper presented to the 2nd Int. Congress on Personal Construct Theory, Oxford. (In press.)

Thomas, L. F. and Harri-Augstein, E. S. (1975). Towards a theory of learning conversation and a paradigm for conversational research. Paper read at B.P.S. Annual Conference.

Thomas, L. F. and Harri-Augstein, E. S. (1976). The self-organised learner and the printed word. S.S.R.C. Monograph. Centre for the Study of Human Learning, Brunel University.

Thomas, L. F. and Harri-Augstein, E. S. (1977a). Education and the negotiation of meaning. Centre for the Study of Human Learning, Brunel University.

Thomas, L. F. and Harri-Augstein, E. S. (1977b). Learning to learn: the personal construction and exchange of meaning. *In* "Adult Learning — Psychological Research and Applications." (M. Howe, ed.) John Wiley, New York.

Thomas, L. F. and Shaw, M. L. G. (1976). FOCUS: A Manual for the Feedback of Clusters Using Similarities' computer program. Centre for the Study of Human Learning, Brunel University.

Thomas, L. F. and Shaw, M. L. G. (1977). PEGASUS: A Manual for "Program Elicits Grids and Sorts Using Similarities". Centre for the Study of Human Learning, Brunel University, 1977.

Thomas, L. F., McKnight, C. and Shaw, M. L. G. (1976). Grids and group structure. Paper presented to the Social Psychology Section of the B.P.S. University of Surrey.

Thomas, L. F., Shaw, M. L. G., and Pope, M. L. (1977). The repertory grid — a report of a feasibility study of personal judgement in staff appraisal. Centre for the Study of Human Learning publication, Brunel University.

Tiedeman, D. V. (1967). "Thought, Choice and Action: Processes of Exploration and Commitment in Career Development". Vol. 1. Free Press, USA.

Tuckman, B. W. (1976). The Tuckman teacher feedback form (TTFF). *J. Educ. Meas.* **13**, 3, 233–237.

Tuckman, B. W. (1976). Teaching: The Application of Psychological Constructs. *In* "Teaching. Vantage Points for Study" (R. T. Hyman, ed.), pp.295–307. Lippencott, Philadelphia.

Tully, J. B. (1976). Personal construct theory and psychological changes related to social work training. *Br. J. Soc. Work* **6**(4), 481–499.

Vannoy, J. S. (1965). Generality of cognitive complexity — Simplicity as a personality construct. *J. Personal. Soc. Psych.* **2**, 385–396.

Wall, W. D. (1969). "Adolescents in School and Society." N.F.E.R., Slough.

Wardle, F. (1978). "PACER Model: Skills and Personal Characteristics of Alternative Elementary Free School and Open School Techers." O.U.P., London.

Warner, J. W. (1971). The journal of introspection and its place in the graduate elementary teacher education programme. *J. Teach. Educ.* **XXII**, 3.

Warren, N. (1966). Social Class and Construct Systems: Examination of the cognitive structure of two social class groups. *Br. J. Soc. Clin. Psych.* **4**, 254–263.

White, R. W. (1959). Motivation reconsidered: the concept of competence. *Psych. Rev.* **66**, 297–333.

Willey, F. T. and Maddison, R. E. (1971). "An Enquiry into Teacher Training." University of London Press.

Winnicott, D. W. (1965). "The Maturational Processes and the Facilitating Environment." Hogarth Press, London.

Wiseman, S. and Start, K. B. (1965). A follow-up of teachers five years after completing their training. *Br. J. Ed. Psych.* **35**, 324–361.

Wood, R. and Napthali, W. A. (1975). Assessment in the classroom: What do teachers look for? *Ed. Studies* **1**(3), 151–161.

Wragg, G. C. (1974). "Teaching Teaching." David and Charles, Newton Abbot.

Yates, A. (ed.) (1966). "Grouping in Education." John Wiley, New York.

Author Index

Subject Index

EDUCATIONAL PSYCHOLOGY

continued from page ii

Thomas R. Kratochwill (ed.). Single Subject Research: Strategies for Evaluating Change

Kay Pomerance Torshen. The Mastery Approach to Competency-Based Education

Harvey Lesser. Television and the Preschool Child: A Psychological Theory of Instruction and Curriculum Development

Donald J. Treffinger, J. Kent Davis, and Richard E. Ripple (eds.). Handbook on Teaching Educational Psychology

Harry L. Hom, Jr. and Paul A. Robinson (eds.). Psychological Processes in Early Education

J. Nina Lieberman. Playfulness: Its Relationship to Imagination and Creativity

Samuel Ball (ed.). Motivation in Education

Erness Bright Brody and Nathan Brody. Intelligence: Nature, Determinants, and Consequences

António Simões (ed.). The Bilingual Child: Research and Analysis of Existing Educational Themes

Gilbert R. Austin. Early Childhood Education: An International Perspective

Vernon L. Allen (ed.). Children as Teachers: Theory and Research on Tutoring

Joel R. Levin and Vernon L. Allen (eds.). Cognitive Learning in Children: Theories and Strategies

Donald E. P. Smith and others. A Technology of Reading and Writing (in four volumes).

Vol. 1. Learning to Read and Write: A Task Analysis (by Donald E. P. Smith)

Vol. 2. Criterion-Referenced Tests for Reading and Writing (by Judith M. Smith, Donald E. P. Smith, and James R. Brink)

Vol. 3. The Adaptive Classroom (by Donald E. P. Smith)

Vol. 4. Designing Instructional Tasks (by Judith M. Smith)

Phillip S. Strain, Thomas P. Cooke, and Tony Apolloni. Teaching Exceptional Children: Assessing and Modifying Social Behavior